W9-BCI-456

History of
American
Schoolbooks

History of
American
Schoolbooks

by Charles Carpenter

Philadelphia

University of Pennsylvania Press

To

Susan, Billy, Christine, Shelley

Phil, *and* Charles.

Preface

IN THE PAGES that follow it has been the desire of the writer to present a general portrayal of American textbooks, and along with this, as a requisite accompaniment, a picture of the pioneer-day school system—this latter only insofar as it had to do with schoolbook production and early usage. An effort has been made to show how the first textbooks came to be, to make passing mention of text writers, and to trace through the bulk of the material presented as nearly as possible the changes that most of the textbook authors brought about.

No attempt has been made to present a comprehensive bibliographical treatment of the subject; a number of volumes would be required to cover anything like all the schoolbooks that have come and gone. To treat of them in their entirety, even if it were within the range and capacity of one person, would be a herculean project, to say the least. Edwin Grant Dexter, an education historian, referring to schoolbooks of the nineteenth century alone in his *History of Education in the United States,* said, "Their titles alone would fill a volume."

The subject matter set forth is confined to books used in what are generally designated as common schools—the elementary, secondary, and high schools. This limitation arises from the nature of such institutions, including the early academies. It

would not be appropriate to refer more than incidentally to
texts used exclusively in universities and colleges in such a study
as the present one. It is fitting, perhaps, to deal briefly with
texts that were utilized in both the lower schools and colleges
in the early nineteenth century, and this has been done, particularly in the two chapters on the science texts and the one on
mathematics books.

A number of texts which became well known for brief periods
have been touched upon lightly here and there. In places there
had to be a curtailment of subject matter and total omissions
were necessary now and then in order to make the volume a
practicable one. The examples of schoolbooks which fitted best
into the context of the material as a whole were used as a guide
in excluding others less closely related. It is hoped that no
outstandingly important texts or classes of texts have been in-
advertently omitted.

The collections of schoolbooks and books pertaining to
education history in numerous libraries have been studied and
the facilities of the libraries utilized. The chief sources have been
the Library of Congress, the New York Public Library, and the
writer's own collection of schoolbooks, the last now consisting
of about three thousand volumes—the fruit of a long period
of selective assembling. Naturally some assistance has been
derived from the volumes of Clifton Johnson, Alfred Hall-
Quest, and others who in the past have written on schoolbooks,
and from the histories of several textbook publishing firms; but
the writings on the subject are limited considering the importance of the subject and the volume of the output.

The writer especially acknowledges his indebtedness to Dr.
Oliver P. Chitwood, Professor Emeritus of History at West
Virginia University, the author of a number of important historical volumes and colonial histories, for going over some of
the chapters. Dr. Chitwood made a number of valuable sug-

gestions, which have been followed in this volume. Thanks are likewise due to Dr. J. P. Brawner, Dean of the Department of English of West Virginia University, and John W. Howard, Professor of Literature in the Dental School of the same university, both of whom were generous with their help. Mr. Frederick R. Goff, Chief of the Rare Book Room of the Library of Congress, has assisted with some early bibliographical questions, and his personal assistance and that of members of his staff who are not known by name to the writer are much appreciated. Gratitude is due, also, to the genial members of the staff of the New York Public Library, the West Virginia University Library, the Clarksburg, West Virginia, Public Library, and others who lent a helping hand.

In such a detailed work one can hardly hope to have escaped without errors, but the writer has done his best to avoid them by checking and rechecking every date cited and verifying each statement which seemed open to question. Should errors have occurred notwithstanding these precautions, the writer is wholly responsible, as those mentioned above as assisting with portions of the manuscript did not check the accuracy of dates or statements of fact.

CHARLES CARPENTER

Contents

The illustrations appear as a group after page 146

History of
American
Schoolbooks

I

The Early American Schools

THE LINEAGE OF AMERICAN school texts, like that of our educational system, goes in a general way back to Europe, mainly to England. The first schoolbooks used were printed in Britain; later, American presses reprinted foreign texts. American school texts in the beginning could not have derived from any other source, the circumstances of our early settlement being as they were. The first colonial printers turned out schoolbooks, and most of the other early printers, following in their steps because of necessity and convenience, did this line of work. The pioneer printing presses, however, could not supply all the books needed, and for a time it was still necessary to import texts. The influx of schoolbooks from the outside lasted, all together, for a period of some two hundred years. But it must be noted that European schoolbooks, either printed abroad or copied in America, were used only until technical developments reached a point where texts could be produced at home in sufficient number to meet the demand. It is apparent that from the first there was a desire to produce the required schoolbooks on home soil — a goal that quickly became a reality when conditions were favorable.

With millions of books easily and quickly to be had today, it seems strange to look back to a time when they were scarce; in fact, we can hardly conceive of such a situation. The scarcity of books, and especially of schoolbooks, however, was acute during the whole of the colonial era and for a time afterward. The result of this shortage was that in schools here and there half a dozen texts, or even less, had to do for classes of considerable sizes. The students took turns in studying, as well as in reciting from them. Handwritten texts and other prepared-at-home substitutes were in widespread use.[1] The shortage of books and materials required in the educational process may have retarded for brief periods the advance of education in some localities, but this seems not to have been true from an over-all standpoint.

Because of the lack of schoolbooks in some places during colonial days and afterward, substitutes were a necessity, but this condition seems to have prevailed mostly in remote settlements and in thinly populated areas. Richard Smith Elliott, who attended school in central Pennsylvania during the first half of the nineteenth century, tells of some of the makeshifts that had to be gotten along with in schools well into the century.[2] A historian writing along the same line said that during the early part of the nineteenth century in parts of Kentucky few textbooks were used because hardly any were available. This writer stated that homemade wooden boards on which A-B-C's were marked were utilized for teaching the alphabet to beginners.[3]

In colonial days, when no schoolbook was at hand, the Bible, a volume of Addison or Goldsmith, or some other book a teacher possessed, might be put to use. In some instances these may have made usable texts, but it is quite conceivable that such books

---

[1] For an account of manuscript schoolbooks, see *Papers of the Bibliographical Society of America,* Vol. 32, 1938.

[2] Richard Smith Elliott, *Notes Taken in Sixty Years* (Boston: Upham & Co., 1884), p. 4.

[3] Z. F. Smith, *History of Kentucky* (Louisville: Printice, 1895), p. 174.

were not very practicable for the general run of beginning pupils. Several historians have commented upon the use in schools of books other than textbooks because of the shortage, but the real extent of this practice can hardly be estimated today.

Well into the nineteenth century textbooks with different presentations of subject matter were occasionally used in schools by students in the same class. There is considerable documentary evidence to support this statement. Half a class might study from an old book, while the other half used a later and different text. Until well after the Civil War most states had some sort of official directive that old texts be utilized as long as possible. Soon after the free school system of West Virginia was established, following the Civil War, the General Superintendent of Schools directed in his annual report (Wheeling, 1866, p. 120) that "Teachers will use such old books as their pupils may have. Whenever books are purchased those in the foregoing list [itemized recommended texts] should be ordered." A number of other states had similar directives during the same period and until along in the 1870's.

In sections of the West the lack of school materials was felt much later than in the East. Effie Mona Mack and Byrd Wall Sawyer, writing of the early schools of their region, said that any sort of schoolbook might be used that the settler owned.[4] Other authors of histories of western states have had something to say along the same line, covering periods late into the nineteenth century. It must be borne in mind, however, that schools in much of the western country did not begin until far along in the middle of the nineteenth century and later, and that shortage of school materials because of sparse settlement and

---

[4] Mack and Sawyer, *Our State Nevada* (Caldwell, Idaho: Caxton, 1948), p. 263.

transportation difficulties occurred considerably later than such shortages in the eastern section of the country.

During colonial days and afterward the education and training of school teachers had a marked bearing on the development of schoolbooks. The improvement in texts and the very slow change in subject matter from time to time were conditioned by the qualifications of those teaching schools as much as by general conditions in the country.

It can hardly be assumed that school teachers, as a body, were what we would designate as well qualified during Colonial times and for a long time afterward. Few took up education as a permanent profession, because there was not sufficient incentive to do so. The technical study of education, as far as lower schools were concerned, had not yet begun. Only a comparatively small number of books on school methods and the teaching of children were available up to the nineteenth century, and these few were not available to many who desired to become teachers.

Teaching more often than not was merely "taken up" or, in many cases, learned like a trade. In order to become teachers, young people were often apprenticed for given periods, to be coached by another teacher. The indentured-servant system was a limited source of schoolmasters; Elwood P. Cubberly in his *History of Education,* as well as other education historians, have commented at length on this practice.

Another phenomenon of the time, lasting into the nineteenth century, was the "wandering school teacher." These were schoolmasters who went from place to place — a sort of equivalent to the contemporary scriveners and wandering tradesmen, some few of whom survived until our own generation. A notable example of the latter were printers. The roaming teachers must have been plentiful in rural sections where conditions were such as to encourage his presence. Although some of them may have been fairly well fitted for their school work, many were inevitably poorly equipped.

Until 1830, a date that marked a turning point in American education, the schools of the country as a whole admittedly had been poor. This is the common opinion expressed by historians and other writers on early American social conditions. Albert Bushnell Hart said, "The public schools up to 1830 were places where people might be educated rather than where they must be."[5] I. M. F. Williams, speaking of the same era, stated that it was "the culmination of a half century of retrogression in the schools."[6] There were few good schools during this early era simply because of the shortage of capable teachers, and there were few good teachers because of the shortage of efficient training.

It would be manifestly wrong to say there were no competent teachers during the early years of American school history. It stands to reason that some were well qualified for their work. Among the teachers of colonial times and around the beginning of the nineteenth century there were a considerable number who stood out and certainly not to be listed as inefficient, Noah Webster, John Filson, of Kentucky, Ethan Allen, Benjamin Thomson, who became well known as Count Rumford, John G. Percival, the early poet, and others certainly must have been capable of effective teaching.[7]

---

[5] Hart, *National Ideas Historically Traced* (New York: Harpers, 1907), p. 223.

[6] Williams, *Horace Mann* (New York: Macmillan, 1937), p. 86.

[7] Many persons, afterward famous, both in this country and elsewhere, have taught school. Among them may be mentioned Bret Marte, Havelock Ellis, Walter H. Page, Chester A. Arthur, William McKinley, Oswald Spengler, Louis Phillipe, H. G. Wells, D. H. Lawrence, Louis Pasteur, Edwin Markham, Walt Whitman, General Pershing, the noted

It may be pointed out, also, that there were two or three Colonial schoolmasters who lived before those referred to above, among these Anthony Benezet and Christopher Dock, who were excellent teachers because of natural talent. Christopher Dock, who taught in Pennsylvania, was the first resident of our country to pen a book on school methods. This was his School-Ordunung. This treatise was reprinted in 1908 in Martin G. Brumbaugh's *Life and Works of Christopher Dock,* and reveals good ideas on school conducting. It has been thought by some that Dock's book was a revamping of a former *School-Ordunung* printed in Tubingen, Germany, in 1583, but an examination of the two books, both extremely rare today, shows there could have been no copying.

From among the early American school teachers, including many people well equipped and others poorly equipped for their work, came most of the country's first writers of schoolbooks. A few of them were professors in colleges and a certain number had no teaching or school connections; but the majority must be designated as school teachers. The first outstanding American schoolbook writer, Noah Webster, was a man who turned to this work through his early employment as a schoolmaster, and other teachers followed his lead.

Russian scientist Elie Metchnikoff, the Russian novelist Leo Tolstoy, and the famous Samuel Johnson. There is a widespread belief, not confirmed that Shakespeare and Cervantes taught school for a time. See Walton, *Living Thoughts of Cervantes* (London: Cassell, 1948), p. 3.

II

The New England Primer

ONE OF THE primitive examples of school texts used in our land was the hornbook, something that goes quite a distance into the past of our forebears, those of England and elsewhere. The hornbook, not at all familiar today to most people, was a paddle-shaped affair of wood with a piece of paper attached, covered with a transparent sheet of "horn," or in rare cases made of wood or metal with the lettering cut or pressed into the surface. The hornbook usually carried the alphabet, numerals, and sometimes religious figures or wording. The larger ones often contained the Lord's Prayer or brief religious admonitions. Many, especially those with the lettering carved into the wood or pressed into the metal, had only the alphabet or the alphabet and the ten digits. The handle of the hornbook generally had a hole through which a cord could be passed, so that it could be attached to a girdle or otherwise to the person. John Carter states that hornbooks are "rarer than First Folio Shakespeares."[1] and two chances to one he is right.

Andrew W. Tuer stated: "There can be no doubt that the hornbook has been extensively used in America."[2] This state-

---

[1] Carter, *Taste and Technique in Book Collecting* (Cambridge University Press, 1949), p. 1.
[2] Tuer, *History of the Hornbook* (London: Leadenhall Press, 1897),

21

ment seems open to question. The best information we have on the subject, as far as our country is concerned is contained in Plimpton's book.[3] The author, long the head of Ginn and Company, was of the opinion that the hornbook was used to a certain extent in colonial days but that "most of those used here were imported from England." It seems unlikely that very many were even brought in from overseas. Dr. Gordon, in his large volume of data on early American medical science, says that Dr. Stephen Hales, the noted eighteenth century English philosopher, inventor, and physiologist, a prominent man in his day, collected, along with some school books, two hundred hornbooks to be sent to the colony of Georgia,[4] but it seems impossible to find a confirmation in historical records that these were ever brought to this country, and probably they were not. Hales was never in America. Dr. Gordon does not give the source of his information. After years of searching, George A. Plimpton and those assisting him found only five hornbooks that had been used in the United States or the colonies, and but one of these is thought to be of American origin.

The battledore followed the hornbook. It was a minor makeshift used to some extent in the early American period. It consisted of a sheet folded once, or in some instances twice, and covered as a rule with lettering similar to that on the hornbooks. These almost forgotten objects are now nearly as scarce as hornbooks, hardly any remaining except a few in the larger institutional libraries. Those of American printing are exceedingly rare.

I, 162. This is a large, well-illustrated book, which was "By command dedicated to the Queen and Empress [Victoria]." A second edition, "a popular version" of small size, was issued in 1899.

[3] George A. Plimpton, *The Hornbook and Its Use in America* (American Antiquarian Society of Worcester, Massachusetts, 1936.

[4] Dr. Maurice Gordon, *Aesculapius Comes to the Colonies* (Ventnor, N. J.: Ventnor Publishing Co., 1949), p. 488.

The *New England Primer,* whether or not a type of book developed from the hornbook and battiedore, stands in the forefront of early American schoolbooks. Charles E. Heartman, the once well-known book dealer and bibliographer, has related how the *Protestant Tutor* developed through a gradual metamorphosis into the *New England Primer.*[5] To comprehend the genesis of the *New England Primer* we must go back to the *Tutor.* This latter book has been referred to by some writers as a "religious primer," but it can properly be called a school primer. The *Protestant Tutor* was strongly anti-Catholic, and had more religious than secular matter in it; but many of the elementary schoolbooks of the time contained hymns, the catechism, the Lord's Prayer, and related matter, and could equally well be designated as religious texts. To speak of any of these early schoolbooks as religious is not exactly correct.

The *Protestant Tutor* was first published, as far as we know, by B. and F. Harris in London, in 1607. Other editions were printed in England, and later, after Benjamin Harris came to America, copies were issued in Boston. It is not known what the year of the first American printing was, but it is supposed to have been around 1685. A number of early schoolbooks pose hopeless bibliographical questions, and the *Protestant Tutor* happens to be one of them. It is not likely that the puzzle of its early publication will ever be finally cleared up.

Probably the first issue of the *New England Primer* was printed in England by John Gaine; but this is not certain. It may be that the name John Gaine was a pseudonym used by Benjamin Harris or someone else. Charles Heartman explored

---

[5] Heartman, introduction to *Bibliography of the New England Primer Prior to 1830,* first privately printed in 1922. The preface of the bibliography was issued in a slightly different form under the title "The *New England Primer:* A Short Essay," and appears in *The Biblio,* II, No. 3, September, 1922.

the details connected with this probable first printing, but his conclusions are hardly more than conjectures. Heartman tells us of the official registration of the "John Gaine" issue, and he thinks this printing might have been the beginning of the *New England Primer*. A Stationer's Register of London, under date of October 5, 1683, read:

Mr. John Gaine
Eodom Die et Annon. Ordered then for his book or copy
Entituled the New England Primer or Milk for Babes. vjd
                                   Jno. Gain
Witt Mr. Scoresby

If this registration, which was an official requirement for all books prior to sale in England, had reference to the first *New England Primer,* so far as we know there has been no copy of it recorded elsewhere.

In Newman's *News from the Stars,* an almanac printed in Boston late in 1690, an advertisement of an American printing of the *New England Primer* appeared. This is the earliest known American mention. The advertisement read:

There is now in the press, and will suddenly be extant, a second impression of the *New England Primer* enlarged, to which is added more *Directions for Spelling:* The Prayer of K. Edward the 6th, and Verses made by Rodgers *the Martyr, left as a legacy to his Children.*

Sold by *Benjamin Harris, at the London Coffee-House in Boston.*⁶

Benjamin Harris was not only fitted from a business stand-

---

⁶ This advertisement is reproduced from George Livermore's *The Origin, History and Character of the New England Primer* (New York, 1915). The story of the early coffee-houses is well told in Aytoun Ellis's *The Penny University: A History of the Coffee-House* (London, 1957). At the close of the seventeenth century there were two thousand coffee-houses in London, and a few were being established in America; Benjamin Harris' London Coffee-House in Boston may have been the first.

point for bringing out the first American printing of the *New England Primer* but was well-equipped intellectually for the task. He evidently was a staunch believer in the forces which were strenuously fought against in the Primer — the devil and evil in general — as they were viewed in early colonial days. Harris personally brought out some of the early publications on witchcraft. Lawson's *Brief and True Narrative,* issued in 1692, which had to do with the Salem witchcraft cases, was "Printed for Benjamin Harris . . . to be sold at his Shop, over against the Old-Meeting House," and the book had a prefatory note from "The Bookseller to The Reader," signed by Harris. We may conclude that this early Boston Coffee-house proprietor and book publisher was in harmony with the thinking of colonial New England, as reflected in some of the contents of the *New England Primer.*

The earliest copy of the *Primer* known to exist today is the 1727 Boston edition, now in the New York Public Library. A 1735 copy is in the Henry E. Huntington Library at San Marino, California. The fact that there are no known copies of printings between 1727 and 1735 indicates how little attention was paid to the preservation of schoolbooks from a bibliographical standpoint prior to the nineteenth century, since it is probable that copies were issued during this period. Evidently no one had sufficient bibliographical interest in the *New England Primer* at the time to make even a diary mention of the bibliographical side of it. It is well known that university libraries in the early days did not consider the various issues of the *New England Primer* worthy of preservation. When copies of books of this era were placed in libraries, even such a one as the Bodleian in England, they were often discarded when new editions came out. This was a general rule in the institutional libraries of the time. That the Bodleian Library disposed of its First Folio Shakespeare for a "later issue" is a matter of record, and the incident tells us more about book preservation during the early day of the *New England Primer* than any other information we have.[1]

The majority of the early issues of the *New England Primer* were similar in having an illustrated alphabet at the beginning. This lesson was generally on four pages, with a blocked-off woodcut picture for each letter. In the earliest issues the alphabet rhymes were of a religious nature. Later, in certain editions, they were in part secular, and still later some editions contained no religious matter. The following are examples of the religious jingles:

A   In Adams Fall
      We Sinned all.
B   Heaven to find,
      The Bible Mind.
C   Christ Crucufy'd,
      For Sinners dy'd.
D   The Deluge drown'd
      The Earth around.
E   Elijah hid,
      By Ravens fed.

Such jingles continued throughout the alphabet. The secular verses were similar to the following:

L   The Lion bold
      The Lamb doth hold.
M   The Moon gives light
      In Time of Night.
N   Nightingales sing
      In Time of Spring.
O   The royal Oak, it was the tree
      That saved his royal majesty.

---

[1] McCray, *Annals of the Bodleian Library* (London: Rivingtons, 1868), p. 41. McCray cites quite a number of examples of "mistaken elemination" of books, chiefly first editions, in the celebrated library.

However, in some instances these fairly cheerful jingles were followed in the partly religious editions with such pictures as that of a man lying in a coffin, with a woeful verse appended. The following, for the letter X, is an example:

Xerxes did die,
And So must you and I.

Death was mentioned and portrayed so frequently in the *New England Primer* that pupils perhaps became hardened to the sound of it, and the idea of final dissolution expounded in the primer must not have had much effect upon the average school child. One tends to grow calloused and unfeeling toward disagreeable things he sees too much of, and this must have been the case with some of the material in the *New England Primer*.

In numerous editions lessons were made up wholly of admonitions of a religious character and the sentiments in general were extremely morose. Many of them contained such lines as:

Liars shall have their part in the Lake
which burns with Fire and Brimstone.
Upon the wicked world God shall rain an
horrible Tempest.

Others pictured even worse things in store for the sinful human race. One lesson was a short story of Christ attempting to lead a youth away from sin. This young man postponed his conversion, thinking there would be plenty of time later on. Then Death comes and surprises him, saying:

Youth, I am come to fetch thy breath,
And carry thee to th' Shades of Death,
No pity on thee can I show
Thou hast thy God offended so.
They [sic] Soul and body I'll divide,
Thy body in the grave I'll hide,
And thy dear soul in hell must lie,
With Devils to eternity.

The word and syllable lessons in the *New England Primer* were of the sort that had become standard in schoolbooks of its day and which educators perhaps believed could not be improved upon.[8] The syllable lessons were most likely very bewildering to young children, and many of them no doubt brought no worth-while enlightment.

Lists of words for spelling drill appear amazing to modern minds in the swift progress expected of the pupils from brief words to long ones. The words for spelling were almost always divided into syllables—sometimes into more than the accepted laws of philology warrant. In some editions there were two or three pages of words with increasing numbers of syllables. A lesson of this kind, beginning with two-letter and one-syllable words, ended up with words of six syllables, such as a-bo-min-na-ti-on or mor-ti-fi-ca-ti-on.

In many editions an assortment of names appeared, with a statement that the list was intended to teach children to spell their own names. In one list of male names were Abijah, Banalas, Berzillai, Eleazer, Gamalial, Gershon, Jahez, Noadiak, Peletiah, Shubal, Uzzal, and Zadock. Among the female names were Abigail, Bethiah, Gillet, Ketura, Kezia, Lettice, Mahetable, and Ursula. The female list in some editions ended with the two Bible names Zipporah and Zibiah. A large proportion of the names were from the Bible, including some frequently used. Others were apparently invented through transposing letters, and were thus names not formerly in use. Many of the names given to children among the New England population

---

[8] Wolfgang Ratichius, 1571–1635, a German educator, was the first to emphasize the need of repetition in beginning schoolbooks, something that was frequently overdone in our early primers and is today often derided. Ratichius, introducing new educational methods, was overshadowed by his contemporary, Comenius. See Compayre, *History of Pedagogy* (Boston: Heath, 1891), p. 121. Compayre calls the German Ratich.

during colonial times may well have come from the *New England Primer.*

What must have been of more interest to children than anything they had formerly encountered were the story lessons in later editions. One of these, included in a number of issues, had the title "History of Master Tommy Fido." This appeared as early as 1767, and was in numerous issues after that. While the "Tommy Fido" composition was much in the spirit of a great deal of the children's literature of the time, there appeared in a Philadelphia edition of 1797 a brief reading lesson, in a somewhat facetious style, which appears to have been too liberal and too learned to find a place in the *New England Primer.* This piece shows a knowledge of mythology and a comprehension of Copernican astronomy that were not too characteristic of the schoolbook compilers of the time. It read :

Mar-ry! says Bil-ly, what do you think the world stands on?
I don't know, says Mar-ry; but I can tell you what our Tom says : Old Tom says the world stands on a great tur-tle; but he could not tell me what the tur-tle stood on. Well, says Bil-ly, I will tell you what my pa-pa says; My pa-pa says that the world don't stand on an-y thing; but is ba-lanced on its own cen-tre, and goes around the sun, in the o-pen space, once e-ve-ry year.[9]

These lines present evidence of a much keener sympathy with the new learning of the time than is found in previous issues of the Primer.

In the 1737 edition, printed in Boston by T. Fleet, the noted "Now I lay me down to sleep" verse, known everywhere, appeared for the first time in America, as far as is known. Only two or three copies of this edition are in existence today. The familiar little prayer follows :

---

[9] T. Dobson, *The New England Primer, Much Improved* (Philadelphia, 1797). In the words beginning with s, the old-style long s type was used.

Now I lay me down to sleep
I pray the Lord my soul to keep
If I should die before I wake
I pray the Lord my soul to take.

The simple rhyme sounds like one that some mother might have composed when she was putting her tot to bed for the night, and it is sometimes thought that it originated with the 1737 *New England Primer,* but this is not true. The prayer is known to have existed in a similar form hundreds of years prior to that date. The oldest known record is found in the *Enchiridion Leonis* of the year 1160. It is not known whether Leoninius, who was a canon of the church of Saint Victor in Paris in the twelfth century, composed the poem or not, but he might well have done so. The "Leonine Rhyme," in which the final syllable of a line rhymes with one in the middle, did come down to us from Leonius, for whom it was named. Another of his often-repeated rhymes is : "Pepper is black, though it hath a good smack."[10]

The illustrations in the *New England Primer* demand more than passing notice. The portrayal of the burning of John Rogers, included in many editions, more often than not had no merit as a drawing. This picture, however, is one of the most important from a historical standpoint that has come down to us from colonial days, and it must have had a strong hold on the contemporary imagination, of grown-ups as well as of children. The popularity of the picture lay in the hatred of the general run of people of New England for the Catholics. One noticeable characteristic of nearly all the John Rogers cuts was the absence of fear and horror in his expression. Some few of the cuts almost make it appear that his burning was enjoyed by the victim as well as those witnessing the tragedy. An example, copied in

[10] Brewster, *Readers Handbook* (Philadelphia : Lippincott, 1882–many times reprinted), p. 548.

numerous editions even as late as the 1843 issue, showed Rogers apparently free of suffering from his martyrdom." In most of the woodcuts the family of Rogers stand as if posed for a photograph. Generally, back of the family, or beside them, are two soldiers, a faulty perspective making them appear twice the size of the family figures. The soldiers or guards in nearly all the cuts are smiling as if amused at the performance before them."

If we examine closely the assortment of pictures in the *New England Primer* we can notice in them a fairly well-represented reflection of the thought of the period.

The picture of the English kings, which replaced the Rogers portraits and the scenes of the martyrdom, marked an effort toward creating an adherence to the not-too-strong British rule in the colonies. Later, after the colonies declared themselves free, the choice of portraits of Americans showed the trend toward American patriotism. With the struggle to free the colonies came a total end of praise of things British, and particularly the use of pictures or mention of the British monarch. Instead, rhymes like these appeared :

Queens and kings
Are gaudy things.

Britain's king in spleen
Lost states thirteen.

" There is a bit of old lore to the effect that Rogers, when asked to intercede to save a woman from burning, replied that "it is a gentle mode of death," and that his petitioner replied, "I hope that you yourself will some day have your hands full of this gentle death." Besant, *South London* (New York: Stokes, 1898), p. 122.

" In the early nineteenth century a chapbook, without date, was published in Philadelphia by William Beastall, of 507 Market Street, under the title *The Executioner, Being a True, Impartial and Most Extraordinary Account of What Happened to the Man Who Burnt the Rev. John Rogers*. The publisher, a "chemist and pharmaceutist," according to advertising in the little volume, sold books, stationery, perfumes, and various medical remedies.

At this time, along with the patriotic illustrations, came a sprinkling of pictures showing books being handed to children or read to them. These betray the fact that there was occurring a weakening of puritan zeal and a stirring, however slight, of the idea of learning among the people. It is true that most of the "bookish" illustrations were accompanied by verses from the Bible; but still there was an indication in them of a growing regard for the printed word in the advancement of knowledge. It is apparent that by 1800 there was no longer a conviction, as there had been formerly, that the things of earth were always vile as compared with the treasures of heaven.

On the last page of the Boston, 1737, T. Fleet edition of the *Primer,* is a picture of the Queen of England that invites special mention. It was evidently made from a block which was used in playing-card printing, and has quite the likeness of many of the pictures used on the "queens" of present-day packs. Collectors of our time have found old playing cards of the *New England Primer* era that unquestionably came from the same block used in certain issues of the *Primer*. Paul Leicester Ford said :

> To find such a print in the Godly New England Primer is perhaps the most curious fact yet known pertaining to the primer, and can only be accounted for by the probability that its purchasers were so ignorant of the appearance of the "Devil's picture cards" that they did not recognize its prototype.[13]

During the first years of the nineteenth century new material was being added to the *Primer*. A great deal of old subject matter was dropped and new material added that was thought more suitable. Some editions of this period came to be fairly practical schoolbooks, and these were as a rule not badly printed.

[13] Paul Leicester Ford, *The New England Primer* (New York: Dodd Mead, 1899), p. 107.

By the end of the first quarter of the century the ferment was at work that would result in a new class of texts that would totally displace the *New England Primer*. The noted text's use began to taper off during the first years of the century. It is true that more editions appeared during the first three decades of the nineteenth century than at any other period, but this was due to increased production and distribution of books rather than popularity of the text. Even when printing of the *New England Primer* was at its peak, educators were beginning to realize that the book had served its purpose. The *Primer* was one of the extraordinary successes of early American publishing, and the publishers retained the title, for its sale value, long after the contents had been changed.

The Southern colonies and states never used the *New England Primer* as did those of the North. A few, but not many, were used south of Pennsylvania. Maryland was originally a Catholic colony and, although religious freedom was granted, such a book as the *New England Primer* could not make much headway there. A number of printings were issued in Baltimore, but these came late. Likewise in Virginia, where the social structure was somewhat unlike that of New England, books of a different kind were wanted, as a general rule. Still farther south, school-book usages were somewhat akin to those prevalent in Virginia. In 1802, Joseph Israel, a wandering printer, who carted his press about on a wagon, printed a *New England Primer* in Washington, Pennsylvania. This man later had a shop fifty miles away in Clarksburg, Virginia (now West Virginia), where he printed a few items, one of which has become well known — Alexander Wither's *Chronicles of Border Warfare,* issued in 1831. There is no record of Israel's printing any school material at Clarksburg but it is possible that he could have done so, as the demand in this vicinity would have been about what they were at nearby Washington, in Pennsylvania.

In 1811 an edition of the *New England Primer* appeared in Pittsburgh, and twelve years later, in 1823, an edition was printed in Wheeling, Virginia, published by Davies and M'Carty. These Pittsburgh and Wheeling printings were for the Ohio Valley population, increasing rapidly at the time, which migrated from New England and the northeast seaboard as much as from south of Pennsylvania. Again in 1845 an issue was printed at Wheeling. Previously an edition had come out in Cincinnati, in 1831, and a very late printing appeared at Judson, Ohio, in 1854.

It is believed that of some two million or more copies of the *New England Primer* printed, not more than three thousand have come down to our time. Today when we look upon one of the comparatively few remaining copies, a diminutive and crude little curiosity, it is hard to credit the fact that the *Primer* could have held such a dominating place in the primary education of a population destined within little more than a century to become one of the most powerful of all peoples — one wealthy beyond the dreams of Croesus and equipped technically and scientifically for amazing production.

III

Nineteenth-Century Primers

THE *New England Primer* and contemporary texts of its class, as has been shown, were not exclusively reading and word-lesson books. Before evolving in that direction, numerous primers were issued similar in substance to the *New England Primer* to the extent that they were composite texts — books of a miniature *school collection* nature.[1] These books were built on the *New England Primer* model, and in most cases copied a portion of its material.

The first issues of the *Royal Primer,*[2] the *Boston Primer* and the *New York Primer* were almost identical with the *New England Primers*. A number even used that wording in some way on their title pages, to show that they were adaptations of the older text.

Some of the American primers that were widely used were

---

[1] The term *school collection* came to designate a text which covered general subjects. Many of the early American schoolbooks were so called, although the term originated in Europe. In Arabia and some other countries where there is not too high a standard of elementary training the school collection type of text is still used.

[2] The American editions were lineal descendants of the *Royal Primer* printed in London by John Newbery, the early English publisher of children's books, whose name has been honored through the American annual Newbery medal.

first published in the latter part of the eighteenth century, and became popular after the beginning of the next century. Among these were the *American Primer* and the *Columbia Primer,* both of which went through numerous printings. Of these, the *American Primer* was more widely used. An edition of this text was put out in Philadelphia in 1779, and one in Boston in 1792; and from 1800 to 1830 it was issued in a number of places. Copies are still in existence showing Cincinnati; Salem; Amherst; Norfolk, Connecticut; and Brookfield, Massachusetts, as the place of printing. It is quite likely that the title brought the text its wide acceptance. The book's peak of success coincided with the beginning of the popularity of the word "American."[3]

Near the beginning of the nineteenth century, changes began to appear in primers. After the turn of the century a number carried the compilers' names on their title pages, and soon this became common practice. In itself, this was to an extent a new feature in the schoolbooks for beginners. The authors whose names began to appear on title pages not only represented a new class of writer but in most cases utilized fresh ideas. Not many years passed before tenets of the education philosophers, especially Pestalozzi, were utilized by the new compilers of lower-school texts.

In 1826 a primer bearing the name of Pestalozzi appeared — the *Pestalozzian Primer,* compiled by John M. Keagy, who taught in a number of Pennsylvania schools, among them the

---

[3] It was during this era that much effort was expended toward creating an "American" or "National" university. George Washington was one of the chief backers of the contemplated institution, bequeathing some of his estate toward it. The story of this long-planned institution is well told in Samuel Blodgett's *Economica,* published in 1807, the first work on political economy written in the United States. Agitation for the university kept up until the middle of the century. Barnard's *Journal of Education* for May, 1856, had an informative article, "A National University," urging the creation of such an institution.

Friends Academy in Philadephia. His was the earliest primer to dwell upon "thinking" in connection with reading, and the first to treat of "the child's environment" as an integral part of schoolwork. The Keagy primer carried the following subtitle : *First step in teaching children the art of reading and thinking.* Thirty pages covered syllable and "thinking lessons" before words, as separate units, were reached. In this text an early groping for new ideas was apparent, but some of Pestalozzi's principles were carried to harmful extremes, particularly his precepts relating to observation and syllable study.

Samuel Worcester's *Primer of the English Language,* which appeared in 1828, was the first to get away from the syllable-reading system, and in this the author initiated the word method of reading in this country. Worcester's primer was published only a little more than a decade after J. J. Jacatot introduced the word system of reading in France — its first use in schools. The defects of the letter-syllable method were pointed out four hundred years ago by the German educator Ickelsamer, but it was not until 1818 that Jacatot originated the analytical-synthetic style of teaching the beginning of reading — the method in which words are taught instead of letters. Franklin T. Baker, in writing of the letter and syllable method, said that for centuries it had been the practice to teach children by beginning with the names of the letters of the alphabet and then combining these names into words, the child having to reach by inference the right sound of the letter in its place in the word. Commenting on this system, Baker remarked that it is strange "that teachers should so long have overlooked the obvious source of difficulty, failing to see that the child at first tends to make that combination of sounds which he actually hears."[4]

---

[4] Carpenter, Baker, Scott, *The Teaching of English* (New York: Longmans, 1921), pp. 98–99.

A fairly successful class of early-nineteenth-century primers were those having localized names. Among them, besides those bearing the names of Boston and New York, already touched upon, were others using the names of Albany, Philadelphia, Massachusetts, New Jersey, and Pittsburgh. The first edition of the *New York Primer* appeared before the Revolution, but no copy of the first issue is known to exist. Other printings of this brief text were put out in 1811, and editions appeared until about 1823. The bibliographical record of the *New York Primer*, like that of the *Protestant Tutor* and the *New England Primer* at the time of the latter's first issues, is clouded. It is possible that certain editions advertised to be published were never printed. This was the case with a number of texts, especially primers, at the time the *New York Primer* began its career.

The *Albany Primer* was issued at Albany, New York, in 1823. It was not widely used in schools, perhaps due to the fact that so many other new primers were appearing at the time it was first brought out. This was an era of ups and downs in school-book production, and any trifling factor might decide the fate of a primer. The *Albany Primer*, like a number of the contemporary school publications, was generally poorly printed on inferior paper. This might have been the chief cause of its failure to enjoy more than a comparatively brief period of usage.

The *Boston Primer* met with as much acceptance as any of the "local name" primers. First issued in 1808 as an "improvement of the *New England Primer*," it followed closely the pattern of its forebears. It went through a dozen editions within ten years. It was of a strongly religious character; in fact some of the lessons were as admonitory as the *New England Primer* had been during its most puritanical days. A lesson with a wood engraving above it read: "All good boys and girls say their prayers every night and morning, and ask their parents blessing, for which God Almighty loves and blesses them." Below this, following a printed border line, was the "Good children must" verse met with in so many of the early primers. The success of the *Boston Primer* might have been due in part to the fact that the city of Boston was considered as an intellectual center of the country and the use of its name thus an asset to the primer.

First published in 1809, *The Evangelical Primer* was one of the last of the almost wholly religious ones. This text went through many printings for twenty years. Here again perhaps the name was in its favor. Copies showing printings dates of practically every year during the second and third decades of the century are in existence. This primer carried in its own pages recommendations by Noah Webster, by Jedidiah Morse, the geography compiler, and by the president of Yale College.

A number of early-nineteenth-century primers bore the names of noted persons in their titles, two or three of them achieving considerable circulation. At the top of this class stands the *Franklin Primer,* first published in 1802. Editions of this text were printed almost every year until 1831. Most of the *Franklin Primers* were put out in a larger size than other primers, and this may have had something to do with the book's wide acceptance. Even so minor a thing as a slightly enlarged page possibly had an influence on the popularity of a primer during the first half of the nineteenth century. Anything new in the structure or the format that would improve the appearance of these small texts might have been a factor in their popularity. The *Franklin Primer,* in the beginning, was clearly an offspring of the *New England Primer,* following the latter's pattern to a considerable extent.

The *Franklin Primer* was written by Samuel Willard, who was born in Massachusetts during the first year of the Revolution. The book contained alphabets, verses, a brief history of

the world, lessons from scripture, hymns, the oft-used catechism
of Dr. Watt, and that of the Assembly of Divines. In content, it
was much like the larger New England primers, and its subject
matter of sufficient coverage to make it a school collection text.
An illustration of a Benjamin Franklin bust was used in an early
edition as a frontispiece, and the great Philadelphian was cited
as "a man whose manner of life from his youth up, is worthy
the most minute observation, and imitation of the rising generation." This was the edition published by J. N. Dunham, in
Boston in 1802. In a later edition published by B. True and
J. M. Dunham in Boston in 1806, the legend under the Franklin bust read : "A man whose manner of life, from youth's first
dawning morn to man's meridian day, is worthy the imitation
of all who wish to thrive upon the World's vast theatre." The
Franklin Family Primer of 1807 contained an epitaph of
Benjamin Franklin following the title page. This edition had a
number of bible-scene illustrations, among them representations
of "Noah's Ark," "Moses in the Bullrushes," and "Moses
Smiting the Rock." Samuel Willard, the compiler of the *Franklin Primers,* was blind during the last thirty years of his life.
During that period his texts were not widely used, possibly
because of his inability to push them.

The *Child's Primer,* the first issue of which was published
in Philadelphia in 1800 ("Printed for W. Jones, Stationer"),
deserves special notice because it was the first primer that carried
a large proportion of material of interest to children. It was the
earliest to carry well-known nursery rhymes — verses that were
to become known everywhere and universally beloved by children. The *Child's Primer* was one of the first to go a long way
toward eliminating gloomy material from schoolbooks. For
that reason, this little text has a niche all its own among American schoolbooks. Nothing is known today of the compiler of the
Child's Primer aside from the fact that he was a "bookseller and

stationer" in Philadelphia. At one time a William Jones of that city was a partner of David Saur (or Sower), a descendant of Christopher; but it is not certain that he was the same man that compiled the *Child's Primer*. A number of primers were issued later by different publishers in various places under the title *Child's Primer*, but none approached the 1800 Philadelphia issue in interest.

It is hard to understand why compilers of early primers so long neglected the nursery rhymes, popular stories, and other such materials that appeal to children, and prose that first found a place in the early Philadelphia *Child's Primer*. Perhaps it was because this form of literature was not considered of any significant value. It was not until 1842 that James Orchard Halliwell, then a youth of twenty-two, published *The Nursery Rhymes of England,* which first called attention to and emphasized the usefulness of such material. A good treatment of the gradual growth of interest in nursery rhymes and stories is to be found in Iona and Peter Opie's collection.[5] What the Opie's say is especially enlightening in any study of early schoolbooks.

For a time during the first half of the nineteenth century, through the efforts of Samuel Goodrich, the "Peter Parley" books were coming out like the products of our present day assembly lines. The *Peter Parley Primer* was issued during that era, and went through numerous printings. It deserved its success because of its excellent format most of all. The book was printed in good type, and had a nice page arrangement and all-round attractive appearance — an outstanding format for its day. This primer was much longer than most others, running to ninety-six pages in some editions.

The *Peter Parley Primer* probably exerted more than a little influence toward improving contemporary primers, and other

---

[5] Iona and Peter Opie, *Oxford Dictionary of Nursery Rhymes* (London: Oxford University Press, 1952).

schoolbooks, as well. There seems little doubt that Goodrich, through his numerous children's books, was a factor in bringing about a change for the better in the appearances of school texts, even though it is not certain that he effected any improvement in their subject matter.

IV

Special Primers

A NUMBER OF out-of-the-ordinary primers were published from time to time which stood slightly apart from regular class-texts but which were so used. Many of the A-B-C books printed during the last half of the eighteenth and first half of the nineteenth century were basically primers, containing subject matter common to the general run of these texts. To cite an example, the *Picture Alphabet,* printed at Concord, New Hampshire, in 1834, with the sub-title *Easy Road to Learning for Good Boys and Girls,* was a book of this sort. Another was *The Pretty Alphabet,* published in Boston a little later. Still another, *The Instructive Alphabet,* printed in New York in 1814, had a temperance slant. Under an illustration of a jug filled with "ardent spirits," it was stated that "this article . . . slays even more than the sword."[1] *Tom Thumb's Picture Alphabet,* a Boston publication, was a text on the order of the rhyme alphabets in the *New England Primer.*

Some of these little books were extremely plain and simply printed publications, but a few had attributes which were ex-

---

[1] The temperance movement started about this time, in an era when Boston had a licensed saloon for every twenty-one males over the age of sixteen. For information on the beginning of this movement see Chard Smith, *Yankees and God* (New York: Heritage, 1954), pp. 327–328.

ceptional and of much interest. In this class belongs the *A-B-C with the Church of England Catechism,* printed in 1785 by Young, Stewart and McCulloch in Philadelphia. The book is peculiar in having blank spaces where the word "king" was to have appeared in the text, and contained the explanation that "that form of expression does not suit our Republican Government," and that "the teacher will be pleased to fill up the blanks with what words he may deem expedient." At the time of the printing, 1785, the final treaty giving the United States independence was only in its second year, and perhaps many of the population were not certain which title in the end—king or president—would be appropriate.

The Young Child's A-B-C or First Book, the initial volume issued by Samuel Wood, the New York printer of children's books, was of the combination school-study and home-amusement type, as many of his publications were.[2] This first Samuel Wood A-B-C has the distinction of being not only the first volume issued by a noted publishing house but also one of the earliest books carrying woodcuts by Alexander Anderson, the first American to produce engravings of excellent quality and often referred to as the father of American engraving. Born at Beekman Slip, near New York City, in 1775, he did copper engraving when a boy, turning to wood engraving later. His work ranked with the best engravings appearing in early American schoolbooks.

An A-B-C book published by Kimler and Conrad in Philadelphia was somewhat unique. It had twelve lessons, with

---

[2] Samuel Wood began printing children's books in 1804 and continued this sort of publication throughout his life. When he took his sons into the business, the firm became known as Samuel Wood and Sons. Still later, when the founder passed away, it became William Wood and Company. The latter firm specialized in scientific books, chiefly medical, and has survived to our own day through a consolidation.

a woodcut on each page. An alphabet and syllabary were included, and at the end, as if placed there on impulse, was the kind of religious indoctrination so often found in early schoolbooks, in the lines :

All of us my son are to die
If we do no ill we go to joy.
The eye of God sees us
All the day.

With no break in continuity these lines were followed by a commercial advertisement of Kimler and Conrad's *Universal Primer*, no record of which the present writer has been able to find elsewhere.

Until after colonial times any A-B-C book used in school work was to all intents and purposes a primer. Scarcely anything in their make-up differentiated them from primers. There was a time, however, in England when the primer and the A-B-C book must have been considered as entirely different. During the reign of Henry VIII, when the monarch was at odds with the Catholic Church, he had "primers" issued that were to be "used to the exclusion of others in England" and "set forth by the King's Majesty and his clergy to be taught, learned and read, and none other to be used throughout all his dominions." Separate A-B-C books were used in connection with these primers. That this distinction between the A-B-C books and the primers persisted in England to a certain extent into the Elizabethan period, is suggested by mention found here and there in annals of the Elizabethan era. In an Alderham, England, town statute of 1595 having to do with schools, ushers were bidden to "train up young beginners in A. B. C., Primer, Catechism and other English bookes."[3]

---

[3] Stowe, *English Grammar Schools* (New York: Columbia University Press, 1908), pp. 109–110. Considerable information on the primer of this era is to be found in "The Curriculum and Text-Books of English

There is no indication that the A-B-C books and primers were thought of as different texts at any time in America, or that they were used as first and second books, as they may have been in England. If this practice was followed in any isolated cases it was doubtless the result of individual schoolmasters' personal ideas.

A number of A-B-C educational texts were printed in German from the time of Christopher Sower until about the middle of the nineteenth century. These German-language publications belong in the special primer category. The German element in the American population during colonial times and for a century after the Revolution had, as a number of historians have attested, an influence on the history of our country, and some of the products of the colonial German-American presses in Pennsylvania stand out. This particularly applies to a few of the items from the Sower press.

Publications of this press appeared both under the names of Sower and Saur, the latter German spelling. The differentiation in the spelling does not seem to mark a date in the policy of the press. As early as 1756 some books appeared with the Sower spelling, and as late as 1770 some used the name Saur. Isaiah Thomas, the well-known historian of early American printing, in *A History of Printing in America,* says that Sower was a distiller, tanner, bookbinder, apothecary, and a manufacturer of ink, clocks, stoves, and machinery — all these besides being a printer and publisher. He came to America in 1724 and opened a printing establishment in Germanstown, Pennsylvania, in 1738. This was not the beginning of printing in that state. William Bradford started the first printing press at Phila-

Schools in the First Half of the Seventeenth Century," by Foster Watson, originally printed in the *Papers of the Bibliographical Society* (Feb. 1, 1902), and later enlarged and printed in book form.

delphia in 1685, but because of trouble with local authorities left for New York late in 1692 or early in 1693. Bradford's offense consisted of printing an address by George Keith, who was employed by the Society of Friends to supervise the schools of the colony. Part of the address offended the authorities, who arrested Keith, Bradford, and two others implicated in the printing, charging them with publishing libelous matter. The trial resulted in a fine for Bradford and release of the others. Directly after this incident Bradford left for New York.

The first book to come from the Sower press is said to have been an *A-B-C and Spelling Book,* issued in 1738. It is not certain whether it was printed in German or in English, or in both, as no copy is known to exist today. Later an A-B-C book was issued by the Sower press in both German and English, and this one has come down to us. To some it may seem noteworthy that as practical a man as Christopher Sower started his printing career with a schoolbook and that he later printed many others. Evidently a liberal-minded man, he also printed playing cards at a time when they were considered by many as instruments of evil.

In 1806 Ambrose Henkel, a Mennonite preacher, and his brother Solomon, a doctor, started a printing establishment at Newmarket, Virginia, a small town not far from Winchester. This was one of the first printing shops set up south of the Mason-Dixon line that endured for any length of time. A number of A-B-C books, printed both in German and in German and English, came from the Newmarket press. The *A-B-C und Bilder Buch,* issued by the Henkels in 1819, was a picture primer of eight pages, containing text matter in German and English. The usual alphabet and syllable lessons were presented. The board covers carried a woodcut, as did practically all the German-print beginners' texts. About half a dozen variations of the Henkel press A-B-C books have come down to our time.

A number of German and German-English A-B-C books were printed in Philadelphia, there being a large German population in that region in the eighteenth and early nineteenth century. *Hoch-Deutsches A-B-C and Namen-Buch* was printed in Philadelphia in 1816, by Conrad Zentler. This book had twenty-four excellent wood engravings, depicting, among other things, a camel, a bear, a dragon, and a spouting whale. In 1822 the *Hoch-Deutsches A-B-C und Namen Buchlein* was printed at Reading, Pennsylvania, and carried a crude woodcut of Martin Luther as a frontispiece. It was bound in the customary German A-B-C–book illustrated boards.

The German schoolbooks out-numbered other non-English texts printed in this country. However, a large number of A-B-C books, formal primers, and other texts in foreign languages besides German were published for use in non-public schools. Such books, in Greek, Italian, Yiddish, and a dozen other languages, were put out during the nineteenth century, and a lesser number have appeared in the present century.

Indian primers stand in a place of their own. A number were printed in a combination of Indian languages and English, and some in Indian tongues alone. Records still exist of a primer in the Massachusetts Indian language, supposedly printed at Cambridge by Samuel Green in 1654, and of a later edition of the same text by Samuel Green and Marmaduke Johnson in 1662; but no copies of the actual primers are known to exist today.[4] If these primers were actually printed they predate all other books of their kind. In the absence of copies of them, however, John Eliot's *Indian Primer,* printed in 1669, must be considered the earliest of its class.

The full title of Eliot's little book is *The Indian Primer, or*

---

[4] Heartman, *Non-New England Primers Prior to 1830* (New York: privately printed, 1935), p. 68.

The Way of Training Up of Indian Youth in the Good Knowledge of God, in the Knowledge of the Scriptures, and in an Ability to Read. This book was printed on the press at Harvard University under the supervision of Samuel Green. Only one copy, now in the library of the University of Edinburgh, has come down to our time. The text was reprinted in 1877, under the editorial supervision of John Small of the University of Edinburgh, and a second edition of the reprint came out three years later.

When Eliot conceived the idea of educating the Indians and converting them to Christianity he studied their dialects with the aid of an Indian boy he had taken into his home to live. Eliot perfected himself in the Indian language sufficiently to preach intelligibly in their tongue. A parallel to the New England divine's work among the Indians in colonial days was that of Alexander Whitaker, in Virginia. Around 1618, Whitaker, a resident of Jamestown, converted some Indians to Christianity and tried to found a college for both whites and Indians at Henricus. The college was well on its way toward establishment when the Indian massacre of 1622 ended the project.[5]

An Indian primer written by Col. Daniel Claus, a colonial Indian agent, was printed in Montreal in 1781, followed by an edition printed in London in 1786. This book was intended for use among the Indians in New York state and lower Canada, and bore the title *A Primer for the Use of Mohawk Children.* Its original edition had ninety-seven pages, and it was an all-round schoolbook for beginners. It was perhaps the lengthiest of all the Indians primers and was fairly well gotten up. As

---

[5] Elias Boudinot (part Indian himself), Jedidiah Morse, and a number of others fairly well-known in American history, attempted to establish Indian schools; but their work was done during the latter part of the eighteenth and the early part of the nineteenth century, many years after that of Eliot and Whitaker.

Col. Claus had worked among the Indians for a considerable period, he knew enough about their ways to write a text suitable for their education.

In 1839 the *Nez-Perces First Book* was printed at Clearwater, Idaho, on a mission press temporarily set up there. This slight volume of eight pages had the following on its title page, beneath the title: "Designed for Children and new beginners." The book contained a newly made Nez-Perces alphabet and lists of words suited to teaching Indian children to read the religious texts that were to follow. Before the eight-page text was taken from the printing office the publication was abandoned because of faults in the alphabet as presented. After further study of this western Indian language another alphabet was formulated and a twenty-page book with the same title was printed.[6]

The twenty-page edition of the *Nez-Perces First Book* was long considered to be the first book printed in United States territory west of the Rocky Mountains, but the eight-page issue of the same text was actually the earliest one.[7] The account of its migrations over land and sea of the Clearwater Press is almost incredible.

For nearly a hundred years the eight-page issue of the *Nez-Perces First Book* was unknown. Finally some of its pages were found pasted to the covers of the later twenty-page edition,

---

[6] Something akin to this is reported to have happened in Utah, where the mormons devised a "desert" alphabet in the early days of Salt Lake City, and a primer was printed, or at least planned, in this alphabet. H. H. Bancroft, *History of Utah* (San Francisco: The History Company, 1891), p. 714. No copy of the primer is known to exist today.

[7] An account of the printing of the *Nez-Perces First Book* is related in *Quarterly of the Oregon Historical Society,* March, 1922. A story of the press itself is to be found in Hubert Howe Bancroft, *Literary Industries* (New York: Harpers, 1891), p. 299.

where they had been placed to stiffen the cover. Wilberforce Eames, the well-known bibliographer of the New York Public Library, discovered the four outer pages of the primer in 1914 when the cover of the later edition was steamed apart. Pages five and six were found elsewhere afterward, but pages three and four have not yet been located.

Other such discoveries, equally unusual, have been made. In 1693 or a year later William Bradford printed a *Catechism for Children and Adults,* which was advertised in his almanac for 1694. No copy of this catechism is known to have survived, but fragments of it, indicating that it was primarily a primer, were found in the binding of a copy of Leed's *Temple of Wisdom,* printed by Bradford in Philadelphia and bound later in New York, as evidence in the binding indicates. This discovery was made by R. Hildebrun.[8]

While California was still under Mexican rule a printing press was set up in that territory by Don Augustin Vicente Zamorano, a Catholic monk. A sixteen-page pamphlet entitled *Reglemento Provisional* (Rules and Regulations of the Province) was printed by Zamorano. This publication bears the date of 1834 and shows the place of printing as Monterey, and it is considered by some as the first educational text printed on the American Pacific Coast. However, Kate Sanborn stated that Don Antonio Coronel, whom she designated "the last specimen of the grand old Spanish regime," had in his possession the first schoolbook printed in California, and she gave the date of the volume as 1835. She spoke of it as "a small catechism."[9] Herbert Fahey says Zamorano in 1836 printed two small schoolbooks, one being a *Catechism No de Artoolegia,* or *Manual of Punctuation,*

---

[8] Wilberforce Eames, *First Years of Printing in New York* (New York: New York Public Library, 1928), p. 25.

[9] Kate Sanborn, *A Truthful Woman in Southern California* (New York: Appleton, 1900), p. 60.

and the other *Tables for Children Who Are Learning to Compute*.[10] It may be that the first of these was the book which Kate Sanborn told about, but the whereabouts of any copy dated 1835, does not seem to be at present known.[11]

In 1834, while New Mexico was still a part of Mexico, a schoolbook was printed at Santa Fe under the title *Cuaderno de Ortografa*. It was a small text, with rules for use of the alphabet, punctuation, and other beginners' lessons—in substance, a primer. The book is believed to have been compiled by Antonio José Martinez, a catholic priest who at one time conducted a school at Taos. Oswald in his valuable treatise on printing tells of Father Martinez's book and of the early printing in New Mexico, when it was still Mexican domain,[12] but of course information on such a press must necessarily be very scanty.

A number of Indian primers besides those already mentioned were compiled and printed in various sections of the country for use among Indian children and in their schools. Late in the nineteenth century, however, where Indian children were taught at all they used regular school texts—books not especially designed for the use of Indians.

Until the present generation many of the Indians energetically resisted the idea of school learning, believing that teaching among their own people of their ancient ways was more desirable. In an article in the *Atlantic Monthly* of July, 1925, "Soldiers, Indians and Schools," by Leo Crane, an Indian agent in the West, it is told how until recently parents hid their children to prevent them from being sent to schools. Crane's

---

[10] Herbert Fahey, *Early Printing in California* (San Francisco: Book Club of California, 1956), p. 24.

[11] G. L. Harding, *Don Augustin Zamorano* (Los Angeles: Zamorano Club, 1934), contains much data on the early California printers.

[12] Oswald, *Printing in the Americas* (New York: Gregg, 1937), p. 415.

article is enlightening in its account of the extremes gone to by the Indians to prevent their "wary, watching children" from being given the traditional American schooling, considering that it ran contrary to their traditions. The noted Kiowa Indian chief, Santanta, who because of his eloquence was given the title "Orator of the Plains," in an address at a peace conference in the Kansas Territory, in 1867, said:

> I love the land and the buffalo . . . . I dont want any of the medicine lodges [schools and churches] within the country. I want the children raised as I was . . . . I have heard that you intend to settle us on a reservation near the mountains. I don't want to settle. I love to roam over the prairies. There I am free and happy, but when we settle down we grow pale and die . . . . A long time ago this land belonged to our fathers; but when I go up to the river I see camps of soldiers on its banks. These soldiers cut down my timber; they kill my buffalo; and when I see that my heart feels like busting.[13]

The primers issued in the South during the period of the Confederacy not only stand in a category of their own, as primers, but comprise a series of books with characteristics all their own, otherwise. These publications, along with other Southern schoolbooks, in text material and makeup, naturally could not have derived from any other period of our history. The primers were issued in a considerable number considering the short span of time in which they appeared and the circumstances which brought them into being. While some of the editions were small, a number ran up to several thousands. Those in charge of schools and education in the Confederacy particularly desired that the children of the region should not have to utilize texts printed in the North or those that had even a Northern textual ancestry or authorship.

---

[13] *Hermann Stieffel, Soldier Artist of the West,* U. S. National Museum Bulletin 225, No. 12, 1960, p. 13.

A few primers had been issued in the South prior to the war, but with the beginning of hostilities between the states a marked increase took place in their production. During 1861 three or four newly compiled primers appeared with Confederate imprints, and in 1862 about the same number were issued. During the third year, 1863, more than half a dozen additional primer texts appeared, and in 1864 there was a still greater number. Because of the unsettled condition during the first part of 1865, the months before the Confederate surrender, printing in the South tapered off and production of schoolbooks almost ceased. By this time there was scarcely any paper to be had.

In the fall of 1861 the *Confederate Primer,* by Richard M. Smith, professor of language and natural science in Randolph-Macon College,[14] was published in Nashville, Tennessee, by the Association of Southern Teachers. This primer was one of the popular ones and met with enough favor to go through four printings during the war period. The first edition, a moderate-sized booklet, was printed in Richmond. This Richmond issue had illustrations, but some of them evidently were from plates that had been used for other purposes and were hardly appropriate for a schoolbook. Their use must have been a "broom stick wedding" kind of event. Such illustrations were frequently used in early school publications. The 1845 Wheeling *New England Primer,* already mentioned, had a picture of a stallion on the front cover, a cut previously used in the *Wheeling Gazette,* advertising "the full blooded Stallion, Surprise," for stud service. In many of the little printing establishments of the day a chance to utilize any available piece of the somewhat meager material was hardly to be neglected.

The Southern Primer or Child's First Lessons in Spelling and

---

[14] Randolph-Macon of Ashland, Virginia, founded in 1830—not the better-known present-day Randolph-Macon Women's College of Lynchburgh, which was not started until 1893.

Reading, published in Charleston, South Carolina, in 1841, and Richmond, Virginia, in 1860, was the most "southern" of all primers issued prior to the war. The Richmond issue at the start of hostilities was a ready-to-hand Confederate text. On its front cover were small-size cuts representing six southern states, showing within a circle outlined by these a cotton field "along the Mississippi." Editions of several thousand copies of *The Southern Pictorial Primer* were issued during the period of strife, and these were lineal descendants of the pre-war *Southern Primer.* The text of *The Pictorial Primer* was well assembled and its quaint illustrations fitted in well.

Early in the Civil War the *Primer* (no other words in the title) of Mrs. Adelaide Dev. Chaudron was issued in Mobile, Alabama. Mrs. Chaudron's readers reached three thousand copies and her spellingbook, according to advertisements, went into its fortieth thousand in 1865. There is no information available as to how many copies of the Chaudron primer were printed, but it was a well-put-up text and must have easily met any competition, if such a thing existed in the South at that period. Mrs. Chaudron, a native of Mobile, wrote a considerable amount and translated from the German some of the historical romances of Clara Mundt, better known by her pen name, Luise Muhlbach.

A text, adapted from a primer previously issued in England, *Our Own Primer,* by Richard Sterling and J. D. Campbell, was the introductory number of a series of *Our Own Readers,* and *Our Own School Arithmetic.*[15] The primer was printed in

---

[15]A copy of *Our Own School Arithmetic* is on permanent display in the Confederate Museum in Richmond, along with hundreds of relics of Lee, Jackson, and others of the South. By the side of the arithmetic is a copy of *A System of Modern Geography,* "adapted to the present condition of the World, for the use of schools and children in the Confederate States of America."

Greensboro, North Carolina, by Sterling, Campbell and Albright, first in 1862; but some of the copies of this primer and some of the readers of the series were printed in Edinburgh, Scotland. It is difficult to determine at present where some of these books first saw the light of day — in Edinburgh or in North Carolina.

The Confederate primers, aside from the regional touches, were in a general way similar in text outline to those of the North. They were, however, nearly always in a less substantial format, most of them being in pamphlet form, and almost none of them had board backs. A number were bound in wallpaper. The covers of those so bound were more rigid than the ordinary paper covers, but neither could withstand much wear and tear or bear more than very moderate handling. Most wallpaper becomes brittle as it ages, and that of the Civil War period was no exception to this rule. Practically all the fragile wallpaper-covered primers that have come down to our day have been preserved through special care, in collections where they have been subjected to but little handling. Some of the wallpaper-bound primers had the design on the outside of two pasted-together sheets, while others had the design pasted inward, thus making it necessary to hold the backs of the books to a light in order to discern the wallpaper pattern.

V

Beginning of Readers

E. VON RACHOW, a German, in 1776 published two books, one of which marked an epoch in a particular class of school texts. The first, a volume of "Moral Tales," was something of a primer, a book that enjoyed a long popularity. The second, *Der Kinderfreund,* or in English *The Child's Friend,* was the first school reader in the sense in which we use the term today. It is true that books from which children learned to read were used as far back as the middle ages, but they were publications considered from long usage to be adapted to such ends, and were not specifically designed textbooks. Examples were the *Distichia Catonis,* the *Liber Proverbrum,* the *Proverbia Wiponis,* the *Aesopus Moralistatus (Aesop's Fables),* and other volumes containing literature which appealed to children.[1]

The Child's Friend went through numerous editions over a period of about one hundred years—a long life for any school text. In Germany it met the approval of both Catholics and Protestants—something in itself unusual for a schoolbook of the era. Von Rachow apparently had certain gifts and traits of

---

[1] Paul Abelson, *The Seven Liberal Arts, A Study in Mediæval Culture* (New York: Columbia University Press, 1910), pp. 16–17. Also Edith Rickert, *Chaucer's World* (New York: Columbia University Press, 1948), pp. 123–125.

mind that most of those concerned with education and with
schoolbooks in his time did not possess. Herman Suderman, the
noted German playwright and novelist, related an interesting
little incident that has to do with *The Child's Friend.*[1] He told
of his mother's promising him a *Child's Friend* during his early
school days if he worked hard and tried to read. He did not
know what "a child's friend" was, but having earned it, and
loving books, he was, according to his own words, entranced
with the volume, and read and reread it with continuous delight;
which bespeaks the fact that von Rachow's book was not an
ordinary one.

The first American school reader, a text along the lines of
Der Kinderfreund, was Noah Webster's *Grammatical Institute
of the English Language, Part 3,* issued in 1785. Although the
word "reader" was not in the title of the first edition, the book
was specifically a reader, a manual intended basically as a text
from which to learn to read. With the third edition the title was
changed to *An American Selection of Lessons in Reading and
Speaking . . . . Being the Third Part of a Grammatical Institute.*
Because of this book the honor of producing in this country
the first of the vast number of school readers belongs to Webster.
Horace Scudder said that Webster "had a singular faculty of
being the first in time in many departments of literary industry,"
adding that he had a way of anticipating other people.[3] The
Grammatical Institute, Part Three, was not published until
eight years after *The Child's Friend,* and there is no hint that
Webster followed von Rachow's text. There is but little chance
that Webster ever saw a copy of Rachow's books, which were
in German, before publishing the *Grammatical Institute, Part
Three.*

---

[2] Suderman, *Book of My Youth* (London: John Lane, 1923), p. 6.

[3] Horace Scudder, *Noah Webster* (Boston: Houghton Mifflin, 1882),
p. 68.

Webster wrote his first book, the spelling text, while teaching at Sharon, Connecticut, and near-by Goshen, New York, in 1781 and 1782. He took his manuscript to a former schoolmaster of his, Ezra Stiles, then president of Yale College, for an opinion on the work. Stiles urged Webster to name this, and two other proposed texts, *The Grammatical Institute, Parts 1, 2 and 3,* feeling, perhaps, that such titles would increase the prestige and sale of the volumes. This accounts for the extraordinary and, to present-day ears, freakish titles of these early texts. Webster's youth at the time perhaps accounts for his acceptance of such a suggestion, coming as it did from a man of much influence.[4] It is not at all likely that the title *Grammatical Institute* for an American school text in any way increased its usage. As Clifton Johnson has pointed out, the unusual title of Webster's early texts "furnished vulnerable points of attack," and critics referred to the compiler in derision as Mr. Grammatical Institute and Mr. Institutional Genius.[5]

The Grammatical Institute, Part Three by the standards of the day was not a small text, and Webster had room to present numerous rules of reading. In line with the compiler's argument that American schoolbooks ought to be more American, he included a certain amount of native material. The volume contained some geographical information and a few items concerned with United States history, among the latter being Freneau's "Our General Washington,"[6] Warren's "Oration On The Boston Massacre," Hancock's speech on the same event, and Washington's "Farewell to the Army."

---

[4] In 1763 John Ash's *Grammatical Institutus, An Easy Introduction To Lowth's English Grammar,* was published in England, and later reissued. It was reprinted in New York in 1799.

[5] Clifton Johnson, *Old-time Schools and School-books* (New York: Macmillan, 1904), p. 171.

[6] Philip Freneau, early poet and one-time school teacher, was one of the originators of the George Washington legend.

Webster explained in the first part of his book that "clear and distinct" articulation was necessary in reading, and that the pupil should notice "the stops and make no pause where the sense required none."; he also observed that it was necessary to "pay the strictest attention to accent, emphasis and cadence," and urged that "the sentiment you express be accompanied with proper tones, looks and gestures." He went on to say that "a good articulation consists in giving every letter and syllable proper pronunciation of sounds," and that "every word ought to be read as if the sentiments were the reader's own." In another section, concerning the elocutionary phase of reading, he wrote : "If a person is rehearsing the words of an angry man, he should assume the same furious looks; his eyes should flash with rage, his gestures should be violent, the tone of his voice threatening. If kindness is to be expressed the countenance should be calm and placid, and wear a smile, the tone should be mild, and the motion of the hand inviting." In another place he wrote that "fear opens the eyes and mouth, shortens the nose, draws down the eyebrows, and gives the countenance a wildness" and that "boasting is loud and blustering."

Webster's initial reader, the *Grammatical Institute, Part Three,* and the revised reading book which followed did not take hold. With this evidence of a lack of public interest he gave up for a time further efforts to produce readers, putting his labor instead into revisions of his spelling book, the first text he had issued, and in other pursuits with which he was always busy. Webster is often thought of as a man almost wholly engaged in things philological, but such is not the case. While his schoolbooks and dictionary were in the making he served in the Connecticut House of Representatives, was a county judge, organized a newspaper, ran a magazine, and delivered numerous lectures. The scope of his mental activities is revealed by even a brief bibliography of his published works.

When Noah Webster in 1784, then a young practicing lawyer, married the daughter of William Greenleaf of Boston,
Webster's friend John Trumbull wrote from New Haven to his
acquaintance Oliver Wolcott, then in New York :

> Webster has returned and brought him a pretty wife. I
> wish him success; but I doubt, in the present decay of
> business in our profession [law], whether his profits will
> enable him to keep up the style he sets out with. I fear he
> will breakfast on Institutes, dine upon dissertation, and go to
> bed supperless.[']

Webster nevertheless got along very well and ate regularly.

Contemporary with the reading texts of Webster were those
of Caleb Bingham, the Boston schoolmaster. His books in most
cases had a strong following. Bingham was Webster's strongest
competitor in both grammar and reader sales until the coming
of Lyman Cobb. Bingham's *Child's Companion, Columbian
Orator,* and *American Preceptor* were all readers, though the
first of these was designated a spelling book and the *Columbian
Orator* was sometimes called an elocution text. (Bingham was
professionally an elocutionist.) The *Child's Companion* was
most certainly as much a reader as was Webster's *Grammatical
Institute, Part Three,* notwithstanding the fact that it was
specifically intended for and advertised as a spelling book.

The *Columbian Orator,* first printed in 1797, contained lessons on a variety of subjects, some of which were longer than
those in most earlier schoolbooks. Addison, Jefferson, Franklin,
and others well known, were represented. There is no suggestion
that there was any designed plan or "system" in presenting the
subject matter. A selection from some well-known author might

---

['] William G. Webster, "Memoir of Dr. Webster," *Explanatory and
Pronouncing Dictionary of the English Language* (New York: Mason
Brothers, 1858), p. ix.

be followed by a lesson of an entirely different character, and
some of the material was even frivolous.

American Preceptor, issued in 1794 was the most popular of
Bingham's texts. It went through sixty-eight editions, selling
around 640,000 copies. The final edition had over two hundred
pages and was well arranged. The selections in this volume were
well adapted for the technical exercises in reading and, differing
from Bingham's previous books, the literary merit of the material
was high.

It is apparent that Caleb Bingham stood apart from other
early schoolbook compilers, being a man of uncommon talents.
Active in many public affairs, he was called upon to aid in a
number of community projects, including the founding of the
Boston Public Library,[8] to which he gave a part portion of his
book collection, which was probably extensive, since he was a
booklover and for a long period had been the proprietor of a
bookshop. He also mixed in politics, running for public office on
a number of occasions, usually without success due to the fact
that his Jeffersonian political party was not dominant in New
England. Bingham was well versed in literature, foreign as well
as American. He made a number of translations from the
French, the best-known being his rendering of Chateaubriand's
Atala into English, first printed in Boston in 1802. In 1930 the
Stanford University Press reprinted Bingham's translation of
Atala, the first volume of a series designated "The Stanford
Miscellany."

Lindley Murray's *English Reader* was published in 1799, a
Sequel to the English Reader in 1801, and the *Introduction to
the English Reader* in 1805. The *English Reader* eventually

---

[8] This library was a forerunner of the present Boston Public Library,
which was founded in 1852 through the generosity of Joshua Bates, a
Boston banker.

became the most popular reading text of its day and remained so throughout most of the first half of the nineteenth century, until about the time the McGuffey texts appeared. It was some time before Murray's readers took the lead over those of Bingham, but finally completely outstripped the latter. Murray's texts on the whole were superior to Bingham's, and this fact, coupled with their superiority over other competitive texts, lent extraordinary prestige to Murray's books.

By the time all three of Murray's reading texts, which followed his grammar, had appeared, the reader as a school manual had become fixed in form. Throughout the nineteenth century there were not to be many further technical changes in the general structure of the school reader. Some minor differences in quality of material selected, in the manner of presentation, in points of elocution, were common; but, all in all, readers during the first half of the century became fixed in over-all structural form. To be successful, readers had to fall more or less within commonly accepted lines.

Among the prose selections of Murray's *English Reader* were writings from Hume, Addison, Goldsmith, Samuel Johnson, and Hugh Blair. The lessons from Blair, more numerous than from all the others mentioned, taken together, were from his sermons and miscellaneous writings. Five volumes of Blair's sermons were published—four during his lifetime and one after his death. These books were widely read both by the lay public and by clergymen, who also sought profit from them; and most of the early reader compilers apparently thought it was to their interest to include material from Blair's writings, or to quote him in connection with questions that had to do with reading points. Murray used three selections from Samuel Johnson's *Rasseles,* but no mention was made to indicate from what work they were taken. The material from Samuel Johnson displayed a story element, but the Blair Selections, on such topics as

Patience, Impartiality, The Misfortunes of Man, Rank and Riches, were in the nature of sermons and were sometimes polemical.

The poems were selected mostly from the works of poets whose names are but little known today. There were selections from Thomson, Pope, Cowper, and a few other well-known poets, but none from Shakespeare, John Donne, and many others of the greatest writers of English verse. Murray selected poetry more for its religious message than for its lyrical beauty.

Murray's *Sequel to the English Reader* possessed certain superiorities over the earlier *English Reader*. The second edition, the one most used, had almost four hundred pages—a large schoolbook for its day. The prose selections were longer in the *Sequel,* and were chosen from a greater number of authors. Hugh Blair was not so strongly represented and Samuel Johnson was more so. Murray seemed to have a penchant for stilted Latinized prose, such as that of Johnson and his followers, and this type of writing had a noticeable place in the *Sequel.* More space was given to verse than in the *English Reader,* but the poetry was still about as superficial in quality.

The last pages of the *Sequel* were given over to an appendix consisting of Biographical Sketches, covering the authors represented in the *Introduction to the English Reader,* the *English Reader,* and the *Sequel to the English Reader,* "with occasional strictures on their writings." In a few instances these sketches were in none too clear a form, but they constituted an innovation in a school reader and must have proved educational to the students. Of fifty such biographical sketches, forty-five were on the lives of British writers. Two were on Frenchmen, two on ancients, and one on an American, Benjamin Franklin—but none of the latter's writings were included in the *Sequel.*

Murray's readers for a time were as popular in England as in the United States. The texts were compiled from an English as much as from an American viewpoint, since Murray was a resident of England at the time he was compiling the books. He was born at Swatara, Pennsylvania, on April 12, 1745, coming of a well-to-do family of the early-American merchant class. The family moved from Pennsylvania to New York City. They owned a large tract of land in what was then the upper part of New York City and which later became known as the Murray Hill section, as it is still designated. Lindley seems to have been of an adventurous nature when a boy, and he wanted to become a sailor. The family overruled this ambition and prevailed upon the boy to study law. He practiced this profession in New York until 1783, and during this time started writing, his first book being *Power of Religion on the Mind,* a volume that still is met with occasionally in antiquarian bookstores, but rarely elsewhere. Some years elapsed before he turned his attention to school texts. Going to England in 1784, he spent the rest of his life there, engaged in writing and marketing his schoolbooks. For some reason, Murray was long thought to be a native Englishman and has often been so referred to by writers.[9] No biography of Murray was included in Barnard's *Educational Biography* issued in 1859, which covered every other well-known American schoolbook writer up to that time. It seems likely that Barnard, as many others did, thought Murray was an Englishman. Clifton Johnson wrote of Murray as an "English compiler,"[10] and as good a historian as Paul Monroe spoke of him as "English born."[11] Other writers have referred to Murray as an "English quaker."

---

[9] Early in the nineteenth century a rumor persisted that Washington Irving had been born in England. See Williams, *Life of Washington Irving* (New York: Oxford Press, 1935), I, 379.

[10] Johnson, *Old Time Schools and School-Books* (New York: Macmillan, 1904), p. 287.

[11] Monroe, *Cambridge History of American Literature* (New York: Macmillan, 1933), III, 401.

With regard to American school readers, Murray has stood second only to William Holmes McGuffey in popular esteem. Perhaps he merits acclaim equal to McGuffey's, for Murray was one of the pioneers and McGuffey was not. Murray has a singular place in the history of the creation of specialized reading texts, whereas McGuffey built his reputation on the foundation which Murray and contemporaries working along the same line built from the ground up.

VI

Following the Initial Readers

FOR A TIME AFTER their appearance the Caleb Bingham and Lindley Murray texts did not have a great deal of competition from other readers. Later, however, a considerable number of such texts by various people appeared in different sections of the country—in some cases in quarters in which one would hardly have expected them. School teachers, previously unknown except locally, compiled reading manuals; ministers and others with spare time turned to this work, and thus a number of readers came into existence. Most of the books were issued under the compilers' names, but a few were anonymous.

Samuel Wood, in the second decade of the nineteenth century, issued the *New York Readers,* consisting of the numbers one, two and three. The compiler's name did not appear, but the name of Samuel Wood as publisher assured a friendly reception. Like most of the other Wood publications, the *New York Readers* were all better printed than the general run of schoolbooks of the time. They were intended originally, it was announced, for local use, but they came to be used fairly widely elsewhere. Inscriptions in existing copies show that they were used in Virginia and in other places as far south as Georgia. It is known that tutors in well-to-do families in the South used the *New York Readers* in their teaching.

Only a few lessons in the *New York Readers* directly indicated that they were planned primarily for sale in New York City and its vicinity. The one lesson in the number two book, for instance, geographically slanted, was about the Niagara River and Falls, and another selection was from the *Long Island Star,* a local newspaper on which Walt Whitman worked; but this latter was not an example of descriptive writing. The lesson formula in the Wood readers was quite like that in the Murray texts, and it appears likely that the compiler or compilers imitated the Murray pattern.

Two lessons in the *New York Reader, Number Two,* were indexed as being "by a girl, aged 16 years," and "by a girl, aged 13 years." Both of these bits were closely akin in style and apparently came from the same hand. The first lines of the lesson "by a girl, age 13 years," read:

> Good nature is a quality so amiable in itself, that all ranks and conditions of men, whether they do really possess it or not; wish to have the world to think they do. A good natured man goes through the vale of tears with more ease than a peevish one; everyone seeks his friendship, and his own placid disposition smooths the rugged path which he meets in life.

The lesson from the *Long Island Star* was on drunkedness, and ran to about five hundred words — lengthy in comparison to all the others in the book. The writer went a long way to tell of the serious evils of drink. About half way through the lesson the author asked a series of questions: Who hath Wo? [sic] Who hath Sorrow? Who hath contentions? Who hath words without cause? Who hath redness of eyes?" The answer was, "The Drunkard."

The three *United States Readers* compiled by William Darby, published by Plaskitt and Cugle of Baltimore in 1829 and 1830, and later revised, were representative texts of their period, and must have compared favorably with any readers of their time, including those of Murray. By 1839 the title page of the *United States Reader Number Three* indicated that it was the fifteenth edition, and the other numbers were reissued approximately the same number of times. A *United States School Primer* was put out by George F. Cooledge and Brother, New York, about 1830, and another *United States Primer,* quite different, in Cooperstown, New York, a few years later; but these latter had no connection with the Darby books.

Darby was primarily a geographer and writer on kindred subjects, and his reader texts contained a good deal of geographical matter — more than any other previous or contemporary readers. Between 1816 and the time of the appearance of the *United States Readers,* Darby turned out a number of works of a geographical nature. Among these were a *Geographical Description of the State of Louisiana, The Emigrants Guide to the Western States and Territories,* and a number of publications with lesser circulation, and it was natural that he carried his geographical interest over into his readers. In the *United States Reader, Number Three,* he included lessons on the White Mountains, and the Natural Bridge of Virginia; and Jefferson's "Description of the Passage of the Potomac at Harpers Ferry" was reprinted. This geographic material seems to have been instrumental in having many other selections of this type appear in other readers, whereas, before, there had been little or no such material. During the next decade or so selections on American geography were a prominent part of many readers. It was an era in which the American people were developing a deep interest in their continental geography.

William Darby was born of Irish parents in Dauphin County, Pennsylvania, on August 14, 1795. At eighteen he was teaching school. He was a self-taught surveyor, and from 1804 to 1809 was a deputy surveyor for the United States Government in Louisiana. Later he was a member of General Andrew Jackson's topographical staff and served during the War of 1812. Darby married a wealthy Louisana widow and remained in the South until his wife died in 1813. He then returned to Pennsylvania, where he lived in the vicinity of Harrisburg for many years.

The readers of John Pierpont, the first of which was the *American First Class Book* appearing in 1823, represented a slight departure from previous texts of their class. The Pierpont readers were compiled, it was stated, with the intention of making them "American" texts — this in a category of books that had all along had too strong a leaning toward England. The readers were in fact an effort to supplant the Murray compilations. In some of Pierpont's prefaces he plainly stated that it was planned that they should displace Murray's readers. On the title page of the *Introduction to the National Reader* was an assertion that the text was "designed to fill the same place in the Common Schools of the United States that is held by Murray's *Introduction,* and the compilations of Gay, Mylius and Pinnoch in those of Great Britain." Evidently Pierpont did not think that there was any need to mention compilers of the United States other than Murray, who at the time dominated the American scene.

In his *American First Class Book,* Murray said he was trying to get away from English influence in his readers; however, the fact remains that much of the material *was* English. At the time, American material was not as plentiful as it is now, but much more good writing could have been included had it been sought for and carefully selected. About a dozen English poets were represented in the *First Class Book* and much more than half of the prose came from outside America. Four or five British magazines were drawn upon — four lessons being from

Blackwoods. At this time *Blackwood's Magazine* was friendly toward the United States, while the *Quarterly Review* and the *European Magazine,* and one or two others, were critical of all America stood for. Pierpont included no material from the unfriendly magazines with the exception of one article from the *Quarterly Review* on a Pacific island.

Seven lessons were chosen from Shakespeare for the *First Class Book,* and from then on most American readers, particularly those intended for advanced pupils, had something from the Immortal Bard. The Pierpont lessons from Shakespeare were from *Julius Caesar, Macbeth, King John,* and *Hamlet.* Naturally the "Address of Antony to His Countrymen" was included, and it became one of the favorite Shakespearian selections in later reading texts. A large part of the American population of the nineteenth century must have gotten their first taste of Shakespeare from the early school readers.

A "Dialog between Bacon and Shakespeare," from *Blackwood's Magazine* made up a lesson in the *First Class Book,* and is of special interest because of the claim, later exploited, that Bacon wrote the Shakespeare plays. The dialog in Pierpont's reader is set in Lord Bacon's study, where Shakespeare had come to see Bacon, at the request of Queen Elizabeth, about a book of sonnets she had penned. A page announces to Bacon, "The Queen has sent unto your lordship Mr. William Shakespeare, the player." Bacon replies: "Indeed .... I have wanted to see that man. Show him in." Some remarks are exchanged on Shakespeare's mission, and then Bacon proposes: "Let us sit down, and discourse a while. The sonnets will catch no harm by our delay, for true poetry, they say, hath a bloom which time cannot blight." Shakespeare returns: "True my Lord. Near to Castalia there bubbles .... a fountain of petryfying water, wherein the muses are wont to dip whatever posies have met the approval of Apollo; so that the slender foliage, which originally sprung forth in the cherishing brain of a true poet, becomes hardened in all its leaves, and glitters as if it were carved out of rubies and emeralds." "Such will be the fortune of your own productions," Bacon replies.

The dialog continues for four pages, and Shakespeare relates something Bacon's chaplain has told him. Bacon interposes: "My chaplain is a worthy man; he has so great a veneration for me, that he wishes to find marvels in the common accidents of my life." Shakespeare retorts: "The same chaplain has told me that a certain arch in Trinity College, Cambridge, would stand until a greater man than your lordship should pass through it." Then Bacon asks: "Did you ever pass through it, Mr. Shakespeare?"

This imaginary dialog appeared in Pierpont's reader in 1823, and it was not until 1857, thirty-four years later, that Delia Bacon, born in the little wilderness village of Tallmadge, Ohio, the daughter of an Indian missionary, started the Shakespeare–Bacon controversy.

Pierpont's *Introduction to the National Reader,* although first issued a year after the *National Reader,* was intended, the compiler said, "as a series of exercises in reading, for the younger classes of our common schools, preparatory to the use of *The National Reader"* — for pupils "who had mastered the reading exercises in his spelling-book." Pierpont stated that he had chosen material that would be "interesting to children," and that would cause the text to be read "both in school and out of school."

In a footnote to the lesson on the "Chase of The Wild Ox in South America," which was taken from Luccock's *Notes on Rio de Janeiro and Southern Brazil,* a book which was never published in this country, Pierpont reproduced what may be the first description in any American book of an object that has had a great deal to do with the history of our country, and which, it may be added, has become the plaything of myriads of American children. It is a description of the lasso as used on the pampas of South America, before it became so widely used on our own western plains, an area that in Pierpont's day was still under the dominance of the Indians and was the feeding ground for vast herds of Buffalo. Luccock's narrative stated :

> The *lasso* is made of narrow thongs, plaited in the same way as the bridles, and is about seven or eight yards long. One end of it is firmly fixed in the hinder part of the saddle, generally on the right side; at the other end is an iron ring, about two inches in diameter. The horseman, about to use the *lasso,* forms a sort of running noose, by passing a portion of it through the ring; this is taken in the right hand, so as the ring may be at the opposite side of the circle; the noose is then swung with care over the head, until the extreme part of it, including the ring, acquires a considerable force. The instrument, thus prepared, as the man advances toward the selected victim, is in due time discharged, carried off the remainder of the string, which before hung loosely in coils on the fingers of the left hand, and seldom fails to entangle the beast.

The compiler of the Pierpont texts was a Unitarian clergyman who, after some disagreement with his Boston congregation, left the pulpit and later became a government employee in Washington. It was during his Boston ministerial period that Pierpont worked up his school texts, and his trouble there was unusual enough to merit attention. While he was pastor of the Hollis Street Church in Boston, pewholders rented the basement of the church to a rum merchant for a warehouse. Pierpont, strong for reform and one of the first anti-liquor crusaders, opposed vigorously the use of part of his church in the distribution of spiritous liquors. (James Russell Lowell wrote that

"There never has been a leader of reform who was not also a blackguard,"[1] but this seems scarcely a fair conclusion.) Certain members of the church resisted Pierpont's actions in the matter and tried to oust him from the pulpit, and, it is recorded, went so far as to defame his character. In the long run, however, the minister won out, got rid of the rum storage, drew his part-due salary, and then resigned.

The noted financier John Pierpont Morgan was the son of the reader compiler's daughter, Judith Pierpont. It is scarcely surprising that such a closely related ancestor of the great J. P. Morgan, who organized the United States Steel Corporation, controlled numerous railroads, and played such a dominant role in the American financial world for many years, should have proved a determined contender against a refractory church congregation.

Lyman Cobb's first reading text was issued in 1830, and others soon followed. They almost at once met with wide popularity. *The Juvenile Reader, Number One,* as originally issued, was substantially a primer, consisting of lessons of no greater difficulty than those in the average primer of the time. The *Juvenile Reader, Number Two* was composed of words of one, two, and three syllables, and was designed "to lead the child by a regular gradation from easy to difficult reading." It was also the intention of the compiler to exhibit in the course of the lessons "all the words of variable or doubtful orthography in the English language" — an astonishingly ambitious program, to say the least. The *Juvenile Reader, Number Three* was made up of words of "one, two and three syllables," with "a greater variety of compositions both in prose and poetry." The fourth text was called *The Sequel Number Four Reader,* and the final one

---

[1] Scudder, *James Russell Lowell: A Biography* (Boston: Houghton Mifflin, 1901), I, 89.

North American Reader, Number Five. The Cobb readers stood apart in being the first truly graduated series of reading texts — the first series of material definitely planned to facilitate continuous progress from the simple to the more difficult.

Lyman Cobb was one of our important early textbook makers of whose youth we know very little. Born in Lenox, Massachusetts, September 15, 1800, he had almost no formal schooling. But he was studious and eventually acquired enough learning to write a dictionary and other fairly important philological works. He wrote a good deal along the lines that Noah Webster followed, and it seems regrettable that the two differed about certain points in each other's work. They would have made a superb team had they worked together, and were sufficiently intelligent to have known the old saying that "snarling curs always have torn ears."

Cobb maintained that *The American Spelling Book* was not compiled by Webster but by Aaron Ely. Cobb's writings, in which he attempted to prove his point, appeared originally in the *Albany Argus* in 1827 and 1828, and his side of all his arguments with Webster were reprinted in a fifty-six page pamphlet in 1831, under the title *Critical Review of the Orthography of Dr. Webster's New Series of Books for Systematic Instruction in the English Language.* Like Noah Webster, Cobb promoted his schoolbooks continuously, and was one of the early believers in advertising. No schoolbooks up to Cobb's time had been so widely advertised as his. It has been said that in pushing his texts he overpraised them, but in this he differed little from most of his competitors.

A number of Cobb's reading texts and his spelling book sold into the thousands, but he nevertheless died a man of meager resources. The exact date of his death seems not to be known for certain, but he passed away in 1864. In such a year, with the Civil War at its height and with the Battle of Gettysburg ended just a few days before, the demise of a bachelor schoolbook author would be apt to attract but little attention.

After Cobb, most compilers designed their texts to assist pupils to progress gradually from the primer level to more difficult reading. By 1840 schools practically everywhere were adopting series of readers, using separate and special texts for certain grades of students only now and then.

The readers of Charles Merriam were among those published at the end of the era of the old non-series texts, and were representative partly of the readers of a day gone-by and partly of the new "graded" ones. In the advertisements, but not on their title pages, they were known as the Springfield Series of Reading Books and were four in number : *The Easy Primer, The Child's Guide, The Intelligent Reader,* and *The Village Reader.* The prefaces to *The Child's Guide* and *The Intelligent Reader* referred to "the compiler" while that to *The Village Reader* referred to "the compilers." However, Charles Merriam is known to have been the creator of all these texts, and any helpers in compiling *The Village Reader* must have been subordinates employed by the Merriam firm, who might have had a limited part in selecting some of the material.

The Village Reader, the final number of the Springfield Series, was issued in 1840. As in *The Intelligent Reader,* a few rules were given on the art of reading, but these were different from those printed in the former book. A set of Rules for Pronunciation, not included in the other Merriam readers, was also given, two or three of which had to do with the relation between "pronunciation and reading." In a few places the matter was spun out to a rather fine thread; for instance, in one reference to the comma it was stated that "in many cases a slight suspension of the voice is required where no comma is printed, and where the pause is slighter than is usually indicated by that stop."

In a number of instances Merriam advocated the use of the dictionary along with the study of reading, saying that this was the only way to comprehend what was read. In this connection, he urged :

> Let the teacher impress upon his scholars the importance of consulting a Dictionary when they meet with words not understood, not only in school but elsewhere. This habit will be of great advantage to them through life. The dictionary, it is to be feared, is too seldom the inmate of the school-house. While other kinds of school books have been so multiplied within a few years, it is said by those who have had the opportunity to know, that the sales of the common school Dictionary have sensibly diminished. If so, the charge of a superficial tendency in the prevailing systems of education may not be without foundation.

This was written by Charles Merriam before he and his brother began to publish dictionaries.

The fame of Charles and George Merriam rests today on their founding of the firm which has published the Webster dictionaries for more than a century. When Noah Webster died in 1843 the Merriams bought the publishing rights of the Webster dictionary, and to our time the firm has continued to issue revisions of the great work. It appears that even while they were still publishing only schoolbooks the Merriam brothers had the dictionary idea in mind.

During the first half of the nineteenth century a number of readers laid stress on subject matter that went beyond the simple objective of teaching reading, these being forerunners of the later "supplementary" readers. John Laurie Blake's *Historical Reader,* issued in 1825, which went through a number of printings, was an early example of this class of text. The compiler stated that "the object of this volume is to enable young persons, when learning to read at school, to acquire a knowledge of some of the interesting and useful portions of history." This reader seems to have been patterned after Alexander Fraser Tytler's *Universal History,* first issued in Great Britain in 1801 and later reprinted in this country by Harper Brothers in 1868, "edited by an American."

Just before the Civil War, Collins and Brothers, of New York, issued three Abbott Readers. These were *The Mount Vernon Reader for Junior Classes, The Mount Vernon Reader for Middle Classes,* and *The Mount Vernon Reader for Senior Classes* compiled by Jacob Abbott, the author of the series of "Rollo Books," popular throughout the country. Some years previously, in 1845, Abbott had compiled *The Mount Vernon Arithmetic,* which met with an extended success, as did many of his books, but the *Mount Vernon Readers* did not win any considerable approval. Too many readers with better scales of progression of difficulty were appearing on the market at the time for such a series as Abbott's to succeed.

VII

The McGuffey and Contemporary Readers

NOTHING NOVEL APPEARED with the introduction of William Holmes McGuffey's reading texts, which were eventually to hold such a very high place in the esteem of the average American. With no noticeable innovations and nothing radically different from other readers current at the time, the initial McGuffey readers, in makeup and general content, could hardly have outstripped any reasonably well-gotten-up competitors on their merits, and it does not seem that they did so. It was only after the readers had been published for several years that they were improved to a point where they began to earn the popularity that was to put them at the top of all American reading texts in volume of distribution.

Before the publication of his initial reader, it seems that McGuffey had in mind the issuance of a number of such texts, and at one time had a manuscript of one volume written. While teaching in elementary schools in Ohio and later during his early days in Miami University, he enjoyed the reputation of being an unusually capable instructor of "reading and speaking"; and, prior to 1833, his brief *Method of Reading* had been printed in London. This all contributed to later developments.

Winthrop B. Smith, a young man from Stamford, Connecticut, was one of the partners of Truman and Smith, a publishing house of Cincinnati, less than forty miles from Miami University. Early in 1836 he developed the idea of printing reading texts, knowing that there was a local need for such publications. Catherine Beecher, with the aid of her sister Harriet, later famous as the author of *Uncle Tom's Cabin,* was at the time conducting a girl's school in Cincinnati, and Smith approached her about undertaking the compilation of the readers. Catherine Beecher informed Smith that she would not be able to accept the assignment and instead suggested the name of William McGuffey, whom she knew, and whom she thought would be interested in compiling and publishing readers.[1] The result was that Winthrop Smith contacted McGuffey and an agreement was reached for him to produce a series of readers and a primer. Later a spelling book was arranged for, the latter to be a text which the publisher hoped might, at least partly, displace the long-successful Noah Webster Blue Back speller.

McGuffey contracted with Truman and Smith to receive 10 per cent royalty up to the amount of one thousand dollars on his books, after which the texts were to be the property of the

---

[1] The McGuffeys, Beechers, and Stowes were closely associated at this time. Lyman Beecher, father of Catherine and Harriet, was the first president of the Theological Seminary of Cincinnati, and the two daughters organized the Cincinnati school which they conducted for a number of years. Calvin Stowe, who married Harriet, was Professor of Biblical Literature in the Seminary (later going to Bowdoin), and a close personal friend of McGuffey, the two working together in the affairs of the Western College Teachers Institute. Although the book was not written until after she left Cincinnati, Harriet Beecher Stowe there got the ideas for *Uncle Tom's Cabin* and for the scenic backgrounds in the Ohio Valley and in neighboring Kentucky across the river. Mrs. Stowe's first children were twin daughters, born in Cincinnati, and she named one Eliza, in honor of Calvin Stowe's first wife Eliza Taylor, and the name descended to the "Eliza" in *Uncle Tom's Cabin.*

publishing firm. It is said that Winthrop Smith was never willing afterward to talk with anybody about his McGuffey agreement, likely assuming that it was his own efforts that made the books successful, which was undoubtedly partly true. While the original agreement with the publisher was extremely disadvantageous McGuffey never attempted or appeared to desire to get out of his poor deal. He was a better compiler of schoolbooks and teacher of philosophy than business man. He was not commercial minded, and it is plain that Noah Webster was shrewder than McGuffey in handling the publication of books. Had McGuffey made such contracts as did Webster he probably would have become one of the wealthy men of the country. Such a result would have depended, of course, upon whether the publishers would have pushed the books as hard as they did, and had McGuffey continued to receive royalties.

The McGuffey *First Reader* appeared in 1836, with the *Second Reader* soon following. The first primer issue did not come out until the next year, 1837. Later in that year, the *Third Reader* came from the press. At this time the publisher of the *Worcester Readers* brought a suit against the producers of the McGuffey texts, charging them with "over-imitation in the McGuffey second and third readers." After a mutually arranged agreement out of court, a few lessons were removed from the McGuffey texts which the Worcester publisher claimed had been unfairly appropriated. There seem to have been no further legal entanglements; but other compilers from time to time, in newspaper letters or otherwise, accused McGuffey of unfairly utilizing material from their books. The McGuffey *Fourth Reader* was printed in 1837, soon after the *Third*. The *Fifth* was not issued until seven years later, in 1844, and the *Sixth* did not appear until 1857. The early years of the McGuffey readers, their ups and downs, claims of violation of copyrights, and the general difficulties of getting the readers accepted were in sharp contrast to the smooth sailing of the series in its latter days.

The first change in the material of the texts came when the *Worcester* people brought their litigation for "over-imitation." After this the books went through a number of alterations, some of them complete or almost comple revisions. The *Second Reader* was "newly revised" in 1844. Seven years later the entire series was revamped, with much fresh subject matter added. In 1879 there was another extensive revision, chiefly because of the appearance around this time of a number of other well-gotten-up competitive reader series. The last changes were in 1920, when the readers were recopyrighted and meager alterations made for the purpose of legalizing the renewal of the copyrights.

In the second year of the Civil War the *McGuffey High School Reader* appeared, but not many were printed. The *McGuffey New Speaker,* and the *New Eclectic Speaker,* a larger text, were issued as auxiliary books to the McGuffey Series. The *New Eclectic Speaker,* appearing in 1858, was put out by five publishers and comprised exercises for "reading or declamation." The volume was advertised for use as a "reader and speaker," but oddly enough it did not meet with sufficient approval to warrant even one reprinting.

In the 1880's the *McGuffey Alternate Readers* appeared. These were issued in the exact format of the regular McGuffey readers, carrying no compiler's name but each title headed *The Alternate McGuffey Reader,* first, second, third, and so on. It was stated in the preface of one volume that:

The experience of many excellent teachers has convinced them that their pupils should have more reading matter in each grade than is contained in the text-book used. Children make rapid progress when they find words with which they are familiar, used with new words in the expression of fresh thought, and should not be required to repeat familiar words which have ceased to interest them.

This may seem to many like a weak contention, and perhaps it was not a statement of fact.

The *Alternate Readers* carried the same class of material that the regular McGuffey books did, and used as nearly the same sort of spelling-lists and illustrations as was possible. Titles of lessons in *The McGuffey Alternate Second Reader* were "The Bird Set Free," "The Kind Boy," "What the Squirrel Said," "The Mischievous Boy," "The Foolish Lamb," "Charles and His Father," "Good for Evil," and so on, on the same line as those in the parallel regular *McGuffey Reader*.

In 1879 the McGuffey texts underwent an extensive revision, and from then on the books were uniformly bound in the brown-printed boards, a binding which was to become familiar to people all over the country. Twice a certain number of the readers were bound in green decorated boards, in the same design as the regular brown binding, but not many of them were issued. These green bindings are very rarely met with in antiquarian bookstores today. Perhaps the great success of the McGuffey texts in their last decades was due to some extent to their uniform brown bindings of hard, durable boards. This format was one of the early examples of mass appeal—something today recognized by all advertisers as essential in increasing distribution.

Alexander Hamilton McGuffey, youngest brother of William Holmes, came to Miami University as a student while the older brother was teaching there. Alexander assisted in the compilation of all the original readers, and he is credited with being the sole compiler of the original *Fifth Reader,* and of the first McGuffey spelling book.[2] Professor T. S. Pinneo, who taught

---

[2] Mrs. Alice McGuffey Ruggles, *The Story of the McGuffies* (New

Natural Philosophy in Marietta College, was associated in editing and assembling all the mid-period McGuffey readers, and had an exclusive hand in the revision of some of them. Henry Herbert Vail was a co-compiler of the 1857 and 1859 revisions, and in 1878 became wholly responsible for editing the series. This was after Sargent, Wilson, Hinkle and Company, of Cincinnati, had taken over publication. Vail became a partner in this firm and afterward vice-president; he later wrote a history of the McGuffey readers which has long been considered by many as the most important one. Minnich's *William Holmes McGuffey and His Readers,* published in 1936, however, contains more information on the readers than does Vail's work.

From the time of the first issues of the McGuffey texts, seven publishing firms have issued them, the last being the American Book Company. This company has of late years printed the readers from time to time, chiefly for the purpose of supplying those wishing to obtain the volumes for bibliographic purposes or for relics of our educational past. In 1928, Henry Ford, the automobile manufacturer, issued a series of reprints of the readers, seemingly as much for personal sentimental reasons as for an advertising project. These were reprints of the 1857 series, the issues that Henry Ford himself had studied in school, and the Ford Motor Company distributed a large number of the sets. At this particular period there was a strong revival of popular interest in the McGuffey books, and the compiler's name gained a more substantial fame than had been his before. Prior to that time McGuffey had not been much written about. Herbert Quick's *One Man's Life,* in which considerable tribute was paid to McGuffey, did not come out until the year that the Ford reprints appeared; and Mark Sullivan's *Our Times,* in

---

York: American Book Co., 1950), a semi-fictional biographical account of the McGuffey family, gives considerable information on Alexander McGuffey. Mrs. Ruggles is Alexander's granddaughter.

which McGuffey was set upon a sort of pedestal, was not published until the year before. The *Encyclopædia Britannica* up to 1928 made no mention of McGuffey, nor did any other encyclopedia of importance.

It has been estimated that from the time of the first publication until 1920 one hundred and twenty-two million copies of McGuffey's texts were issued.[3] Sixty million copies were sold in the 1870's and 1880's. In 1895 they were being rapidly displaced by other readers, but for a time even after this they hung on heroically here and there. Since 1920 a quarter of a million copies have been sold.[4] The success of the McGuffey readers far exceeded that of any other school texts bearing a single person's name. No others, with the possible exception of the Spencerian copybooks have approached the more than one-hundred-million mark of the McGuffey readers — and the Spencerian books were only small pamphlets of a few pages.

These readers prospered so outstandingly because of certain factors that can be pointed out. First, they were published by firms who were aggressive salesmen and advertisers — establishments with which it was difficult to compete. They specialized in schoolbooks and worked closely with school management, leaving no stone unturned to further the use of McGuffey readers. After a time the sale of the books seemed to roll on under its own momentum, like a snowball rolling downhill and gathering volume as it goes.

Further, the readers fitted in appropriately with their time. They were ethically in step with the era in which they were published. It was an age in which the "Virtues" were highly

---

[3] This estimate is that of President Dillman of the American Book Company. See *Textbooks in Education* (New York: American Textbooks Publishers Institute, 1949), p. 45.

[4] Livinggood, *Our Heritage* (n.d., n.p.), p. 23 — a brief history of the American Book Co.

and generally extolled, philosophically if not in everyday practice. It was the time of the Scottish medical doctor, Samuel
Smiles, who across the sea preached most emphatically the
homely virtues in books on self-help, character, thrift, and duty
— the same moral entities that McGuffey fostered in his readers,
and all the books of Smiles went through numerous editions.
McGuffey's readers fitted into the time exactly as did Samuel
Smiles's books, and, we might say, as did Elbert Hubbard's brief
publication, "A Message To Garcia," printed in the millions
early in the present century.

While it is supposed by many that the McGuffey readers had
almost a monopoly on the reader market during the last half
of the nineteenth century, this was not actually the case. A
number of well-known reader series published during that period
were more than passingly successful. Louis Osgood, Epes Sargent, Charles W. Sanders, William Swinton, Richard D. Parker,
David B. Tower, Marcius Willson, Lewis B. Monroe, George F.
Holmes, J. Madison Watson, and George S. Hillard all compiled readers which were widely approved and which went
through numerous printings. The sales of some of them ran into
millions. There was a demand for "good reading," and reading
texts found a ready market. It must be borne in mind, too, that
the period of competition with the McGuffey readers covered
half a century, and it is only to be expected that during this
extended time there would be a number of other popular reader
series.

The Charles W. Sanders readers appeared near the same time
that the first McGuffey book was printed, and for some years
were more popular than the latter. Sanders' first series consisted
of a primer and four reading books. Most of the *First, Second,*
and *Third Reader* was made up of the compiler's own compositions. The *Fourth Reader,* issued in 1842, was comprised

of lessons from numerous pens, some of them well-known selections that had appeared in earlier texts and which were destined to appear in later ones.

Early in the 1880's a new series of Sanders' readers, running to a fifth, were published and were widely used—much more so than the series first issued. They were of a high order and were made up of material with a wide appeal. In the new series were popular selections that had appeared before, together with much new material of an enlivening freshness. These last Sanders readers came to be greatly loved—as much so as were the McGuffey texts some time later. In the Dictionary of American Biography it is stated that from 1838 to 1860 thirteen million of the Sanders readers were sold. After a long life of schoolbook compiling, Sanders died on July 5, 1889. Shortly after his death the *Omaha Herald* printed an editorial memorial honoring his name. It was reprinted in many newspapers over the country, and read in part :

> Charles W. Sanders is dead . . . . Sanders has made you weep, he has made you laugh, he has kept you from play, and he has helped to knock some ideas into that stupid head of yours . . . . There was the First, and the Second, and the Third, and the Fourth, and the Fifth Readers, and they took you from the time you were six till you were sixteen to get through them. And Sanders' name was the head of every page.[5]

How could one have known anything about the boy who saved the dykes of Holland, or the little match girl, or the bad boy who would not give his sister a drink of cold water on the night before she passed over the silent river, or the

---

[5] This is a frequently repeated error. The *Dictionary of American Biography,* in its article on Sanders, say every left page had his name on it. The early Sanders readers carried the compiler's name only on the title page and on the backstrip of the binding; the later ones, only on the left-hand pages.

industrious boy who picked red rasberries and took up the mortgage on his widowed mother's house, if it had not been for Sanders? How few would be able to repeat, "Sister, thou wast mild and lovely," if it had not been for this same benefactor, or which of you could have told anything sensible or rhythmical about the "Battle of Blenheim," or "The breaking waves dashed high," etc., but for Sanders?

"The rose has been washed, just washed in a shower, which Mary to Anna conveyed," Sanders told us with the assistance of Cowper. And did Sanders hint that it was the shower that conveyed Mary to Anna, considered from a grammatical standpoint? He did not. He showed himself a man who could be trusted. He had ideas, too, about the functions of the imagination. He thought the imagination should be awakened . . . . He printed stories in which violets converse fluently with oaks and grasshoppers were entertained by humming birds. He meant to give milk to babes. Then there were the select stunners of the Fifth Reader— "jewels five words long, which on the stretched forefinger of all time glitter forever." There were words that it was a positive gymnastic exercise to pronounce, and which were looked upon with such awe that they were carefully avoided during the remainder of life . . . .

And Sanders is dead—that guide, philosopher and friend. What if he made hot tears flow over his obstinate spelling pages and caused the impatient blood to surge to the head on dread examination days? It is all forgiven and forgotten. He was a close companion and a safe one for many years.

The Hillard readers, a series of six books, came out just before the Civil War. These were printed over a period of a quarter of a century by several publishers. George S. Hillard, a general writer, turned out several books besides his school texts and had connections with publishing firms at various times, as reader, adviser, and so on. Hillard, a lawyer, was a versatile man and not all a scholarly recluse. He wrote a great deal of interesting material, his most important and scholarly work being the two-volume *George Ticknor — Life, Letters and Journal,* published in 1876, which is of permanent value as a trenchant record of a prominent nineteenth-century literary figure — one who not only wrote of, but lived in the world of literature.

The Hillard readers, published contemporarily with those of McGuffey, were something on the order of the McGuffey texts, a number of the same lessons being used; in some of the editions most of the subject matter was closely similar. It is only natural that publishers should turn their eyes toward the McGuffey readers at this particular time, the period following the Civil War, because of the fact that they were becoming an unprecedented wonder of the publishing world. Notwithstanding the heavy competition they encountered, the Hillard readers were widely used.

Just before the Civil War Hillard's *First Class Reader,*[*] which was not a part of his regular series, was issued; it ran to five hundred pages. It was no doubt intended as much for a general literature text as much as for a reader, as no elocution matter was included and nothing on the technical side of reading was mentioned; the material was of the anthology type. The volume covered such a wide range of topics that it stood out from a literary standpoint, and was quite different in this respect from the general run of its competitors. Selections were utilized from Robert Curzon's *Visits to Monasteries in the Levant,* George Ticknor's *History of Spanish Literature,* and P. B. Brydon's *Tour through Sicily and Malta* — little-known books of high

---

[*] The *North American First Class Reader,* by David B. Tower and Cornelius Walker, appeared a few years before, and one or two other texts bore the title *First Class Reader.*

merit and deep interest which other compilers had not drawn from.

Hillard's *Intermediate Reader,* first issued during the Civil War and afterward reprinted a number of times, included Clement C. Moore's "Night Before Christmas," one of the first times it appared in a schoolbook. The title was listed as "Christmas Time" and the author's name as C. C. Moore. Two lines were omitted from the Hillard book :

He had a broad face and a little round belly
That shook when he laughed like a bowlful of jelly.

Although such a word as "belly" was used without self-consciousness at the time Moore wrote his celebrated poem, by the time of Hillard's compilation, through some strange distillation of human thought, it had come to be considered too coarse for use in a schoolbook for both boys and girls. Eliminating the offensive lines, as charming as any in the whole composition, was a convenient way out of the dilemma for the compiler.

The George F. Holmes readers, known as The University Series, published by the University Publishing Company, were the last to be put out by an old-type "all-around" compiler. They first appeared in the 1870's and were reprinted for almost a quarter of a century, chiefly because they were most excellent texts. All the Holmes books—readers, arithmetics, spelling books, and histories—were well put together from a textual standpoint and were widely approved. The compiler was for a long period professor of history and literature in the University of Virginia and he seems to have possessed an almost faultless knack for textbook making.

Some day George F. Holmes may well become the subject of an interesting biography. He was born in British Guiana, where his father was Judge Advocate of the colony, and at two years of age was taken to England to live with his grandfather.

While attending Durham University, he was sent to Canada because of some misunderstanding with his family. From Canada he drifted after a time to Philadelphia, then to Virginia and to other southern states. He studied law and was later admitted to the bar and practiced his profession, although he never took out naturalization papers. At the age of thirty-seven he was teaching foreign languages in the University of Richmond; two years later he moved to William and Mary to teach history and political science. In 1848 he was made president of the newly founded University of Mississippi, but a short time later was called back to Virginia because of illness in his family. En route to Virginia he lost an eye in a road accident and was handicapped the rest of his life. He never returned to Mississippi but remained instead for some years in Monroe County, Virginia (now West Virginia) where he farmed, wrote, and studied. He carried on a correspondence with the noted French philosopher Auguste Comte, to whom he wrote on one occasion, "I have first to work for bread for my family, then to work for books, and finally to work for leisure and independence." In 1857 Holmes went to the University of Virginia as professor of history and literature, and remaining there forty years, until his death in 1897. He was unconventional in many ways and was said to be indifferent to his personal appearance.

William Torrey Harris was the man responsible for the creation of the Appleton readers, which were published in the 1870's and 1880's and which were extraordinarily successful. For several years Harris was United States Commissioner of Education, and he had a marked influence on the progress of American education. His story is the subject of a volume, *Yankee Teacher,* by Kurt F. Leidecker, issued by the Philosophical Library in 1946, in which, among many other interesting details, the story is told that Harris found it necessary to remove Lincoln's Gettysburg Address from the Appleton reader in order to get the latter adopted in South Carolina. The Appleton readers grew so rapidly in popularity at one period that a competitive firm issued a sixty-four-page booklet entitled "Appleton Readers A Failure" — evidence, we may safely guess, of their success rather than of their "failure."

After the days of George Frederick Holmes, Sarah Arnold, Charles B. Gilbert, William T. Harris, Marcius Willson, and other compilers of the latter part of the nineteenth century, reader construction became a task for the expert in child training, for the psychologist who studied the techniques involved in reading. In the latter part of the century the readers of James Mark Baldwin were issued.[7] The compiler, a well-known psychologist, thought of reading in schools in psychological terms, and his texts were quickly accepted almost everywhere. During the past three or four decades reader compilation has in most cases followed in the footsteps of Professor Baldwin.

[7] Baldwin taught psychology in Princeton and Johns Hopkins universities. In 1900 Oxford conferred an honorary D.Sc. degree upon him — the first it ever awarded. Some of Baldwin's psychological conclusions were based on studies of his young daughter. See Pillsbury, *History of Psychology* (New York: Norton, 1929), p. 252.

VIII

Grammars

THE FIRST AMERICAN-WRITTEN English grammar was that of Hugh Jones, *An Accidence of the English Tongue,* printed in London in 1724. Less than a century had passed since the initial English grammar had been worked out by the poet Ben Jonson,[1] a man who knew and associated with Shakespeare and must have had considerable versatility of mind.[2] No copy of Jones's *An Accidence of the English Tongue* is known to exist in America. It is another of those rarities of print now represented by a single copy — in this instance the one in the British Museum.

---

[1] A reprint of Jonson's *English Grammar* of 1640 was issued in London by the Lanston Monotype Corporation in 1928, with a preface by Strickland Gibson, of the Bodleian Library, that gives a full history of the *Grammar,* with bibliographical data on the various printings, which have been few.

[2] William Bullokar's *Book at Large for the Amendment of Orthography for English Speech,* printed in London in 1580, and John Stockwood's "A plaine and easie laying open of the meaning and understanding of the Rules of Construction in the Accidence," the work of a Tunbridge Wells school teacher, issued ten years later, were works on language structure, inflections and so on, but they were not English grammars. In the day of Bullokar and Stockwood only Latin grammar was taught in the schools. Many Latin grammars were published before the coming of the English grammars. One hundred and eighty-six writers of Latin grammars up to that time were listed in Solomon Lowe's *Grammar of the Latin Tongue,* printed in England in 1726.

How many copies of Jones's book were printed is a question, but it is not likely the number was very large.

In his grammar Jones expressed himself as a purist in language; he thought the mother tongue "should not be corrupted," and believed that a "public standard" of language ought to be "fixed" to "direct posterity and prevent irregularity, and Confused Abuses and Corruptions in our Writings and Expressions." The contents of the text are about what one would expect to find in so restricted a manual and in one appearing early in the eighteenth century.

Hugh Jones came to the College of William and Mary in Virginia in 1717, twenty-four years after that institution was founded, to fill the chair of mathematics. (This was ten years before a similar professorship was instituted at Harvard.) Jones returned to England in 1722, and two years later his book, *The Present State of Virginia,* was published—a description of social, educational, and religious conditions in Virginia during the first part of the eighteenth century. Jones wrote that Virginia "may be justly esteemed the happy retreat of true Britons" and that the country "exceeds all others in goodness of climate." He wrote many other commendations of his adopted land, though sometimes they were at the expense of the other colonies. He looked upon the Maryland Catholics disapprovingly and upon the Indians with dislike, and thought the Negro slaves had a much easier life than was generally reported.[3] Near the time Jones's book on Virginia appeared his grammar was also published. The title page of the little text listed the author as "Hugh Jones, Minister of Jamestown, Virginia," but there was no mention of his academic connections.

The second English grammar of American origin was that of

---

[3] *The Present State of Virginia* was reprinted by the University of North Carolina Press in 1956.

Johnson printed in 1765. This work was originally written by Johnson for his young grandsons, William and Charles, who must have been exceptionally precocious, for Johnson records that one of them at the age of six "was making a rapid progress in Hebrew."[4] It appears that Samuel Johnson, the author of the grammar, was a man of energy and application, in contrast to the indolence that has been attributed to the much more famous Samuel Johnson of England. The American Samuel, Connecticut born, graduated from Yale at the age of eighteen and was later appointed the first president of King's College, now Columbia University.

The third American grammar, *A Plain and Easy Introduction to English Grammar,* was issued in 1773 by Thomas Byerly, a New York school teacher. It must have appeared in a very limited edition, as it is rarely come upon today, even in libraries rich in early American books. It came out at perhaps an unfortunate period for the issuance of a schoolbook to appear —a short time before outbreak of the War of Independence. Four years after the issuance of Byerly's text, Albert Curtin's *Compend of English Grammar* was published—this one right in the midst of the Revolution. Curtis's grammar also ranks with the very rare schoolbooks today.

After the Revolution was over and the American people were facing other problems a fifth grammar appeared and gained more notice than had any previous American grammar. It was Noah Webster's *Grammatical Institute of the English Language, Part Two.* Published in 1784, the book, a practical language text and well promoted, became the forerunner in pattern of a number of American grammars.

Webster acknowledged that Robert Lowth's *Short Introduction to Grammar* was his main source, and, as Lowth had done

---

[4] Chandler, *Life of Samuel Johnson, D. D.* (New York: T. and J. Swords, 1805), p. 76.

before him, divided his subject matter as Latin grammarians
for a long time had done. Some of Webster's material was
copied, and it used the question and answer system extensively,
as he said, "to aid the memory." Notwithstanding Webster's
active promotion of the sale of his books, his grammar never
became popular in school use, though other grammarians cast
designing eyes on it with the idea of borrowing.

The Young Ladies Accidence, published in 1785, Caleb Bingham's first grammar, was a by-product of his teaching. In 1784
he had opened a school for girls in Boston, and his text, as the
title page indicated, was compiled for his pupils. Bingham's
institution became one of the best known of its sort at the time,
and the first serious teaching of English grammar in this country
occurred there. When Bingham was later employed to reorganize
the Boston public schools, his grammars were adopted for use
there and schoolmasters elsewhere later used them in considerable numbers. Bingham's texts, like all the earlier English grammars, British as well as American, contained incongruities. The
chief defect lay in the fact that some of the matter in the texts
was not English grammar but Latin grammar incapable of
adaptation to English.[5] This seems to have derived from Lily's
Latin Grammar, the pattern of which the English grammarians
followed prior to the appearance of American grammarians.

William Lily, born in the last half of the fifteenth century,
went to Italy to study under Latin masters in Rome and did
much to advance Latin studies in England; but his Latin studies

---

[5] Epes Sargent Dixwell, long headmaster of the Boston Latin School, in
his autobiography, writing of the early 19th century, says that the Greek
grammars were faulty because they were based on Latin rules. "Our
grammars [Greek] were quite defective," he wrote; "we were taught to
fit the Latin Syntax and Latin Prosody to Greek words and sentences."
Epes Sargent Dixwell (Boston: George Ellis Co., 1907), p. 42. This autobiography was stored away for almost three quarters of a century, then
found and privately printed by one of Dixwell's descendants.

in Italy, as several writers on the subject have pointed out, did not qualify him to direct what form English grammars should take. George Philip Krapp discusses the evolution of our English grammars from Latin grammars and the shortcomings there resulting in the latter,[6] as does R. H. Robins, in an extraordinarily informative book.[7] Professor Robins states that "the grammar of a language must be worked out from and for that language alone," which was not done by our early English grammarians.

For a generation after its appearance Lindley Murray's *English Grammar* was the dominating text of its class, quickly finding acceptance in England and later in the United States. This book, in its various revisions, in its field ranked in popularity with that of Webster's spelling book. The *Grammar* was first printed in England in 1795 — Murray was living in that country at the time — and the volume was not published by an American press until five years later. A revised edition was issued in 1808 and a number of other revisions were published in fairly close succession. In the same period three revisions of Webster's grammar text were made, but none could ever compete with any marked success against those of Murray.

In Murray's introduction to the 1808 edition of his *English Grammar* he acknowledges his indebtedness to grammarians preceding him, giving Webster credit for one passage. Webster later charged Murray with using thirty or more passages from his work, adding some comments about other alleged borrowings which he said "are so incorporated into his work, that no person except myself would detect plagiarism." This charge was printed

---

[6] Krapp, *The Knowledge of English* (New York: Holt, 1927), ch. 16, "What Is Grammar?"

[7] Robins, *Ancient and Mediæval Grammatical Theory in Europe* (London: G. Bell & Son, 1951), p. 72.

in the introduction to Webster's "Abridged Grammar" in his *American Dictionary* of 1828, two years after Murray died. A like representation was made in 1817 in a letter from Noah Webster to John Pickering, but this was not made public until after Murray's time. The witty Heinrich Heine once said : "In literature, as well as in life, every son has a father who, of course he may not know . . . or knowing, would wish to deny." It is hard to understand why Webster stirred up this matter of alleged plagiarism after Murray had passed away.

The *English Exercises* of Murray was first printed in 1797. In it appears the following sentence for parsing that illustrates a characteristic of Murray's texts :

> Whatever fortune may rob us of, it cannot take away what is most valuable, the peace of a good conscience, and the cheerful prospect of a happy conclusion to all the trials of life, in a better world.

Throughout his texts Murray indulged in such moral peregrinations, which had no integral connection with the study at hand. In the introduction to his *English Grammar* he wrote :

> Even sentiments of a pious and religious nature, have not been thought improper to be occasionally inserted in these Exercises . . . . The importance of exhibiting to the youthful mind, the deformities of vice; and of giving it just and animating views of piety and virtue, makes it not only warrantable, but our duty also, to embrace every proper occasion to promote, in any degree, these valuable ends.

Murray's *Grammar* was used so extensively that a number of "abridgements" and "adaptations" were issued, here and in England. The compiler himself prepared the first abridgement soon after the initial printing of the first edition of the grammar.

In 1838 Alger's *Murray's Grammar,* a reissue of Murray's *Abridgement* to which an "appendix" was added, was printed. The extensive appendix contained new exercises in orthography, parsing, syntax, and pronounciation, "to be used in connection with Murray's large text."

Alger's book was first published in 1833 and went through various printings by more than one firm until the middle of the century. Murray's small *English Exercises,* an auxiliary manual first issued in England in 1797 and later in this country had a number of printings. Both these small books retained their popularity as long as Murray's more comprehensive volumes sold well since Murray advertised them as "adjunct to the larger grammars."

Some of the supplementary volumes to Murray's regular grammar must have been books more or less put together and published merely for profit. That Murray had a sort of intimation that this was the case with his own abridgement is indicated by lines in the introduction of its first issue :

> It may justly be doubted whether there is any ground for objection to the following compilation, on the additional cost it will occasion. The preservation of the larger Grammar, by using the Abridgement, may, in some instances, make amends for the charge of the latter. But were this not the case, it is hoped the period has passed away, in which the important business of education is, too often, regulated or influenced by a parsimonious economy.

We may still hear sly echoes of that last sentence from time to time in various spheres of application.

The *English Grammar* of Peter Bullions appeared in 1851, and it went to a "Thirty-first Edition, Revised," within a decade. Bullions' grammar was the outstanding one around the mid-nineteenth century, possibly due to the fact that the compiler was an exceptional scholar. Of all the early and mid-nineteenth century grammar compilers, Bullions was perhaps the most learned. For a number of years he was professor of language in Albany Academy. In this small early-American educational institution, he was associated with a number of teachers who were later to become well known. The father of Bret Harte, who gained fame as a writer in California, was professor of Greek in Albany Academy, and the young Bret spent some years there. Herman Melville, of *Moby Dick* fame, was destined to attend Albany Academy after Professor Bullions' time. Joseph Henry, the noted scientist, taught in the school six years and there developed in part the ideas upon which Samuel F. B. Morse and Thomas Edison later applied to practical electrical inventions that changed civilization. At the Academy Henry did much of the work which later earned him the secretaryship of the Smithsonian Institution and made his name known all over the world.[8]

Besides Bullions' *English Grammar,* he compiled Latin and Greek grammars. These texts were marked by an excellence found in but few grammars, or schoolbooks of any class, at that time. Bullions wrote his *English Grammar* with the hope that it would supersede Murray's, and it was indeed one of the two or three texts that did most to make Murray's obsolete.

The *English Grammar* of Bullions overcame many of the defects of Murray's, and took a middle path between the over-sized advanced grammars of the day and the abridgements, which gave it a marked advantage. The compiler avoided many outworn rules and definitions that were obviously inapplicable to common-sense language study. For a considerable period Bullions' grammar was the most widely used and it was not completely displaced until Harvey's day. During the Civil War, when Southerners were reluctant to use "Northern" texts, the Bullions grammar was an exception. The *Analytical and Prac-*

---

[8] Cuyler Reynold's *Albany Authors* (privately printed, 1902), gives data on the writings of a number of schoolbook compilers who were teachers at Albany Academy.

tical Grammar of the English Tongue, by Bullions, was printed in Raleigh, North Carolina, in 1864 — one of the few grammars of any kind to be published in the South during the war.

Contemporary with Bullions' grammars a number of texts patterned closely after his work appeared. Some of them met with very little approval, while others enjoyed fair success. Around the same period a number of "beginner" or "primary" grammars texts appeared — something new in the grammar field. One example was L. T. Covell's *Primary Grammar,* which came out in Pittsburgh in 1853. The author taught school in Alleghany, now a part of Pittsburgh, but at that time little more than a village. His text, he stated, was "designed for beginners," and the material was in the simplest form. Its first lesson defined grammar as "the science of language and the art of using it," instead of using a much longer and more loosely constructed definition as was then customary. The first page bespoke the fact that some progress was being made in providing material for beginning school children. The compiler stated that "the chief object of Grammar is to teach the art of Composition, which is to be acquired only by actual practice," evidently assuming that if one could set thoughts down on paper correctly, he could also speak correctly.

The small *Parsing Book* by Allen H. Weld, also the compiler of a larger grammar, was published in Buffalo, New York, in 1853. This small text was scarcely more than an adjunct of the author's larger grammar and much of the text was too complex for the use of beginners. Covell's *Primary Grammar* and Weld's *Parsing Book,* with their mixture of inconsistencies and good qualities, were typical of a number of brief texts which appeared about the middle of the century. In these brief manuals the simplification of grammar and clarification of subject matter that took place after the Civil War had their beginning.

The grammars which followed the war between the North and South were, as a whole, more suited to their purpose than their predecessors, although many were still too complicated. Almost every grammarian attempted some explanation of the rules he set forth, but the explanations themselves were complicated and did not always make their meaning clear.

Grammar writers of the period claimed that it was necessary for pupils to diagram sentences, but failed to give a clear reason, capable of being easily understood by a pupil. The substance of the various statements about diagraming was essentially the same—it was "the breaking up of the sentence."

Rollo LeVerne Lyman, speaking of the whole mid-century period, said that it was "the inductive period" in grammar study, and that grammar was conceived of as the "science of the sentence."[9] The "inductive method" naturally met with quite a lot of opposition. Professor Emerson E. White, writing at the beginning of the present century, said: "There is perhaps no method of teaching more frequently misused as the inductive. Pupils are led to generalize facts without seeing the *reason* for the inference."[10] All in all, the inductive grammar-teaching method of the nineteenth century, we may be certain, was often more than defective.

John S. Hart explained that "the word analysis is from the Greek ἀγάλνσιη, dissolution, taking apart, or separation of a compound into its constituent parts."[11] In support of this definition he stated that "the analysis of sentences is a matter of logic

---

[9] Lyman, *English Grammar in American Schools Before 1850, Bulletin U.S.' Bureau of Education,* 1921, No. 21.

[10] White, *The Art of Teaching* (New York: American Book Co., 1901), p. 75.

[11] John S. Hart, *Grammar of the English Language, With an Analysis of the Sentence* (Philadelphia: edition of Eldridge and Bros., 1874), p. 161.

rather than of grammar," and that "the logical faculty" is the "basis of all sound knowledge." Such a view of the point at issue is typical of many of the then-current explanations by grammarians—even so competent a one as Hart.

Only a few grammarians of the time used the same form of diagraming. Some adopted the horizontal line method, of which there were a number of varieties; others resorted to a bracket system that divided the sentence in a vertical outline. S. W. Clark in his *Practical Grammar,* issued in 1859 and reprinted later, used a form of diagram in which every word was completely encircled, the whole procedure resulting in a confusing disposition of words. Compilers of the era did not agree on *how* the diagraming was to be done, but only that it was requisite. The term "mapping" came into wide use as applied to this branch of sentence study; even such late compilers as Reed and Kellogg[12] used the terminology as did Harvey.

Simon Kerl's grammars, which appeared after the Civil War, were among the first to try to break away to a certain extent from "analyzing" and "diagraming." The *Language Lessons* of Kerl, issued in 1878, was one of the earliest texts to work away from "grammar" to "language." It was too soon, however, to get entirely away from long-used and complicated rules, and a good number of them were included in Kerl's *Language Lessons.* The compiler was much concerned with showing how to avoid incorrect expressions and demonstrating what was right and wrong in word usage and sentence structure.

Goold Brown, a native of Providence, Rhode Island, taught school for a number of years in New York City, later conducting an academy there. During this New York period his first grammars were compiled. He had an effective way of presenting his

---

[12] Reed and Kellogg, *Higher Lessons in English* (New York: Maynard, 1905), p. viii.

material, which perhaps did much in advancing the use of his texts. He avoided to a large extent "spoken language," using extensive excerpts from the works of various authors for his extraordinarily drawn-out subject matter.[13] Brown's *Grammar of English Grammars* was issued in 1851 and reprinted at various times until after the Civil War. This text is unique for its length (more than a thousand pages), which had never been equalled among school texts prior to its time. It has been well called the leviathan of schoolbooks. Hundreds of examples of false syntax were cited from other texts of its day and from those previously used. Brown was not slow to call attention at great length to the numerous faults and errors he found in rival grammars. Although much of his *Grammar of English Grammars* was of value, page after page could have been omitted to advantage. Most of the merits of the book—and there were many—were buried under an avalanche of pedantic verbiage.

In his grammars Goold Brown advocated more energetically than anyone before him the practice of parsing. He stated, in contradistinction to the usual pronouncements of the day, that language is a matter of "putting together parts"—an affirmation that needed to be set forth at the time. Having a considerable influence over other grammarians, Brown perhaps was responsible for the appearance in subsequent texts of more emphasis on pausing than by any line of reasoning was necessary. Goold Brown's influence on contemporary and later grammarians was quite marked, but, as one commentator has remarked, not wholly happy. His sway over grammarians, for both good and

---

[13] Robert Louis Stevenson, not long before he died, planned an English grammar to be based on the English classics. The book got no further than a sketch of the plan; but had Stevenson lived, with his perseverance he probably would have completed the textbook. See Balfour, *Life of Robert Louis Stevenson* (New York: Scribner, 1901), II, 172.

bad, carried through to the twentieth century. One of his texts, *Institutes of English Grammar,* was still in use after 1900.

Thomas W. Harvey's books were as successful as any of the grammars used during the last half of the nineteenth century. His *Practical English Grammar* was originally published in 1868 and later revised a number of times. The *Elementary Grammar and Composition* was a revamping of the original *Elementary Grammar.* His elementary texts, with less material, were otherwise built much on the general pattern of the larger *Practical Grammar.* Harvey, like a number of his predecessors, was a firm proponent of diagraming. He used the vertical line form, which looked simple but which had faults which made it vulnerable to criticism. In treating some of the parts of speech and certain rules of grammar, Harvey was clearer than most of his predecessors; even so, some of his directions were none too lucid. His lesson in the *Practical Grammar* on forms of the verb showed five classifications: the common, the emphatic, the progressive, the passive, and the ancient. These were to be considered, he explained, as "the subdivisions of the tenses."

In his last *Revised English Grammar,* Harvey somewhat modified certain of his views. His drill plans came to be built more on the word than they formerly had been, particularly on the grammatical relation of one word to another. Taking the work of Harvey as a whole, it may be said that he aided in bringing a touch of simplicity into school language study.

The texts of John S. Hart already mentioned, appeared at about the same time that Harvey's did, and during their early days were Harvey's strongest competitors. They did not, however, retain their popularity as long. The Hart grammars consisted of a beginners' *Class Book,* followed by an *Elementary Grammar,* an *English Grammar and Analysis,* and two volumes on composition, the last of which was *Composition and*

Rhetoric, an advanced text of some excellence. Hart was one of the first grammarians to help direct the emphasis of grammar teaching toward "composition." In his *First Lessons in Composition,* in the beginning sentence of the preface, he said: "Nothing in school is usually so poorly taught as composition," and he urged its intensive study as one of the vital needs of the day.

Hart was for a number of years principal of the Philadelphia High School, and his work in this institution made his name well known. Many of the lectures he delivered were published, and some of them, particularly those on language and English literature, were widely circulated. The Philadelphia High School had a remarkable growth from both a scholastic and attendance standpoint during Hart's administration, and his reputation gave a momentous impetus to the high school movement all over the country.

The grammar texts of George P. Quackenbos, contemporary with those of Hart, were extensively used, but they did not possess the clarity that was characteristic of the Hart texts. Some of Quackenbos' lessons were marred by being put into question-and-answer form—not quite appropriate for a late nineteenth-century grammar text. He was one of the first of the grammarians of the Civil War period, however, to look ahead to much less use of parsing and diagraming. In his *First Lessons in Composition,* first issued in 1851 and reaching an output of two hundred thousand copies by 1888, he made one statement that deserves to be cited in any historical treatment of American grammars. He said: "Parsing is secondary to composing, and the analysis of our language almost unimportant when compared with its synthesis." This was penned at a time when the general run of grammar compilers were crowding more and more matter on parsing and diagraming into their pages.

Quackenbos' *Illustrated Lessons in Our Language,* published after his *Composition,* stood largely in a class of its own, a small text in which the compiler advocated "Language before grammar,' sticking fairly close to this declaration throughout the book. The little volume, put out by Appleton in 1876, was well illustrated with engravings by A. R. Waud—quaint pictures that could not fail to catch the eye of pupils of the age for which the text was designed. This meant something in a language-study book of the time, when such illustrations were rare.

What may perhaps be designated as the last grammar of the nineteenth-century genre were the several texts of Alonzo Reed and Brainard Kellogg. Reed was at one time instructor of English in the Polytechnic Institute in Brooklyn, and Brainard Kellogg was a professor of English language in the same school. Their closely connected work in the school led to a long period of collaboration.

Reed and Kellogg's *Higher Lessons in English* appeared in 1877, and went through numerous printings and a number of revisions during three decades. This book would perhaps rank among the first half-dozen school grammars from the standpoint of extended popularity. Up to 1897, but not in the revised editions after that, the authors stated in their preface to the *Higher Lessons* that the book "was not written to air crotchets or to resolve grammatical puzzles, but for everyday use in the schoolroom." They said also that "while shunning no difficulties that lay in our path, we have not turned out of our path to encounter any." There were but few grammarians up to their time who were averse to inserting here and there a few "grammatical puzzles"—in a little different form, if possible, from those found in other texts.

The first lesson in the *Higher Lessons in English* started out with the story of language origin, and not with the definitions

which had so long had an accustomed place in such texts. The
compilers told of a language "that we never learned from a
grammar or book of any kind"—one that was not "taught by
parent or teacher." This was the "Natural Language" of "cries,
laughter and tones"; the "language of gestures," and so on. The
compilers were here dealing with the new theories of language-
origin only recently advanced by Frederick Max Muller, the
Anglo-German philologist, and those of his school. While this
had no true alliance with the study of grammar, introduced as
it was it perhaps created a language interest.

Reed and Kellogg, it appears, attempted to make themselves
believe they were compiling texts in which unnecessary rules
had been thrown overboard, out-of-date methods had been
dropped, and new principles had been introduced; but this was
hardly true. These two grammarians of the last part of the
nineteenth century remained hedged in by technical grammatical restraints common to most of the century. They seemed
unable to get away from quite a number of antiquated teaching
practices. But it is a fact that the two Brooklyn grammarians,
like Harvey somewhat before them, played some part in the
early movement to sweep the cobwebs out of the structure of
grammar teaching.

The Augean stables of American grammar study were not
wholly cleaned until after the dawn of the twentieth century.
During the last decade of the nineteenth there was a minor
flushing of the defilement that had accumulated over a good
many more years than the thirty of King Augeas—but not
more than a minor flushing. Only during the present century
has the purifying and cleansing stream thoroughly washed away
the cluttering debris so carefully guarded by such nineteenth
century grammarians as Lindley Murray, Samuel Kirkham,
William Wells, Charles Ingersoll, and a dozen or so others.

The failings of nineteenth-century grammar study in our

schools have been elaborated upon by George Philip Krapp.[14] Professor Krapp stated that the older grammars "marched under false colors. They pretended to give genuinely precise and scientific definitions of words as structural elements of speech, though in reality they did nothing of the sort." He said further that our early grammars "contained the appearance of a scientific system, but their system was not derived from observation of the actual process of speech."

In our own day Professor Charles Carpenter Fries, of the University of Michigan, chiefly in his *American English Grammar* (1940), has likewise called attention to the defects of the old grammars and in addition, of those used at the present time. Professor Fries sanctions more and more liberality and more simplification in language teaching and usage. There are, however, opponents of these ideas. Professor Harry R. Warfel, of the University of Florida, has vigorously attacked Professor Fries's views, stating that it is not to be expected that "every child write his own grammar." Professor Warfel says: "Language is a tool like a kitchen stove . . . . That a child should be encouraged to play with a gas range without an awareness of some fundamental rules seems unwise," going on to assert that language teaching without benefit of rules seems to him unsound.[15] It must be confessed that complete abandonment of grammar would bring about undesirable results something like those arising from "modern art." It would encourage too many shortcomings and condone too many abuses of English. There is already too much laxity in that direction.

---

[14] Krapp, *The Knowledge of English* (New York: Holt, 1927), pp. 228–251.

[15] Warfel, *Who Killed Grammar?* (Gainesville: University of Florida Press, 1952), p. 16.

IX

Rhetorics and Foreign Language Books

AFTER HIS RETIREMENT from a professorship in Edinburgh University, Hugh Blair, in 1783, published his *Lectures on Rhetoric*. Two or three cut-down editions of the text were first issued in America, and it was soon afterward reprinted in the original form. The first full edition in America was put out by Robert Aitken in Philadelphia, in 1784. The book, both in its curtailed form and in the full editions, was for more than a century a widely used text in England and in the United States, in schools, colleges, and in individual study. The book contained lessons on the writing of English, the structure of the sentence, use of metaphor, character of style, analysis of eloquence, the anatomy of discourse, and other kindred topics. Blair delved into the nature of poetry, compared ancient writings with modern, and dwelt upon the great epics of literature. He also touched upon the writing of history—a moot subject which is as much argued today as it was two hundred years ago. A century ago the historian Leopold Ranke was thought to have freed history from "philosophy" and brought it down completely to the realm of reality; but other conceptions of history have developed, and in our own time Benedetto

Croce and others have advanced ideas that are thoroughly at variance with the conclusions of Ranke.

Blair set down every word of his ideas with a sureness that is evident — an attribute of most of the "philosophers" of his time. It has been observed in some writings that Blair was not original in his thinking, and this may be partially true. But he had a vast erudition and used it effectively and, in many cases, appealingly. He seemed to be able to elaborate at great length upon every phase of any subject that took his fancy. One may get an idea of the remarkable range of subject matter that Hugh Blair was able to handle by examining the index in one of the well-edited issues of his *Rhetoric*. This book is almost a miscellany for general reading — a modified *Anatomy of Melancholy,* one might venture to say.

As originally put out, Blair's book became the basis upon which a number of other rhetoric texts were compiled, and it influenced the content of the first American school rhetorics. This was admitted by virtually every compiler of the nineteenth century.

George Campbell's *Philosophy of Rhetoric* was first printed in England in 1776 and afterward in this country. It was reprinted from time to time until after the middle of the nineteenth century. This was a work that ranked with Blair's in worth, and, while not used so widely, it still enjoyed a very considerable success. Campbell, a Doctor of Divinity like Blair, was as much the versatile handler of varied material as the latter. Campbell as a rule was not quite so drawn-out in presenting his subject matter as was Blair, but there were times when he did not reach perfection with respect to brevity.

On one occasion Campbell went to extra lengths to explain the "Calculations of Chance," and in handling the topic he dwelt in detail upon the throwing of dice, the manner of letting them leave the hand, and the terms and motions involved. On the quest of how often a given number "ought" to come up he came to a definite conclusion : "I say, therefore, that the chance is equal for every one of the six sides." (He did not seem to entertain the idea that dice are sometimes loaded.) A little further on he confided that "calculations may be founded on experience, as well as upon chance," showing a rather more extensive technical knowledge of the kinetic shifting of dice than is generally thought to be within the sphere of the average Doctor of Divinity.

Campbell touched on art, and quotes the Frenchman De Piles's *Principles of Painting* in a statement surprisingly like some of the present day defenses of modern art. De Piles, according to Campbell, wrote almost two hundred years ago : "Nature in herself is unseemingly, and he who copies her servilely, and without artifice, will always produce something poor, and of mean taste." This same argument is frequently advanced today by advocates of modern art. Although Campbell himself did not accept the Frenchman's criticism of art, it is interesting to note how closely akin it was to much modern criticism. Sprinkled here and there through Campbell's *Philosophy of Rhetoric* are casual lines that reveal the discerning wisdom of the author.

From the penetrating works of Hugh Blair and George Campbell and a few of their followers the early American school rhetorics were evolved; but these new texts omitted the peregrinations and philosophical dissertations of which Blair and Campbell, especially the former, were so fond of.

One of the early completely American rhetoric texts was Ebenezer Porter's *Analysis,* first printed in Andover, Massachusetts, in 1827 and later reprinted in other places. This was almost as much an elocution text as a rhetoric text, and despite some tepid subject matter it was considerably used. Its success might have been due to the inclusion of literary selections at a time when that was not a common practice, almost half of the volume being so taken up. Like most of his predecessors in the compilation of English rhetoric texts, Porter was a clergyman, and at the time he produced the *Analysis* he was teaching in a Massachusetts theological seminary and was widely known.

Samuel P. Newman's *Practical System of Rhetoric,* published in 1834, was one of the early American productions that was wholly a rhetoric. The compiler was Professor of Rhetoric in Bowdoin College and his work was reprinted over a period of quarter of a century, a sixtieth edition being issued in 1859. In the seventh edition a note at the beginning of the volume indicated that at the time the text was also being printed in England. The book was simplicity itself as compared to those of Blair and Campbell, or even to that of Ebenezer Porter, which may perhaps account for the fact that it fared as well as it did.

James R. Boyd's *Elements of Rhetoric* appeared shortly after the early editions of Newman's text, and it was in a smaller size. It achieved sufficient popularity to justify its revision two years after its original appearance. The text, as was stated in the introduction, was patterned after the works of Blair and Campbell, but "presents a more correct method and from the best portions, at least, the most useful points of their works." Boyd issued a series of annotated English classics for school use, and edited what was perhaps the last American school edition of Lord Kames' *Elements of Criticism,* which was in substance a rhetoric. The Kames book as revised by Boyd was issued in 1855 and was reissued some years later.[1]

---

[1] Henry Home Kames was a Scottish lawyer who wrote on philosophy and other subjects and took an important part in various public affairs. He was knighted in 1752. He was a close friend of Benjamin Franklin during the latter's last stay in England and the two were much given to

Elements of the Art of Rhetoric, by Henry H. Day, an Ohio schoolteacher, appeared in 1850 and within a decade went through four editions. The author, like Boyd, turned to a new style, his book being almost a composition-writing manual — one of the earliest of its kind. John S. Hart's *Composition and Rhetoric* came out in 1870 and went through many printings during the next two decades. This text dealt primarily with composition, and was along the line of the many that were to appear within the next three or four decades under the title of *Composition* or *Composition and Rhetoric.*

A number of much-read and highly respected books of a philological nature are in substance rhetorics, although perhaps not many have thought of them as belonging in that category. Among volumes of this class can be mentioned William Mathews' *Words: Their Use and Abuse,* a book that went through edition after edition for a quarter of a century. The well known *Words and Their Ways in English Speech,* by Greenough and Kittridge, is another book of this sort. Kittridge became more or less a legend in the academic world, and nothing he wrote succeeded better than his *Words and Their Ways.*

Late in the nineteenth and early in the present century the evaluation of rhetoric as a school study changed. What had formerly been covered in the rhetoric texts was now included in texts emphasizing composition, and no more rhetorics appeared.

The foreign-language books, chiefly grammars, are in a class of their own. The Latin grammars, a heritage from the distant past,[2] were the first of these books used in American schools. In

---

playing jokes on each other. See Fay, *Franklin: The Apostle of Modern Times* (Boston: Little Brown, 1929), pp. 282, 283, 344.

[2] Far in the past many opposed the study of Latin grammar — in other

the seventeenth and eighteenth centuries no one was considered educated above the most elementary stage unless possessed of a knowledge of Latin, at least to the extent of being able to read it and to know its syntax.

In the American colonies Latin was considered of such importance for pupils above the lowest rank that many schools were arranged on that basis. In Virginia the early institutions known as "free schools" were organized especially for Latin instruction.[3] A number of Latin Grammar schools were established in New England. The first was the Boston Latin School, arranged for in a Town Meeting in 1635, just a decade and a half after the landing of the Pilgrims. These early New England institutions were for boys only, there being a newly passed law that such schools were "improper and inconsistent . . . as ye

words, the study of grammar of any sort. It is well known to students of medieval history that Pope Gregory the First, the founder of papal supremacy, was a strong opponent of the study of grammar. He was against grammatical observance and the bickering that arose from it. Hallam, *Literature of Europe* (New York: Widdleton, 1870), I, 28. The English writer Helen Waddell, author of *Mediæval Latin for Schools*, in one of her recent learned and intriguing studies of the Middle Ages, relates on the authority of a ninth-century author that Gregory used bad grammar and defended such usage as being "partly due to indigestion as well as to holy zeal." Waddell, *The Wandering Scholars* (London: Constable, 1949), p. xix. H. O. Taylor in *The Mediæval Mind* (New York: Macmillan, 1919), 3rd edn., II, 149, defends the early grammar, saying "Grammar was most instrumental in preserving Mediæval Latin from violent defections which would have left the ancient literature as the literature of a forgotten tongue." Horne Tooke, in his vastly learned and witty, though sometimes eccentric, *Diversions of Purley* (London: Printed for the Author, 1798), p. 5, said: "I think grammar difficult, but I am very far from looking upon it as foolish; indeed so far, that I consider it as absolutely necessary in search after philosophical truth; which if not the most useful perhaps, is at least the most pleasant employment of the human mind."

[3]Ames, *Reading, Writing and Arithmetic in Virginia 1606–1699* (Williamsburg: Virginia 350th Anniversary Celebration, 1957), pp. 10 and 22.

law enjoins" for female attendance.[4] A Latin school was founded in New Haven, Connecticut, in 1684, "the erection of ye said schoole," according to the record that has come down to us, "being principally for ye instruction of hopeful youth in ye Latin Tongue, and other learned Languages."

With the abolition of Latin as the usual language of the learned it lost some of its prestige from the standpoint of lower-school education, but for a period it continued to be thought of by many as the foundation for the acquirement of knowledge. Early in the nineteenth century the German philosopher Arthur Schopenhauer said in his cynical way: "If a man knows no Latin, he belongs to the vulgar, even though he be a great virtuoso on the electrical machine and have the base of hydrofluoric acid in his crucible."[5] Even then numerous educators were beginning to attach little value, or at least less value than before to the study of Latin.[6]

There being at an early date a substantial demand for Latin grammars in the colonies, they were of necessity brought from England. The first book of this class produced in America was Ezekiel Cheever's *Accidence, A Short Introduction to the Latin Tongue,* written before 1650 and sometimes referred to as the

---

[4] The first American high school, established in Boston in 1825, was for boys; one for girls was opened four years later.

[5] Schopenhauer, *Essays* (New York: Burt's Home Library, n.d.), p. 316.

[6] In medieval times and later students in all universities had to be competent in Latin since virtually all lectures and textbooks were in that language. Even as late as the sixteenth century much higher education consisted almost entirely of Latin and Greek studies. Charles O'Malley, *Michael Servertus* (Philadelphia: American Philosophical Society, 1953), p. 53, speaking of the early sixteenth century period, says: "In a large measure a medical education at that time could be and frequently was constituted of little beyond a proficiency in Latin and Greek."

first American schoolbook. An "abridgment" was printed in 1709, one year after Cheever's death, and a third edition, "Revised and Corrected by the author," was put out in Boston in 1724. From what we can gather now, it seems probable that the text was used in manuscript form before it was printed. The book as it finally came from a press was a small volume of less than a hundred pages, wholly the product of Cheever's early teaching days. He began conducting a school in New Haven when he was twenty-three, remaining there twelve years; he then went to Ipswich, which is some miles northeast of Boston, to establish a school; and later removed to Boston, where he remained a teacher until he was in his nineties. An informative biography of Cheever was published in the third number of Barnard's *Journal of Education,* and reprinted in the editor's *Educational Biography* in 1859. Elizabeth P. Gould's *Ezekiel Cheever, Schoolmaster,* printed in Boston in 1904, is a good account of the noted New England teacher.

At the little town of Ipswich the first protest of Americans against an action that "infringed their liberties" took place in 1687, when Governor Andros levied an arbitrary tax during the time Cheever was resident there. The story of this Ipswich incident has come down to us through Cotton Mather's curious but entertaining *Magnalia,* originally issued in London in 1702, reprinted in Hartford in 1820, and issued in other editions since. This book contains a great deal of information on pioneer New England education, and particularly on Harvard, the latter written, as one witty biographer of Mather has said, when Harvard "had not yet had the opportunity to displace him."[7] It was while teaching in his first school at New Haven that Cheever compiled his *Accidence,* which was last printed at

---

[7] Peabody, *Cotton Mather* (New York: Harper, 1902), p. 108.

Boston in 1838 in a twentieth edition. It is notable that this initial grammar was used over a longer period than was any later American Latin grammar.[8]

In 1779 a *Short Introduction to Grammar,* "Being a new addition [sic] of Whittenhall's Latin Grammar," was published in Philadelphia, "Printed by Joseph Cruikshank, in Market-Street, between Second and Third Streets." This book showed on the title page that it was the "Third Edition," "For the Use of the College and Academy in Philadelphia." No compiler's name was anywhere shown; it was merely explained in the preface that "the Ground Work is Whittenhall's Latin Grammar," a book previously published in England. This early American Latin text may be another of those books on which a printer made all or most of the revisions. It is evident from an examination of the two books in the American and English editions that there were extensive revisions.

Among the grammars of Peter Bullions, published about the middle of the century, was his *Principles of Latin Grammar,* which became one of the most frequently printed texts of its class. The book was based, the compiler stated, on Adams' *Latin Grammar,* a long-time favorite in England. Bullions in his usual efficient manner made an excellent text out of the older volume, adding "Corrections and improvements suggested by subsequent writers, or the result of the author's own reflections and observations during many years as a classical teacher." Bullions' Latin text was printed over a long period and, along with it, Jacob's *Latin Reader* was issued by the same publisher,

---

[8] The first "modern school text," Comenius' *Orbis Sensualium Pictus,* while not a Latin grammar, was primarily a Latin text since one side of every page was in that language. It was meant to advance knowledge of Latin while imparting useful general information. The book was printed in this country in the nineteenth century in editions of limited quantity, but there seems to be no generally available information that it was ever used here as an ordinary school text.

with cross references to explanations of the Latin structures in
Bullions' *Grammar*.

Small Latin grammars of the mid-nineteenth century widely
used were E. A. Andrews' *First Lessons in Latin,* and George
Stuart's *First Year in Latin.* Andrews' text was of pocket size
and the subject matter was as compact as the volume itself.
There seemed to be just enough material on each phase of
grammar, and the fables and brief stories at the end of the
book for "reading and translation" were of a nature to make
the study a little more interesting than the material in some
kindred texts. Stuart's text, like Andrews', was down-to-earth,
the compiler selecting practically all his Latin phrases and sentences from Latin authors.

A number of French grammars, as well as a few in Spanish,
German, and other languages, were published during the nine-
teenth century for American school use; but the study of these
languages never progressed sufficiently in the common schools
for any of the texts used to attain outstanding prominence.
Among the earliest of the French grammars was John Perrin's
Grammar of the French Tongue, printed by Hickman and
Hazard in Philadelphia in 1822. It was originally issued in
France, and the first American edition was "From the last
London Edition, Carefully revised by Thomas Wilson." As
early as the second decade of the nineteenth century Cubi's
Spanish Grammar appeared in this country and by 1826 a
third edition was being printed in Baltimore. This edition was a
five-hundred-page volume, and was much superior to the second
edition. Cubi's small *Spanish Dictionary,* published in this
country early in the century, was the first one of its class.

Louis P. Klipstein's *Grammar of the Anglo-Saxon Language,*
published in 1848, was the first work in its category issued in
America. Due to loss of part of the manuscript, some inaccu-

racies appeared in the first printing. The next year a corrected edition was printed. This revised text was one of the most scholarly books on the subject written during the nineteenth century, and Klipstein became recognized as one of the foremost Anglo-Saxon scholars. Already, in 1845, the University of Giessen in Germany had conferred on him a Ph.D. degree *in absentia* for his work in Anglo-Saxon.

Klipstein was born in Winchester, Virginia, in 1813, son of a physician who came over with the Hessian troops and later settled in the Shenandoah Valley. The story of this learned son of a doctor from the Hessian Province is one of the strangest and most tragic in all American schoolbook history. The boy, Louis Klipstein, was brilliant and did well in anything he turned his hand to. He became a schoolteacher in Charlottesville, Virginia, and there, while reading Scott's *Ivanhoe,* developed an interest in its dialog, with its Anglo-Saxon terms. This interest led Klipstein to study the Anglo-Saxon language and its relation to later English, which resulted in his Anglo-Saxon grammar. The book was finished on a South Carolina plantation owned by his wife, whom Klipstein had met and married while there.

The loss on Klipstein's book because of the necessity to reprint it shortly after its first appearance and its failure to win wide acceptance led to quarrels with his wife over her having to help bear the expense incurred, and there was a separation. Klipstein took to drinking, and in the 1870's he was seen begging on the streets of Charleston, South Carolina, a number of times. At this period he was living in shacks with Negroes. His wife disposed of her property at Santee, not a great distance from Charleston, and went to Florida. Klipstein followed her but evidently his wife would have nothing further to do with him, and he reverted to the frustrated and defeated life he had led in his South Carolina days. Louis Klipstein died in Florida, a pauper.

A few Anglo-Saxon grammars, as well as two or three Anglo-Saxon readers, were published after Klipstein's day. Stephen H. Carpenter's *Anglo-Saxon Grammar and Reader,* and his *English of the Fourteenth Century* were published in the 1870's and reprinted until some time in the 1880's. The latter book, a study of English in the age of Chaucer, traced the evolution of the language down to his time. It was designed, as the author stated in his preface, as an "introduction to the study of English Literature," especially insofar that of early England has affected the writings of modern times. Stephen Carpenter was a professor of rhetoric and English literature in the University of Wisconsin, and after retirement from teaching continued to apply himself to Anglo-Saxon studies.

Francis Andrew March, whose interest in Anglo-Saxon was aroused when he was a young man by Noah Webster, published his *Comparative Grammar of the Anglo-Saxon Language* in 1870, and the text was still being reprinted as late as 1899. The year his grammar appeared, March also produced an *Introduction to Anglo-Saxon: An Anglo-Saxon Reader.* He was one of the number of well-known philologists who late in the nineteenth century worked for spelling reform. As several other sons of schoolbook compilers did, Francis Andrew March's became renowned. His son, General Peyton March, served as Army Chief of Staff at Washington during World War I.

By the end of the century Anglo-Saxon was becoming less popular as a school study. It was later to be practically ignored except in philological courses in institutions of higher learning, and even there it was not too much studied.

X

Arithmetics

THE FIRST ARITHMETIC written and published by an American was Isaac Greenwood's *Arithmetic, Vulgar and Decimal,* printed in Boston in 1729. The volume did not carry the compiler's name on the title page, but Greenwood made known in an advertisement in a contemporary newspaper that he wrote the text, and no doubt exists about its authorship. Greenwood's advertisement, in the *Boston News Letter* of May 29, June 5 and 12, 1729, ran:

Just published *Arithmetic Vulgar and Decimal;* with the application thereof to Variety of Cases in Trade and Commerce. By Isaac Greenwood, A. M., Hollisian Professor of Mathematics, and Philosophy. To be sold by Thomas Hancock at the Bible and Three Crowns near the Town Dock, Boston.[1]

The Greenwood *Arithmetic* was 158 pages in length, and had lessons on enumeration, addition, subtraction, multiplication, and division, just as later arithmetics did. Both common (vulgar) and decimal fractions were thoroughly covered, as were square root, cubes, and so on. Ten pages were given over to "pounds" and "the Aliquot Parts of Shillings"; almost a century

---

[1] Simons, *Introduction of Algebra into American Schools* (Washington: *Bureau of Education Bulletin 18, 1924*), p. 68.

was to pass before pence, shillings, and pounds were to disappear from American schoolbooks. Greenwood divided the decimal with a comma, although he stated that the distinguishing mark could be "a Comma, Period, or the like." Instead of "subtraction" he used the spelling "substraction."[2] According to Greenwood a billion was a "million million"; he was using the old European application of the word, which is still used in England. The terms million and billion in the present sense are less than a century and half old; million as used today first appeared in the Italian Berghi's arithmetic in 1494. As far back as Egyptian times there was a symbol for million, but it represented a different quantity from the modern million.[3]

In 1721 Thomas Hollis, a wealthy London merchant, endowed a professorship in divinity at Harvard, and in 1727 provided for ones of mathematics and philosophy. He stipulated that the holder of the last-mentioned professorship should "promote true piety and Godliness by his own example and Incouragement," and that the professor, "while he is delivering his Philosophical and Astronomical lectures, is to make such incidental reflections upon the Being, Perfections and Providences of God, as may arise from the subjects, and may tend seriously to impress the minds of youth."[4]

Isaac Greenwood was the first appointee to the Hollis pro-

---

[2] David Eugene Smith, *History of Mathematics* (Boston: Ginn, 1923–24), II, 95, tells of the evolution of this spelling.

[3] Professor A. S. Eve, of McGill University, in an article "Dizzy Arithmetic," in *Atlantic Monthly,* February, 1925, explains the inception and evolution of the terms millions and billions and shows that there is still a need of adopting internationally, to suit modern scientific needs, a uniform enumeration for quantities designated as millions, billions, and trillions, which is not at present the same in all countries.

[4] Cohen, *Some Early Tools of American Science* (Boston: Harvard Press, 1950), p. 12.

fessorship at Harvard—this in 1727. It was during his early incumbency there that his *Arithmetic* was published. From the record it appears that Greenwood was a splendid teacher of mathematics and science, and got along particularly well for a while, being a sort of protege of Thomas Hollis, the London benefactor. There was one fly in the ointment—young Greenwood's serious and evidently frequent lapses from sobriety. After a time these irregularities caused numerous upsets in his career, and his removal from office was under advisement several times. On April 17, 1738, while Greenwood was still in his thirties, the following was recorded :

> The Honorable and Reverend Overseers having upon the Mathematical Professor's humble confession of his past Miscarriages, deferred the consideration of the vote of the Corporation, relating to the removal from his Office, till their next Meeting, and the Said Professor by that means, continuing in the exercise of his Office, and it being necessary in order to his instructing the Youth in Experimental Philosophy (who by law are obliged to pay for all said instructions) that he have use of the apparatus; and nothing appearing since the last Meeting of the Overseers, but that Mr. Professor Greenwood behaves himself, with sobriety and Diligence in his Office, Therefore voted, That the apparatus be again committed to the Care of the said Professor till further Order of the Corporation.[5]

Later in that year, the fruits of the numerous New England stills[6] being too easily accessible to the mathematically talented

---

[5] Cohen, *Some Early Tools of American Science* (Boston: Harvard Press, 1950), pp. 133–134.

[6] "Newport had twenty-two 'still-houses' at one time and it was estimated that the Massachusets stills consumed 15,000 hogsheads of molasses yearly." Wertenbacker, *The Puritan Oligarchy* (New York: Scribner, 1947), p. 198. Although Professor Wertenbacker states that the largest part of the liquor output was exported, it must be true that much of it must have been consumed locally.

Greenwood, the Harvard overseers found it necessary to replace him. He was taken out of his professorship, and was succeeded by one of his own pupils, John Winthrop. When King's College, later Columbia University, was founded, the first professorship established was that of mathematics. A young student from the class of John Winthrop by the name of Daniel Treadwell was King College's first professor of mathematics. He came to the newly created college "recommended by Professor Winthrop as eminently fitted for the station."[7] Even that far back the Hollis professorship at Harvard, which Isaac Greenwood filled for a decade in spite of his addiction to alcohol, was an influential one.

Greenwood was born in Boston in 1702 and was graduated from Harvard in 1721, receiving the A. M. degree three years later. It appears from the Harvard records that after his dismissal Greenwood still had some connection with the university. It is known that he privately taught after his Harvard professorship, as he had done previous to going there, and from all indications he got along fairly well.

In 1730 an *Arithmetica or Cypher-Konst* was printed in New York by J. Peter Zenger, renowned for his early efforts on behalf of freedom of the press. This first algebra text printed in the United States was written in the Dutch language and based on the compiler's earlier work on algebra published in Holland in 1714. The compiler was Pieter Venema, who had been a teacher in Holland and who is believed to have taught in New York.[8]

---

[7] *A History of Columbia University 1754–1904* (New York: Columbia University Press, 1904), p. 22.

[8] It is thought that Venema died in New York and is buried there, but this point has never been substantiated. See A. Day Bradley, "Pieter Venema, Teacher, Textbook Author and Freethinker," *Scripta Mathematica,* March 1949, No. 1, later reprinted in pamphlet form.

Venema explained that he wrote his combined arithmetic and algebra "because there was here no ciphering book in the low Dutch concerning trade or merchandise and for the sake of the teaching of inquiring youth and of all the lovers of the teaching of arithmetic, I have undertaken to make a clear and succinct ciphering book upon that excellent science which flourishes in the city [New York] and country. To this are added the elements of algebra whereby that which is not understood in arithmetic can be demonstrated by the clear words of algebra."

The *Arithmetica or Cypher-Konst* was a volume of one hundred and twenty pages, with the first seventy-five on arithmetic and the rest given over to algebra, which Venema said was "the key to the obscure propositions of arithmetic." The arithmetic section followed the general pattern of the day, progressing gradually through fractions and "the rules of higher arithmetic." It treated "trade," "partnership," and "the handling of merchandise" in considerable detail. Only two copies of this little text are known today, both in the New York Historical Society Library. A third copy, in the New York State Library, was destroyed in the fire of March, 1911.

Although the first in the United States, Pieter Venema's book was not the first containing algebra printed on the North American continent. As far back as 1556, the *Sumario Compendioso,* a volume with six pages of algebra, was printed in Mexico. A facsimile of this book, with an account of its history by David Eugene Smith, was published in Boston in 1921. It is of course quite well known that printing began in Mexico a century earlier than it did in the Atlantic seaboard colonies and that any number of books came off the Mexican presses before the 1640 issue of the noted *Bay Psalm Book,*[9] the first book printed in the

---

[9] *Bibliography of Mathematical Works Printed in America through 1850* (Ann Arbor: University of Michigan Press, 1940). No class of textbooks has been so well covered in histories of mathematics, documented

United States. Professor Louis Charles Karpinski records five mathematical books printed in Mexico prior to the time of the issuance of the *Bay Psalm Book.*

The first separate algebra text printed in the English language in this country was Jeremiah Day's *Elements of Algebra,* published in New Haven, Connecticut, in 1814. The compiler was a teacher of mathematics at Yale, and his algebra enjoyed a most phenomenal success. By 1850 sixty-seven editions had been printed, totaling 134,000 copies. Of the American school texts which ran through many editions, this is one of the few where exact circulation is known. The record was kept straight by the appearance in the title pages of the respective editions of the number of copies printed.

Until the time of Nicholas Pike in the latter part of the eighteenth century most of the arithmetics used in America were English productions. Chief among them were those of James Hodder, Edward Cocker, John Ward, George Fisher, and Thomas Dilworth. Dilworth's was the most popular of all arithmetics in this country until the appearance of Pike's, with George Fisher's books running it a close second. Hodder's, Dilworth's, and Fisher's texts were reprinted in this country, and many copies of all of them were also imported from England. John Ward's *Young Mathematician's Guide* was used chiefly in Yale and Harvard and other higher schools.

---

treatises, and bibiographies as have the school arithmetics. In a study of the subject the student can go to the several volumes of David Eugene Smith and Louis Charles Karpinski, which contain much interesting material. For the general history of school arithmetics, a number of other books are available, among them Smith's *Rara Arithmetica,* the important Augustus De Morgan publications *A Budget of Paradoxies* and his *Arithmetical Books,* and the first book written by the noted Shakespearian scholar James O. Halliwell, *Rara Mathematica, A Collection of Treatises on the Mathematics,* published in 1839. This last book, printed when the author was not yet twenty, is rarely to be found today, but most of its contents has been absorbed in the other books mentioned.

Hodder's *Arithmetick* was originally printed in London in 1661, and it was the first arithmetic to attain that widespread popularity in schools that many were to achieve in the next two hundred years. James Hodder, the compiler, the date of whose birth is not known, kept a school in Aokahan Yard, Lothbury, England, which was advertised in his 1661 edition as "next door to the 'Sunne,' where such as are desirous to learn . . . may be carefully attended and faithfully introduced." Later Hodder conducted a school at Bromley-by-Bow, which is in County Kent southeast of London.[10] It was while at Lothbury that Hodder's *Arithmetick* was brought out, and by 1690 the seventh edition had been put in type.

In 1719 an edition of Hodder's *Arithmetick or That Necessary Art Made Most Easy* was printed in Boston by J. Franklin, brother of Benjamin. This book was put out, as the title page showed, "for S. Phillips, N. Buttolph, B. Elliot and N. Negua, Booksellers in Boston and sold at their shops." The title page listed the compiler as "James Hodder, Writing-Master"; and it was stated that it was "the Five and Twentieth Edition, Revised, Augmented, and above a Thousand Faults amended, by Henry Mose, late Servant and Successor to the Authour." The Boston edition was an exact copy of that issued in London in 1690 by Henry Mose. Mose, successor to the compiler, taught in a school in Sherborne Lane, London, and apparently inherited the assets of Hodder.

The 1719 Boston Hodder's *Arithmetic* was a small octave of two hundred and sixteen pages, fairly well printed, and the woodcut at the front is believed to be the first illustration to be reproduced in an American book.[11] The "scratch" system of division was used by Hodder — a method presented in all arith-

---

[10] De Morgan, *A Budget of Paradoxies* (New York: Dover, 1954), II, 265.

[11] *The Antiquarian,* August 1931.

metics until the time of Pike. The "Austrian Method" of subtraction was taught, and compound interest was treated in a system of computation dropped two centuries ago. In division Hodder used the method of writing first in a column the beginning multiples of the divisor, the remainders being put in a vertical column without preserving the decimal order. Even to look at a problem so worked out is today confusing.

Cocker's *Arithmetic,* based on Hodder's, was the most popular one in England during the eighteenth century. This exceedingly popular text went through a hundred editions in England within a century. It first appeared in 1678, only seventeen years after the initial issue of Hodder's less-used work. Cocker's text was utilized very extensively in America, and it is hard to understand why it was never printed on our side of the Atlantic. Evan's *American Bibliography* listed an edition printed at Philadelphia in 1779, but did not indicate the source of the datum and, as no such copy has ever been recorded elsewhere, Evan's listing is now believed to have been an error. That Cocker's book was never printed in America was probably due to the fact that it was current at a time when many texts used in American schools were imported from overseas.

During the last half of the seventeenth century and the first half of the eighteenth, freight rates on shipments from England to the colonies were very low because many vessels came to this country light, to haul back tobacco and other agricultural products—a condition which favored the import of British books to America. It is true, also, that they could generally be produced less expensively in England than in the colonies.[12]

Augustus De Morgan in his *Arithmetical Books* says that Cocker's *Arithmetick,* which went through one hundred and

---

[12] For an account of early transatlantic freight rates in relation to book shipments see *The Printer in Eighteenth Century Williamsburg* (Williamsburg: Colonial Williamsburg, 1958), p. 10.

twelve editions, was a forgery by John Hawkins, a London publisher known to have been involved in irregularities in connection with some of his publications. It is claimed that the English dictionary issued under Cocker's name was a forgery by Hawkins, and this charge has been well substantiated. De Morgan asserts that the *Arithmetick,* which appeared in 1667, the year Cocker died, was a concoction from other authors' works put together by John Hawkins, with Cocker credited as compiler, and that Hawkins did much advertising to promote the book. De Morgan said that the *Arithmetick* derived its success more from this exploitation than from its merits, even stating that some of its popularity resulted from the fact that it was mentioned on the stage in a popular play of its day. De Morgan thought that Cocker, who had long been known as a master of penmanship, had a reputation indeed "since a bad book under his name pushed out the good ones." [13]

De Morgan believed that the Cocker *Arithmetick* resulted in a deterioration of arithmetical texts for some time; but it is possible that the London University professor of mathematics erred in some of his conclusions about Cocker. It is true that Cocker dropped much of the confusing long-used terminology and that he condensed some problem solutions. Taking into consideration the shortcomings of all the early arithmetics, it is a little difficult to believe that the book bearing Cocker's name was quite as inferior, in comparison, as De Morgan pronounced it.

Despite the vast, uncounted number of Cocker's *Arithmetick* printed, it ranks, strangely enough, with the very rare books of its class at the present time. Percy Fitzgerald commented on the extreme scarcity of copies of the early editions of this particular book. He said, "So scarce are copies of the editions

---

[13] *Encyclopædia Britannica,* 13th Edition, article on Cocker.

before 1700 that Dr. Dibdin [Thomas Frognell Dibdin, well-known early nineteenth-century bibliophile and bibliographer] was never able to see one prior to the thirty-second, which appeared some time after 1700."[14] Fitzgerald, writing after De Morgan's time, did not seem to doubt Cocker's authorship of the arithmetic, and after his remark about the text, added, "Poor Cocker did not live to enjoy the great renown his book obtained."[15]

The record of "George Fisher" ranks with the two or three most involved bibliographical puzzles having to do with school-books, a few perplexing discrepancies still stand out. Louis C. Karpinski has told the story of George Fisher as nearly as he was able to figure it out.[16] He concluded that the name was a pseudonym. The British Museum listed the name of George Fisher as Mrs. Slack, and so catalogued its George Fisher items. The Library of Congress did the same thing for a period, but in later years the designations on the index cards were marked out with pencil, presumably on the strength of doubts that later developed.

The real Mrs. Slack was the wife of a London printer and publisher who at one time had a establishment on the old London bridge. Mrs. Slack's actual name was Ann Fisher Slack, and it was long thought that she had used George Fisher as a pen name just as Marian Evans used George Eliot. One weakness in this assumption is the fact that an arithmetic was published under the name of George Fisher the year Mrs. Slack

---

[14] Percy Fitzgerald, *Recreations of a Literary Man* (London: Chatto and Windus, 1883), p. 308.

[15] Much information on Edward Cocker not readily found elsewhere is available in *From the Books of Lawrence Hutton,* one of the Harper's American Essayists Series, put out in 1892, pp. 113–116.

[16] Louis C. Karpinski, "The Elusive George Fisher Accomptant and Writer and Editor of Three Popular Arithmetics" *Scripta Mathematica,* October, 1935.

was born. Strangely enough no one up to the present time seems to have thought of the possibility that there might have been a real George Fisher, perhaps an accountant, who had turned to writing mathematical texts.

In 1731, George Fisher's *Instructor* was printed in England. It was destined to go through numerous reprintings both in England and the colonies and, later, in the United States after the Revolution. The first American edition was printed in 1748 and in half a century it went through a dozen editions here. The first American issue was printed by B. Franklin and D. Hall in Philadelphia under the title *The American Instructor*. It is probable that Benjamin Franklin gave it the new designation because he thought it would increase its popularity as an American schoolbook. By 1800 editions had been published in Delaware, Pennsylvania, New York, New Jersey, Massachusetts, and New Hampshire. The popularity of the book derived chiefly from the fact that it was not merely an arithmetic but was something like a general "school collection."

Lessons in reading, grammar, handwriting, and "A Compendium on the Sciences of Geography and Astronomy" were included, and along with these, "gauging according to the most modern and approved practice." At the end of the long title-page legend were the words "To which is added the Rudiments of Drawing, with Several very useful tables Etc." The drawing section had four pages of outstandingly superior figures. There were three pages of script-copy examples and lessons were included on "walling," bricklaying, timber- measuring, carpentry, and "the erection of chimneys." One section covered the manufacture of "transparent colors" and another, "Colors and Dyeing." Three pages had to do with "instructions for marking linen" and were accompanied by two plates of letter and number designs for such use. The number of pages varied in different editions and some matter appearing in early issues was omitted from later ones — the "Poor Planters Physycian," a sort of "doctor-book" composition, for example.

Although John Ward's *Young Mathematician's Guide* was never reprinted in this country, as already mentioned it was for a considerable period used at Yale and Harvard as the main mathematical text. It was prescribed by the university authorities and several mentions of it are to be found in the literature of the time. A "higher arithmetic" and thus in a class of its own, it seems odd that it was not printed in the colonies. Perhaps it was decided that it would not be profitable, since it was a difficult piece of printing requiring special type and since use of it was limited. It was first issued in England in 1707 and forty years later had reached an eighth edition — "carefully revised" and "to which is now first added a SUPPLE-MENT containing the history of Logarithms." The work, as the title page showed, treated in its different sections Arithmetic, Algebra, The Elements of Geometry, Conic Sections, and the Arithmetick of Infinities. Until the final edition, except for added material, the contents were not much changed.

Little biographical information is available on John Ward, but the dedication of his *Young Mathematician's Guide,* which was inscribed to Sir Richard Grosvenor, proves the fact that he was an intelligent man and one well qualified for the tasks he set himself. In his introduction, headed "To The Reader," he had this to say about mathematical studies :

As to the usefulne/s of Arithmetick, it is well known that no Bu/ine/s, Commerce, Trade, or Employment whatsoever, even from the Merchant to the Shop-keeper &c. can be managed and carried on, without the a//i/tance of Numbers.

And as to the Usefulne/s of Geometry, it is as certain, that that no curious Art, or Mechanick-work, can either be invented, improved, or performed, without its a//i/ting Principles; tho' perhaps the Artiſt, or Workman, has but little (nay ſcarce any) Knowledge in Geometry.

Then, as to the Advantages that ariſe from both theſe Noble Sciences, when duly joined together, to aſſiſt each other, and then apply'd to Practice, (according as Occasion requires) they will readilly be granted by all who conſider the vaſt Advantages that accrue to Mankind from the Buſineſs of Navigation only. As alſo from that of Surveying and Dividing of Lands betwixt Parties and Party. Beſides the great Pleaſure and Uſe there is from Time-keepers, as Dials, Clocks, Watches &c. All theſe, and a great many more uſeful Arts, (too many to be enumerated here) wholly depend upon the aforſaid Sciences.

And therefore it is no Wonder, That in all Ages ſo many Ingenious and Learned Perſons have employed themſelves in writing upon the Subject of Mathematicks.

(The above is quoted from the Eighth Edition, brought out in London in 1747, an issue used in this country.)

Dilworth's *The Schoolmaster's Assistant,* if we may judge from the number of American editions, was the most popular of all the English compiled texts in this country. In his English edition of 1743 Dilworth listed fifty-five English teachers who commended his work, and there were plenty who publicly approved his book in this country later on. The fact that *The Schoolmaster's Assistant,* in some cases issued under a different title, went through fifty-eight known printings after its first appearance in Philadelphia in 1781, attests its American popularity.

Just prior to the beginning of the nineteenth century Dilworth's book was being "adapted to the commerce of the Citizens of the United States," and by 1803 another edition, printed at Troy, New York, stated that it was "adapted to the currency of the United States." Dollar currency was established by Act of Congress in 1786, and coinage begun in 1792; but many arithmetics carried the English monetary system into the nineteenth century. Until his death in 1799 George Washington kept his accounts in shillings and pounds, and many other well-known persons did the same. Into the first decade of the nineteenth century facility in figuring pence, shillings, and pounds was generally considered as necessary as was that in figuring dollars and cents. The dollar mark did not appear in an arithmetic until 1797 when it was used in Chauncey Lee's *The American Accomptant: Being a Plain Practical and Systematic Compendium of Federal Arithmetic,* printed at Lansingburg, New York, now a part of the city of Troy.

Some two or three small American arithmetics were published between the time of Greenwood's volume and the end of the eighteenth century, none of which attained popularity. Among these were Benjamin Dearborn's *Pupil's Guide,* printed in Portsmouth, New Hampshire in 1782, and reprinted in Boston a year later. Another was Alexander MacDonald's *Youth's Assistant,* put out in Norwich, Connecticut, in 1785, and reprinted later in Litchfield and in Providence, Rhode Island. In 1743 a volume of 276 pages, with the title *The Merchant's Magazine or Factor's Guide,* by Robert Briscoe, was printed in Williamsburg, Virginia — the first book dealing with mathematics issued in that state. It contained a "Great Variety of plain and easy Tables for the speeding Casting up of all Sorts of Merchandise, sold either by Number, Weight, or Measure; and for reducing Sterling Money into Currency of sundry rates; with tables of Interest and Rebate, and of the Value of Gold and Silver in Virginia."

In 1788 Pike's *New and Complete System of Arithmetic,* "composed for the use of Citizens of the United States," was issued in Newburyport, Massachusetts, printed by John Mycall, later a Boston printer. This book and the *Abridgement of the*

New and Complete System of Arithmetick (the fourth edition of which used the spelling *arithmetic,* while the fifth reverted to *arithmetick*), originally issued in Newburyport by the printer of the first Pike text, were the first generally accepted and widely used American arithmetics. The initial book of Pike had 512 pages, which were reduced to less than four hundred in the first revision. This briefer volume was subsequently cut down still further. Isaiah Thomas, the early American printer, brought out most of the Pike texts after the first two.

In his first arithmetic Pike seems to have attempted to cover every phase of arithmetic that he could recall.[17] Pike's table of contents took up six pages. "Interest," "compound interest," "pensions," "annuities," "weight systems," and "foot measurement" were covered and there were explanations of "barter," "alligation medial," "finding the year of indiction," "measuring of Rhoades," and other topics which today few would know the meaning of. Enumeration up to billions and trillions was gone into, the compiler using the old form in explaining these quantities.

Pike seemed never to run out of rules, and some of the many he used were not too clear. More than a few must have been difficult for the brightest of pupils and some perhaps never succeeded in grasping some of them. He dwelt on the pendulum, the almanac, and included rules on the extraction of the biquadrate root. There was also a rule for determining the date of Easter for any year from 1753 to 4199 — no little feat of calculation even had the knowledge been of any use. Thomas H. Huxley wrote in 1868, "I doubt if one boy in five-

---

[17] In contrast to this wide coverage Erastus Root in *An Introduction to Arithmetic* (Norwich, Connecticut, 1796) omitted fractions entirely, not, as he explained in his preface, "because I think them useless but because they are not absolutely necessary."

hundred ever heard the explanation of a rule in arithmetic,"[18] and one may justifiably wonder whether Pike's were all thoroughly explained or whether any attempt was made to interpret them.

Naturally Pike went into the topic of gauging, as all other early arithmetic writers did. He explained how to gauge a mash tub, and had problems measuring the quantity of beer in containers. The frequency with which early arithmetics incorported problems on beer measurement seems worthy of note and perhaps indicates the difference between the way this beverage was looked upon during colonial times and the way it is looked upon by many today. Thomas J. Wertenbaker says that in New England, "Barley was grown for beer, which was a standard drink."[19] Records still exist of New England workers being paid their wages partly in beer.[20] After all, it is no surprise that Pike, a New Englander himself, included problems on measuring beer and told how to gauge a mash tub — at that time these were not so much problems for specialists as they are today.[21]

Paul Monroe, the well-known education historian, in the *Cambridge History of American Literature* chapter on Educa-

---

[18] Huxley, *Science and Education* (New York: Collier, 1901), p. 86.

[19] Thomas J. Wertenbaker, *The Puritan Oligarchy* (New York: Scribners, 1947), p. 55.

[20] When the great scientist Kepler had to give up his studies and go to Linz in Austria to teach mathematics in order to make a living he sold some of his books in Linz and was paid for them partly in beer. Carola Baumgardt, *Johannes Kepler* (London: Gollancz, 1952), p. 150.

[21] Ernest Earnest, professor of English in Temple University, in his *Academic Procession* (Indianapolis: Bobbs Merril, 1953), pp. 38, 72, 182, touches amusingly and with genial enlightenment on the association of students and beer down through the history of our institutions of higher education. Another volume issued the same year, Straus and Bacon, *Drinking In Colleges* (New Haven: Yale Press, 1953), is more sociological in nature.

tion, states that Pike's arithmetic was "avowedly a patriotic or nationalistic endeavor," and this is true, as borne out by the fact that George Washington and many other notables of the time praised and recommended the text. President Ezra Stiles of Yale, President Wheelock of Dartmouth, and Joseph Willard of Harvard heartily commended it. The Harvard endorsement also carried the signature of the Hollis Professor of Mathematics.

The *Schoolmaster's Assistant,* "being a plain arithmetic adapted to the United States," by Nathan Daboll, which came out after Pike's, was the most popular arithmetic of the first half of the nineteenth century, far surpassing Pike's in extent of usage. It went through more editions than any other American arithmetic. It appeared in 1800 and by 1843, the last date printed, it had gone through sixty-eight editions. Nathan and David A. Daboll's *Complete Schoolmaster's Assistant,* compiled by Nathan Daboll's son and issued in 1836, 1845, and 1849, is considered a revision of Daboll's arithmetic, but these editions are not counted in the sixty-eight mentioned above.

The extensive use of Nathan Daboll's *Schoolmaster's Assistant* was due to its emphasis on the new American money, its small size as compared to that of Pike, its limitations to material that was actually needed in schools, and its all-round practicability. Like the general run of arithmetics of its day, it had some tricky problems; and while a few, like many of Pike's, required a more advanced knowledge of mathematics, most of the problems presented were not difficult. A large part of the text was given over to the new dollar currency; but often the compiler, for no apparent reason, would switch back to pounds and shillings in the midst of a lesson.

Daboll was much given to using wine, rum, and brandy as

subjects of his problems. Some of them began "a gentleman
bought" so much rum, and so on—which leads one to believe
that purchase of such things by gentlemen in the old days was
not uncommon. Gamblers interested the compiler and he put
some of their complicated workings into his problems. Like
beer, gambling was not ill thought of in Colonial days and
afterward. As late as the 1830's religious magazines carried
articles on buying lottery tickets, without expressing disapproval
of the practice. It may be that Daboll took his cue in this
sphere from the numerous other arithmetics makers before him
who had included gambling problems in their pages.

As in practically every arithmetic of the time there were a
few problems in Daboll's text on geometrical ratio. One such
problem was the following :

A rich miser thought 20 guineas as a price too much for 12
fine horses, but agreed to give four cents for the first, 16
cents for the second, and 64 cents for the third horse, or so
on quadruple or fourfold proportion to the last; what did
they come to at that rate?

The answer as set down was, "The twelve horses came to
$223696, 20 cents." Daboll, like Greenwood, used the comma
for separating decimals and left a space between dollars and
cents.

At the end of Daboll's arithmetic was a set of forms showing
how to frame bonds, bills of sale, leases, and notes. These were
all simply stated, as was the rest of the subject matter. If anything was out of proportion it was the number of lessons in
American money. But this was something new and doubtless
seemed at the time to warrant more space than at present seems
to have been justified. Naturally Daboll's name became widely
known. Augustus De Morgan is authority for the statement that
according to Daboll "was a saying that became current in

America during the first half of the century," just as "according to Cocker" had earlier been current in England.[22]

The *North American Arithmetic* of Frederick Emerson stands apart as the forerunner of all the later arithmetics divided into parts, many of which are published today, and because of its illustrated lessons. Emerson's *Primary Lessons in Arithmetic,* only thirty-four pages in length, issued in 1826, seemingly attracted little attention. Four years later the *North American Arithmetic, Part 1,* appeared and by 1834 was followed by *Part 2* and *Part 3.* The great popularity of these texts must have been due to their unique compactness and the attractiveness of the material presented. No arithmetic before the *North American Arithmetic, Part 1* had been so appealingly assembled. Emerson truly said in his preface, "The method employed for illustrating the subject, it will be seen, is original and peculiar." In this respect the *Part 1* was a milestone — the most original of all nineteenth-century school arithmetics. The *North American Arithmetic* and other texts of Emerson were printed until well after the middle of the century, and there were numerous imitators even reaching into our own day.

In 1840 Charles Davies brought out his *First Lessons in Arithmetic,* and so much of the material followed that of Emerson's *Part 1* that Emerson brought a suit for infringement of copyright. The case was eventually settled out of court. It was announced that Emerson was paid a certain sum, and later he made a public statement to the effect that any apparent copying from his text by Davies had been "accidental." Davies was a graduate of West Point, taught mathematics there, and was later professor of mathematics at Columbia University. He compiled a series of school arithmetics and wrote several

---

[22] De Morgan, *A Budget of Paradoxies* (New York: Dover, 1954), I, 42.

volumes on mathematics, particularly on the higher branches.

During 1869 nineteen of Davies' school texts were being published by A. S. Barnes and Company. Besides his arithmetics, his editions of Legendre's *Geometry* and Bourdon's *Algebra* were widely used. Davies' *Legendre* was a revision and special arrangement of the "David Brewster translation," and apparently Davies did not know that it was actually translated by the then young Thomas Carlyle. The translation was made the same year that Carlyle translated Goethe's *Wilhelm Meister*. The fact that he had translated the *Legendre* was not publicly known until after Davies' time. Sir David Brewster wrote the notes and introduction and it was long thought that he had done the translating.[23]

It is difficult to believe that a man of Charles Davies' accomplishments would intentionally appropriate material from a little text such as Emerson's *North American Arithmetic*. Such a thing should have been wholly unnecessary in the case of one so capable, industrious, and dependable as Davies.

In 1821 Warren Colburn's *First Lessons in Arithmetic* was published. In some of the printings it was designated *Intellectual Arithmetic*. The next year the *Sequel to the First Lessons* appeared. These two texts have been considered as responsible for rescuing school arithmetic from "ciphering," an old, rutbound method.[24] Colburn's *First Lessons in Arithmetic*, which has been called "the greatest educational book of the century,"[25] was based on the teachings of Pestalozzi, who believed that

---

[23] See de Morgan, *Budget of Paradoxies,* II, 371, and *Encyclopædia Brittanica,* 13th edition, article on Sir David Brewster.

[24] The term "ciphering" came into widespread American circulation originally through the use in schools of such books as Venema's *Arithmetica or Cypher-Kontz,* already touched upon, and early arithmetics in which the word appeared. It is an old French word for figuring, originally coming from Arabic.

[25] Williams, *Horace Mann* (New York: Macmillan, 1937), p. 94.

children ought to be turned away from mathematical abstraction and that they should first learn the idea of numbers "by observing sensible objects." In his initial preface Colburn said :

> As soon as a child begins to use his senses, nature continually presents to his eye a variety of objects; and one of the first properties which he discovers is the relation of number. He intuitively fixes upon *unity* as a measure, and from this he forms the idea of more and less.

In his very first lesson Colburn tried to make the pupil comprehend number ideas wholly as an observing process rather than a "ciphering" procedure. The first questions of his text were :

1. How many thumbs have you on your right hand? How many on your left? How many on both together?
2. How many hands have you?
3. If you have two nuts in one hand, and one in the other, how many have you in both?

These words, elemental as they may seem, indicate Colburn's ideas of the process involved in a child's learning the beginnings of arithmetic. One sees that his conception was that it is a mental working of the observational element of the mind. There is, of course, not a possibility that Colburn's questions had any intended connection with counting on the fingers.[26]

---

[26] Strangely a few of the great mathematicians used their fingers in calculating in their early school studies. Nobert Wiener, who has done wonderful things along mathematical lines in our own day, says in his *Ex-Prodigy* (New York: Simon and Schuster, 1953), p. 45, that he counted on his fingers and continued to do so long after it was considered unacceptable in his school classes. Raphael's famous drawing of Ptolemy and Boethius with an astrolobe shows Boethius counting on his fingers. Several noted paintings show the same practice. David Eugene Smith in his *History of Mathematics* goes thoroughly into finger reckoning; and as far back as the first century of the Christian era, the Venerable Bede made the earliest known mention of it. Some of the earliest arithmetics, including that of Robert Recorde, carried illustrations showing finger counting.

In his first text Colburn introduced "mental" arithmetic. All the compilers of the "mental" arithmetics during the mid-nineteenth century and later leaned upon Colburn's method. Those of Benjamin Greenleaf, John F. Stoddard, Edward Brooks, Charles S. Venable, and others could almost be called "sequels" of Colburn's *First Lessons*. It is clear that Colburn had a new idea and the success of his texts is not difficult to understand. These arithmetics presented a fresh approach to school teachers and they quickly recognized the worth of the new method. From the time of the publication of Colburn's first book in 1821, his texts went through edition after edition until 1895.

Warren Colburn, a native of Massachusetts, died at the age of forty. He did not live long enough after the publication of his arithmetics to realize their true value to education. Not long after his death the copyright of the texts was disposed of by the family, but the members of the family later bought the publishing rights back. The title pages of the 1863 edition of the *Intellectual Arithmetic,* printed by Hurd and Houghton of New York and H. O. Houghton and Company of Boston, stated that the book was "Published for the heirs of Warren Colburn" and the edition was copyrighted in the name of "Temperance C. Colburn, Widow of Warren Colburn."

Warren Colburn should not be confused with his contemporary Zerah Colburn, the noted nineteenth-century Vermont-born mathematical prodigy, who also died young. In a letter Sir William Hamilton stated that he was influenced to study the branches of mathematics in which he became famous through early conversations with Zerah Colburn, but there seems not to have been any family or other connection between Warren Colburn and Zerah. The latter wrote an autobiographical *Memoir of Zerah Colburn,* published in Springfield, Massachusetts, in 1833, in which he narrates many of his experiences and relationships, but he nowhere brings in the name of Warren Colburn and it seems possible that the two never met. It is certain they had entirely different types of mind inasmuch as Zerah could not work out on paper a simple example in multiplication or division although he could answer the most amazingly intricate problems almost immediately. He once gave the correct cube root of 413,393,348,677 in five seconds.

In 1820 a small arithmetic was published in Dublin, Ireland, *The Use of the Bean Table,* with the subtitle, "An Introduction to Addition, Subtraction and Enumeration With Visible Objects." This book, "sold by R. N. Tims," did not show the compiler's name. The text contained precepts similar to those of Colburn. In the introduction the author stated :

> Children are commonly taught to pronounce the numbers one, two, three etc. in succession, and when by the force of memory they can reckon as far as one hundred, they are supposed to have a perfect knowledge of these numbers; whereas, in truth, they have none. All they know of each number is that it follows what goes before it; for instance, the idea they have of twenty is, that it is after nineteen and before twenty-one. By custom and by reckoning the objects around him, the child requires a more distinct idea of the numbers . . . . The child should always attach to the number the name of the object before him : for instance he should say, *one bean and one bean are two beans,* and not one and one are two; this later belongs to a more advanced stage.

Further along in the Dublin arithmetic the author said : "The simplest form in the science of number is UNITY, the largest number is composed of ones or UNITS, repeated or added together." Other ideas in the book are identical with those of Colburn. Did Warren Colburn see this little Dublin arithmetic before he compiled his own? It is not probable that he did, since it appeared such a short time before his own *First Lessons.* It seems likely that Colburn and the compiler of *The*

Use of the Bean Table worked out their ideas, so much alike, simultaneously and independently, neither knowing of the other. The processes of both the Colburn and Dublin arithmetics were based on Pestalozzi's sense-perception ideas, and it may be that the two compilers merely happened to express in almost similar words the ideas set forth by the noted Swiss education reformer.

According to dependable estimates, more copies of the arithmetics of Joseph Ray were printed than of any other American arithmetic texts. Ray was born November 25, 1807, in Virginia, in what is now the Northern Panhandle of West Virginia. He studied at a small school and later at the new Ohio University at Athens until he ran out of funds. He taught for a period in Cincinnati and then studied medicine, receiving his M.D. degree from the Medical School of Ohio when he was twenty-one.[27] Ray had a pronounced flair for mathematics and after a year of spasmodic medical practice was offered a place as instructor of mathematics in the Woodward High School of Cincinnati, referred to by Ray in some of his arithmetics as Woodward College, which he accepted. Ray became so interested in mathematics and in his teaching that his first school text appeared after the short period of three years.

His first book was *The Little Arithmetic,* which bore the

[27] The Medical School of Ohio was founded by Dr. Daniel Drake, who had had less than a year's medical training at the University of Pennsylvania and who taught in a number of medical schools. He is famous as the author of the American medical classic *Pioneer Life in Kentucky,* which has gone through a number of editions and will see more. This book has been pronounced by J. Christian Bay, one-time director of the John Creer Library of Chicago, as "the greatest of all Kentucky books." The last edition was issued by Schuman in New York in 1948. Alexander H. McGuffey married Drake's daughter, and in Drake's book is a long letter to Mrs. McGuffey in which the schoolbooks of Dilworth, Noah Webster, and the McGuffeys are touched upon.

subtitle "Elementary Lessons in Intellectual Arithmetic and the Analytic and Inductive Method of Instruction." On the title page were the words, "Being an introduction to Ray's *Eclectic Arithmetic*." *The Little Arithmetic* was published in 1834, and three years later the *Eclectic Arithmetic* came out. Within twelve years an even dozen of Ray's texts were in print.

The same year that *The Little Arithmetic* appeared a small *Table and Rules in Arithmetic for Children* was issued, but after four or five printings it was discontinued and the material incorporated in Ray's *Arithmetic, Part First*. This text was first printed in 1842 and was still in print as late as 1913. *The Little Arithmetic* was reissued as *Arithmetic, Part Second* in 1843, as part of "The Eclectic Series Newly Improved." There were several revisions of all the Ray texts and frequent changes in titles. By the middle of the century the *Arithmetic, Part Second* had been revised and made into a book under the same title, with the addition of the words, "a thorough course of mental arithmetic by induction and analysis."

From a technical standpoint the Ray texts were much on the order of Colburn's. The compiler did not draw out simple arithmetical matter to the extent that Colburn sometimes did but throughout his whole series of texts adhered to the simplicity and directness that were an inherent part of his method. Ray did not try to make his arithmetic problems difficult and introduced nothing more puzzling than the natural difficulties inherent in "figure" tangles. The story is told that when Ray published his *Higher Arithmetic,* a text "for high schools and colleges," his brother Mose, who all his life lived in the Pan handle section of West Virginia, where he was born, wrote to the compiler telling him that the text was "suitable for small children and not for higher students."[28] In regard to another

---

[28] Robert Grove Hughes, "Joseph Ray, the Mathematician and Man," *West Virginia Review,* February, 1932.

From *Heath's Fourth Reader*, 1903
Reproduced by permission of D. C. Heath & Co.
Many of the very human pictures in schoolbooks have enhanced reading
interest among pupils.

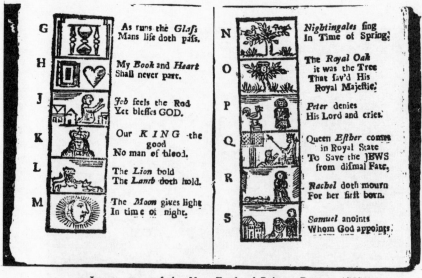

G
As runs the *Glaſs*
Mans life doth paſs.

H
My *Book* and *Heart*
Shall never part.

J
Job feels the Rod
Yet bleſſes GOD.

K
Our *KING* the good
No man of blood.

L
The *Lion* bold
The *Lamb* doth hold.

M
The *Moon* gives light
In time of night.

N
Nightingales ſing
In Time of Spring;

O
The *Royal Oak*
it was the Tree
That ſav'd His
Royal Majeſtie;

P
Peter denies
His Lord and cries.

Q
Queen *Eſther* comes
in Royal State
To Save the JEWS
from diſmal Fate;

R
Rachel doth mourn
For her firſt born.

S
Samuel anoints
Whom God appoints;

Lesson page of the *New England Primer,* Boston, 1727
Courtesy of New York Public Library
Rhyme alphabets similar to this one were included in nearly all editions
of the *Primer.*

Page from Comenius's *Visible World,* Twelfth Edition, London, 1778
This book was the forerunner of all our modern illustrated schoolbooks.

Newton wrote a "Universal Arithmetic."
Portrait reproduced by permission of Scripta Mathematica
Our schoolbook writers have followed in the footsteps of many well-known men: Roger Bacon, Philip Melanchton, Ben Jonson, Thomas Huxley, Jules Verne, H. G. Wells, Rudyard Kipling, Alexander Bell, and Count Leo Tolstoy penned textbooks.

From the *New England Primer,* Baltimore, 1829
This was one of the few editions showing only nine of the ten Rodgers children.

German Language ABC Book, Harrisburg, Pa., 1838
Numerous German-language texts of this sort were issued from
Christopher Sower's day down into the mid-nineteenth century.

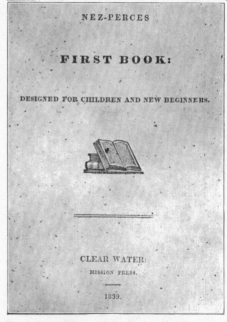

Nez-Percés Primer, Printed in Clearwater, Idaho, 1839
Courtesy The Oregon Historical Society
Produced in what was then part of Oregon, this was the first book
printed west of the Rocky Mountains in United States territory.

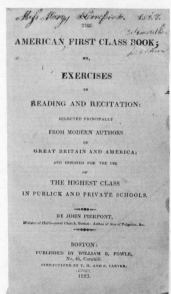

The first Booke of the English Schoole-Master.

CHAP. I.

TEaching all Syllables of two Letters, beginning with the easiest, and joyning them together that are of like found, as you may perceiue by placing (c) betwixt (k) and (s) and coupling them as you fee: and than teaching to reade words of two Letters.

The titles of the Chapters muft not bee taught the Schollers, but onely direct the Teachers.

a e i o u	a e i o u
Ab eb ib ob ub	Ba be bi bo bu
Ad ed id od ud	Da de di do du
Af ef if of uf	Fa fe fi fo fu
Ag eg ig og ug	Ga ge gi go gu
Ah eh *h oh *h	Ha he hi ho hu
Al el il ol ul	La le li lo lu
Am em im om um	Ma me mi mo mu
An en in on un	Na ne ni no nu
Ap ep ip op up	Pa pe pi po pu
At et it ot ut	Ra re ri ro ru
Ac et it ot ut	Ta te ti to tu

Ak ek ik ok uk — Bak bek bik bok buk
Ac ec ic oc uc — Cac cec cic coc cuc
As es is os us — Sa se si so su
Az ez iz oz uz — Za ze zi zo zu
Ai ei *i oi *i — Ia ie ji io iu
Ap ep * ou * — Pa pe ** po **
Au eu * ou * — Va ve vi vo vu
Aw ew * ow * — Wa we wi wo **

Ar er ir or ur — Qua que qui quo **

If you doe ill, fy on vs all :
Ah, is it fo ? he is my foe.
Woe be to me, if I doe fo.

Vp, go on : loe I fee a pye
So it is, if I doe lye,
Woe is me, oh I dye,
Ye fee in me, no lye to be.

B   CHAP.

When your Scholler hath perfectly learned his Letters, teach him to know his vowels: and after two or three dayes when hee is skilfull in them, teach him to call all the other letters confonants, and fo proceed with the other words of Art, as they ftand in the Margent ; neuer troubling his memory with a new word, before hee be perfect in the old.

C, before e, o, u, like (k) but before e, or i, like (f) if no other letter come betweene.

Now you may teach your Scholler, that hee can spell nothing without a Vowell.

Teach him that (r) is put for (i) the vowell, and make him reade these lines diftinctly.

Page from Coote's *English Schoolmaster* of the late eighteenth century A number of the "School-Collections" before Webster and Murray carried marginal information for the teacher. The above told how to teach a pupil to read through the long-used letter and syllable method.

THE
AMERICAN FIRST CLASS BOOK;
OR,
EXERCISES
IN
READING AND RECITATION:
SELECTED PRINCIPALLY
FROM MODERN AUTHORS
OF
GREAT BRITAIN AND AMERICA;
AND DESIGNED FOR THE USE
OF
THE HIGHEST CLASS
IN PUBLICK AND PRIVATE SCHOOLS.

BY JOHN PIERPONT,
Minister of Hollis-street Church, Boston: Author of Airs of Palestine, &c.

BOSTON:
PUBLISHED BY WILLIAM B. FOWLE,
No. 45, Cornhill.
STEREOTYPED BY T. H. AND C. CARTER.
1823.

Pierpont's *First Class Book*
First printed in 1823, this was one of the initial readers with a high order of material. The Pierpont texts enjoyed a long favor.

From *The McGuffey Fifth Reader,* 1879
The train conductor hires the locomotive engineer Martin Kroller. So
famous has this McGuffey story become that "wild" engineers on railroads are still given the nickname of "Martin Kroller."

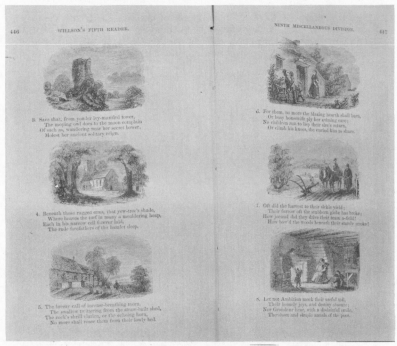

From Harper's *Willson's Fifth Reader,* 1861
The *Elegy Written in a Country Churchyard* is so splendidly illustrated
in this lesson, with a cut for each verse, that the book makes a good
collector's item for any collector of Thomas Gray's poems.

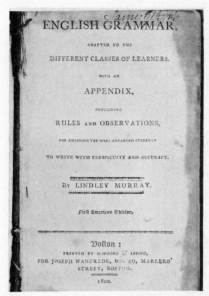

Title Page of Murray's *English Grammar*, 1800
The first widely used American text of its kind.

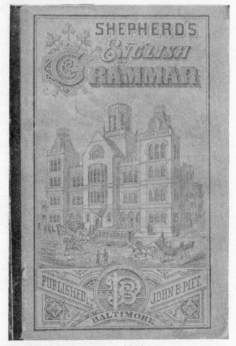

Shepherd's *English Grammar*, 1881
About this time illustrations first appeared in grammar books, helping
to relieve their long-time dullness.

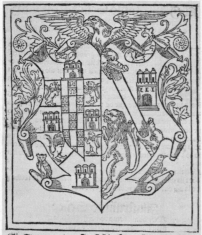

¶ Sumario côpédioso delas quêtas
de plata.y oro q̃ en los reynos del P̃iru son necessarias a
los mercaderes:y todo genero de tratantes. Cô algunas
reglas tocantes al Arithmetica.
❀ Fecho por Juan Diez freyle. ❀

Title page of the *Sumario Compendioso*. Printed in Mexico City, in
1556, this was the first mathematical text printed in the New World.
Reproduced through the courtesy of The Huntington Library,
San Marino, Cal.
The only other known copy is in the Escorial in Spain.

Chap. **V.**   *Division.*   55

I shall not, I(hope)need to trouble myself, or
Learner, to shew the Working of this Sum, or a-
ny other, having, now(as I suppose)sufficiently
treated of Division; but will leave it to the Cen-
sure of the experienc'd to judge, whether this
Manner of dividing be not plain, lineal, & to be
wrought with fewer Figures than any which is
commonly taught : As for Example appeareth.

(8
97 (5
9863 (0
987529 (3
9876418x (0
98765z3609 (8
98765430s987 (6
49382714848769 (4
2469135786376543 (2
zz345678998765432x   (124999999
98765432xxxxxxxx   9876543zr
98765432zzzzzzzz   124999999
98765433333333   249999998z
98765444444   3749999974
987655555   4999999966
9876666   6249999958
98777   7499999940
988   8749999933
9   9999999920
                      11249999915
                      ────────────
                              8

Proof 12345678998765432r
E 2   CHAP.

From Hodder's *Arithmetick*, Boston, 1719
This was the first arithmetic book printed in the English Colonies.
Hodder thought that the above division problem was "plain and
wrought with few figures."

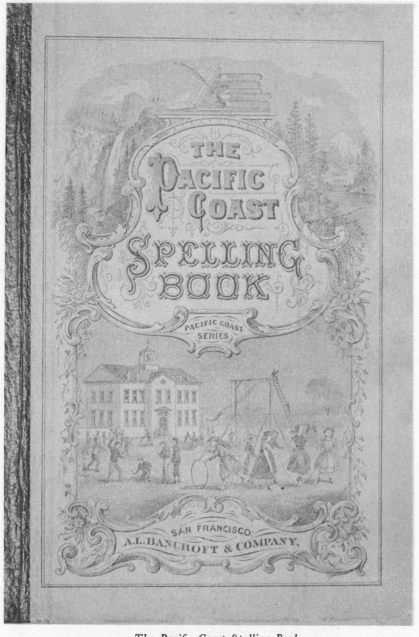

The Pacific Coast Spelling Book
First printed in San Francisco in 1873, twenty-five years after the
discovery of gold in California, this speller was a favorite on the
West Coast.

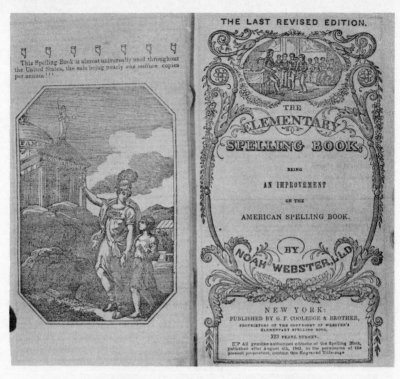

Webster's "Blue Back" *Speller* of 1848
This text with its familiar classical frontispiece was used for almost
a century by millions of American children.

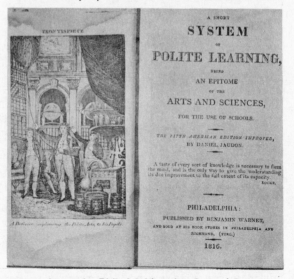

An early Philadelphia-printed special text
Four or five early nineteenth-century special texts were the forerunners
of the many "literature" books that were to be published during the
last half of the nineteenth century and in the twentieth century.

From Ellis's *Primary History*, 1884

Following the Civil War period, much interest was evinced in the opening up of the Western country. Every school pupil must have been fascinated by the picturings of the West.

A Spencerian Copybook of 1864

The "Spencerian System" became a family affair. Besides the name of Platt Rogers Spencer, the names of the sons and sons-in-laws appeared on the cover.

From Worcester's *Geography,* 1830

Alexander Anderson's woodcuts for textbooks were very popular with students.

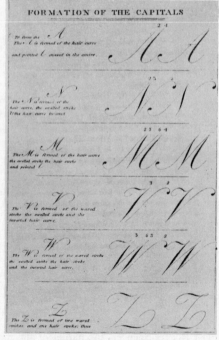

From Jenkins's *Art of Writing,* Boston, 1791

This was both a treatise on handwriting and a copy-model text. Within quarter of a century after it appeared, several other American penmanship books of this sort were in print.

XXIX

RIP VAN WINKLE.

[WASHINGTON IRVING, 1783–1859.

Whoever has made a voyage
up the Hudson, must remember
the Catskill Mountains. They

A post-Civil War *Holmes Reader*
Visual appeal in schoolbooks was noticeably lacking until the advent of
effectively used illustrations.

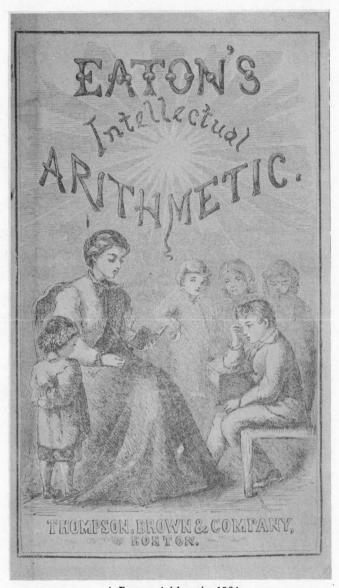

A Boston *Arithmetic,* 1864
The mid-nineteenth-century effort to make schoolbooks attractive, both
outwardly and inwardly, had a strong influence on education.

edition Mose wrote to his brother : "If I couldn't write a harder text than this I wouldn't write any." While Mose Ray could not by any stretch of the imagination be listed as a consummate writer, he must have been expert in mathematics, which evidently ran in the family. It is plain that Mose possessed that admirable human attribute, an abiding sense of humor.

Joseph Ray died in Cincinnati in 1855 at the age of forty-eight, at a time when the popularity of his texts had about reached its zenith. After his death his arithmetics continued to go through numerous revisions and editorial changes. One edition appeared even after the end of the nineteenth century. It is rather remarkable, considering how early Ray's arithmetics appeared, that between 1900 and 1913 the annual average sale was still over a quarter of a million copies.

During the twentieth century there has been little change in school arithmetic methods, teaching processes, or fundamental make-up of textbooks. The school mathematical compilations since 1900 are technically so little different from those of the last portion of the nineteenth century that there seems little reason to go into them from a bibliographical standpoint or to cite the slight method variations. Perhaps the most marked difference is to be found, as is the case in many other classes of texts, in the improved text make-up of most arithmetics produced today.

XI

Spelling Books

IN AMERICAN COLONIAL DAYS a school spelling manual, besides word-drill lessons, contained material for all-around study; reading exercises, samples of script, a brief section on arithmetic, a little religious matter, and almost anything thought to be helpful in the learning process in the school. Most of the well-known early beginning schoolbooks used in England and America were designated *spelling* books, whether that term was in the title or not, or by the more popular appellation *spellers*. The *New England Primer* in its day was frequently referred to in that way. In fact, at the time there was little difference in the make-up of some of the beginning spelling books and the primers, except that the former were generally larger.

Two of the school texts most widely used in the Colonies, outside of the *New England Primer,* were the spelling books of Thomas Dilworth and Daniel Fenning. Dilworth's *New Guide to the English Tongue,* though not titled a spelling book, was generally considered to be one, and was actually more nearly a speller than anything else. This book, first issued in England in 1740, was later printed several times in the American Colonies. In the early editions about half of the somewhat more than one hundred pages were taken up by spelling lists, progressing from words of one syllable to longer ones. The structure of the text,

148

from a practical standpoint, was chiefly directed at learning to spell. Notwithstanding this fact, much of the book's contents was ineffective in that sphere, containing such totally impracticable letter combinations as *Nebuzaradum, Estremadure, Saxigesime,* and *Abelbethmaleah.* At another point, in a single lesson were the words *Aberconiway, Caglian, Clarencester, Compostella, Elezar,* and *Thyatria,* and thirty-four others just as puzzling.

In Dilworth's days the elimination of difficulties confronting pupils did not seem to be a goal in the preparation of texts: on the contrary, difficulty appears to have been an aim worked toward, even in texts printed for the use of the youngest children. It seems quite certain that to confront a student with baffling subject was believed to result in better mental discipline — in other words, to increase a pupil's power to grasp and comprehend. We can find puzzling matter in any number of school texts on various subjects up to the end of the eighteenth century, and, in some cases, well into the nineteenth. In fact, it was not until Pestalozzi's educational views became fairly well disseminated and the great Swiss's pronouncement that "the mechanism of teaching ought to be simple" was broadly approved that planned difficulties and distractions were wholly eliminated from books used in schools — well after 1800.

Daniel Fenning's *Universal Spelling Book,* first issued in England in 1754 and reprinted in our country a number of times, was one of the popular and widely used early spelling texts. It was a book quite on the order of Dilworth's *Guide,* the full title being *Universal Spelling Book, or a New and Easy Guide to the English Language.* Fenning was connected with the Royal Exchange Assurance office in London and at about the time his speller appeared turned out several other texts, including an arithmetic, an algebra, a small dictionary, and a volume on the use of English.

Fenning's *Universal Spelling Book* was issued in Maine, at Falmouth, as early as 1786 — the first book printed in that state; and an issue was put out in Dover, New Hampshire, in 1795. The book was used well into the nineteenth century in American schools, going through a printing in Baltimore as late as 1810, a date which attests to its staying qualities. By this time a number of American spelling books were being published, and Noah Webster's had taken a firm hold. Of course Fenning's book could not continue to overcome such vigorous home-ground competition and it gradually went down hill, finally dropping out of use. Aside from Perry's *Spelling Book,* it was the last widely used schoolbook of British composition.

The first purely American spelling book was Anthony Benezet's *Pennsylvania Spelling Book, or Youth's Friendly Instructor and Monitor,* initially printed in Philadelphia in 1770. A second edition appeared in 1779, and a third in 1782. These several printings indicate that Benezet's book was fairly popular, although it was chiefly used among the Quakers. Like other spelling books of the "miscellany" type, Benezet's contained material for other studies.

The Perry *Spelling Book,* once much favored, was compiled prior to Noah Webster's text and was still being printed long after Webster's book appeared. One of the chief competitors of the Webster text, it was prepared by William Perry, a Scottish dictionary compiler, and first printed in Edinburgh in 1777. It was later reprinted many times in this country — Isaiah Thomas and his successors issued three hundred thousand copies from 1785 to 1804.[1] Its popularity may have been partly due to the fact that Perry's dictionary was well known and much used

---

[1] Oswald, *Printing in the Americas* (New York: Gregg, 1937), p. 85.

both in Great Britain and this country, and partly to the religious content of the text. The manual had lessons quoting morning and evening prayers. the ten commandments, and other religious themes, all of which would appeal to the greater part of the American population of the time. A number of fables, in the usual schoolbook style of the day, were included, and these, too, helped to increase its popularity. The book was well illustrated with good woodcuts. The Perry spelling text was still being printed in 1818, thirty years after the appearance of the Webster blue-back speller, and was the only *real* competitor of Webster's book during the first quarter of the period of its circulation.

The Noah Webster *Spelling Book* appeared in 1783, and bore the title *Grammatical Institute of the English Language, Part One*. The book was originally issued by the printing firm of Thomas and Andrews of Boston, which had for some time been putting out school texts. Three years after publication the title was changed to *The American Spelling Book,* and in 1829 to *The Elementary Spelling Book,* under which title the book went through printings running into many millions. It has been estimated that from seventy-five to eighty million copies were printed. According to records of the Appletons, long publishers of the book, thirty-five million copies were produced from 1855 to 1890. In one year, 1866, sales of the little book reached 1,596,000 copies.[2] Printing presses were worn out printing the book and it was at this time that the term *Blue-Back Speller* became a household word all over the country.

In the beginning it was Webster's goal to displace the Dilworth and Fenning texts, and he said as much. Naturally he hoped also to displace *Perry's Spelling Book,* but he never

---

[2] *First Hundred Years of the House of Appleton* (New York: Appleton, 1925), p. 44.

ventured to say so. It was his hope, he stated, that in writing his speller he was preparing "a book from which children could really learn to spell," something that had previously been, to quote his own statement, "difficult for them in the books extant." Webster also desired to make American pronunciation uniform and contended that only through the use of one standard spelling book could this aim be achieved — and naturally he wanted that one book to be his. He stated that there was popular prejudice in favor of Dilworth and that the American people at one time did not believe the Englishman's text could be improved upon. Webster brought out that he wanted to get away from the inclusion in his spelling book of superfluous words, of which there were so many in both Dilworth's and Fenning's book, and this he did accomplish.

The New England lexicographer went a long way toward accomplishing all that he proposed to achieve in his spelling book. He almost completely avoided the inclusion of impractical words such as those his predecessors had used so freely. Some few long words were included in the lessons near the end of the book, but they were such words as *conscientious, geometrician, surreptitious, cosmographic, etherealize,* and *scholasticism* — all perfectly comprehensible and easily grasped by the pupils. The pronunciation Webster first used was based on Samuel Johnson's *Dictionary,* and so acknowledged; but in the 1832 edition of the *Elementary Spelling Book* it was stated: "The pronounciation here given is that which is sanctioned by the most general usage of well-bred people both in the United States and England. This fact is stated from personal knowledge." Webster wanted it known at this time that he was no longer dependent upon the work of the celebrated Dr. Johnson. He believed that words should have one "fixed correct pronounciation," and stated in the 1832 speller that "there are a few words in both countries, England and the United States, whose pronounciation is not settled beyond dispute. In cases of this kind I have leaned to regular analogy as furnishing the best rule of decision." He was by this time free from influence by any of the dictionary makers, as his own had been published, and he was well upon the road to becoming recognized as America's foremost scholar.

Some editions of the Webster *Spelling Book* carried a number of fables and engravings were usually used to specially illustrate these lessons, which were intended as reading exercises. Some of the editions were particularly well illustrated. The 1844 issue had one hundred and fifty engravings by Alexander Anderson and W. G. Morgan.[3] The dress styles in these cuts were brought up to date, which had not been done in some of the former issues.

A Sequel to the Webster Elementary Speller, or Speller and Definer, by William G. Webster, listed on the title page as "son of the late Noah Webster," was published in 1845, two years after Noah's death. This was a minor dictionary, for school use. At about this time several such dictionaries appeared, and these to a certain extent temporarily displaced spelling books in some sections. The William G. Webster *Speller and Definer* was printed in the same format as was the *Elementary Spelling Book* and was bound in similar blue-board covers — with the hope, no doubt, that such a format would help bring patronage to the new *Speller and Definer.* Some other spelling book publishers of the time also adopted blue-board covers quite like the standardized Webster speller cover.

Around the last years of the eighteenth and first of the nineteenth century a considerable number of new spelling books

---

[3] Anderson had made part of the illustrations for former editions. He also engraved the cuts for the Hartford, Connecticut, *Child's Spelling Book* about the time he made his first ones for Webster.

issued from presses in various parts of the country. Outstanding among them were the texts of Caleb Alexander, Benjamin Johnson, John Comly, and Enoch Hale, and one or two that were printed anonymously. Benjamin Johnson's *New Philadelphia Spelling Book* came out in that city in 1809. It contained illustrations by Alexander Anderson, one of them being a fine cut of the schoolbook favorite, Niagara Falls. The book had lessons on the alphabet, spelling lists, an assortment of homonyms, and other material including "stories from various authors." The compiler stated in his preface that the principal difference between his speller and others was in "the fairness of the paper, size of the type and the beauty of its ornaments," and this was a justified claim.

John Comly's *New Spelling Book* was printed in Philadelphia in 1806, and was a forerunner of his *Spelling Book,* which was used over a period of three or four decades. Comly was a Pennsylvania school teacher who later became a clergyman. For many years he kept a journal which was published by his children in 1853 and proved to be quite enlightening on early social life. In his *Journal* Comly tells of visiting Baltimore in 1829 and reports that "the almost universal subject of the railroad [the B & O], seemed so to engross the attention of all classes, Friends as well as others, that there appears little room for subjects or meetings of a religious character."[4] The book nowhere mentions Comly's schoolbook writing but touches upon some school incidents, only one having to do with spelling. Comly recorded that "the practice in schools then [speaking of still earlier days] was to spell four or five syllables before beginning to read."[5]

---

[4] *John Comly, Late of Byberry, Pennsylvania* (Philadelphia: Chapman, 1853), p. 454.

[5] In the September, 1852, *Knickerbocker* is an article entitled "Byberry," by Yadessal, evidently a pen name, containing information extra-

A fairly good text "By Sundry School Teachers," the *United States Spelling Book,* was first issued in Pittsburgh in 1809, and later reprinted there and at other places, chiefly in the Ohio Valley, numerous times. In 1829 it was produced at Wheeling, Virginia, and afterward reprinted there over a number of years. In most issues the book indicated on the title page that it contained "appropriate reading lessons, being an easy standard for spelling and reading." There was a sprinkling of religious material, but as a whole the material was well balanced, and for a time, the book, especially in the western country, was evidently a serious competitor of Webster's *Speller.* It is not known today who compiled the text, but some of the editions were copyrighted by D. and M. Maclean and J. J. Carpenter. It had no connection with the *United States Readers,* by William Darby, printed in Baltimore.

In the 1830's and 1840's, for some reason not easily comprehended, much bickering took place over spelling systems, spelling books, and so on. At this era, despite the astounding popularity of Noah Webster's *Spelling Book,* many besides Lyman Cobb, who has already been referred to, registered objections to Webster's texts. These remonstrances were not all from persons interested in book publishing or who had reasons of self-interest for trying to detract from the popularity of Webster's publications. So well-known a man as George B. Cheever, Congregational minister and noted publicist of New England and New York (once imprisoned in connection with a libel in some of his temperance writings), protested strongly against Webster's influence. Cheever opposed all "newfangled" ideas in spelling and language and argued that "innovations should be resisted, nor should any mere Lexicographer, nor University, nor knot of Critics, have it in their power to make

---

ordinarily quaintly told, about John Comly, the early schools of Byberry, and so on.

them prevalent." Cheever wrote a number of books that were widely read in both the United States and England and in one of them he claimed that the "spelling trouble" of the time was "owing in a great measure to Dr. Webster's unfortunate orthographical eccentricies, which have set so many spellers and journeyman printers agog to imitate him."[6]

During this era many compilers of spelling books made unjust attacks upon their competitors. But naturally not all of them resorted to such tactics. The Stephen Byerly *New American Spelling-Book* was first printed in Philadelphia in 1836, and at the beginning of his preface, referring to the unfriendly grumblings that were current at the time, Byerly stated, "It has been very common with the compilers of spelling-books to begin with a long enumeration of faults in the system of others," and proceeded to point out that he had no intention of following that practice and that any attempt to improve the art of instructing youth was to be commended, and that he himself was doing what he could in that direction, especially so by "simplifying" his text. The sixteen wood engravings used in Byerly's *New American Spelling-Book,* of a noticeably animated nature, looked as though they might have been the work of some self-taught amateur engraver as far as workmanship was concerned. The condor was pictured in a way that no bird ever resembled and "The King of Beasts," the lion, was portrayed with his mouth hanging open as though he were laughing. Crude though this particular illustration is, it brings to mind the Lion-king so charmingly pictured by Kaulbach in his ever-fresh *Reynard the Fox* drawings.[7] It is quite apparent that the illustrations in Byerly's *Spelling-Book* were copied and not

---

[6] George B. Cheever, *Wanderings of a Pilgrim* (New York: John Wiley, 1846), II, 49–50.

[7] Wilheim von Kaulbach, German artist noted for his illustrations of the works of Goethe, "The Pied Piper of Hamlin," and other books.

too well, from examples in the *Penny Magazine*. The latter was a popular English periodical that was reissued in New York and Boston and from which a number of American schoolbooks profited. It was also a closely-copied model for the early issues of *Harpers Monthly Magazine*.

With the beginning of the issuance of readers in graded series nearly all the compilers provided a spelling text to go along with their reader series. The Osgood, Swinton, Monroe, Sargent, McGuffey, Sanders, Holmes and practically all the other reader series had their respective spelling books, which were printed in the same format as that of the readers. A few of the spelling books accompanying series were by a different compiler, but usually the same person compiled both readers and speller.

During the days of the successful reader series only a few spelling books which stood alone were published. Among the latter were James N. McElligott's *Young Analyser,* 1846; D. F. DeWolfe's *Instructive Speller,* 1862; J. Wilkin Westlake's *Three Thousand Practical Words,* 1874; Geoffrey Buckwalter's *Primary Spelling Book,* 1879; and the anonymous *Pacific Coast Spelling Book,* put out by the noted Bancroft firm of San Francisco in 1873. Some of these enjoyed long periods of success, particularly the *Pacific Coast Spelling Book* — probably because it was a product of the region in which it was chiefly used.

In the last half of the nineteenth century a number of spelling books appeared under the title of *Etymology* or *Orthography,* or used one of those words in the title. In 1880 the *Grammar School Word Book and Etymology,* by Edward Althaus, was published; a short time later Albert D. Wright's *Analytical Orthography* appeared. Calvin Peterson's *Speller, Analyses and School Etymology* came out during the 1880's and this and other texts of its class met with considerable approval.

After the beginning of the present century, spelling books broke away from the reader series and regained their status as separate texts. All the spelling books today stand entirely alone, and sometimes they are merely small manuals of words without any special system. Not so much importance is attached to the ability to spell correctly at present as there was in the nineteenth century. It has been pointed out many times that spelling was over valued at the expense of other studies during the nineteenth century, and that this criticism is justified cannot be denied.

Nowadays we do not take the ability to spell correctly as seriously as did many of our forefathers. In 1830 the Reverend Samuel Arnold was tried in a New Hampshire court for beating his adopted son, Joseph Pray, for failure to "spell and pronounce a word." That same year a volume on the case, under the title *An Astonishing Affair,* was printed in Concord. The book defended Arnold and stated that "he acted conscientiously in inflicting said punishment, and did it out of pure motives."

The "simplified spelling" movement had a vogue early in the present century and some well-known persons lent their backing toward getting it adopted by the schools. Although it may come as a surprise to some, the idea was nothing new. In 1703 there appeared in England a thirty-two page pamphlet, *Animadversions on English Spelling,* credited to the pen of John White, a Devon school teacher, in which simplified spelling was recommended. The *Animadversions* pamphlet was reprinted in 1958 by the Augustian Reprint Society, Clark Memorial Library, Los Angeles. As early as 1793 an American book on simplified spelling, William Thornton's *Cadmus, or A Treatise on the Elements of Written Language . . . . Fixing the*

Orthography and Orthoëpy, was published by R. Aitken in Philadelphia. The volume contained two dedications—one in regular and the other in simplified spelling. Noah Webster, who was in favor of reforming spelling, must have taken some notice of this Philadelphia book.

We may gather from all this that when Theodore Roosevelt, George Bernard Shaw, and some of the better-known philologists voiced approvals of the new spelling in the late nineteenth and early twentieth century they were stirring a long-simmering porridge. Professor Calvin Thomas, of the University of Michigan and later of Columbia, a widely acclaimed authority on language, was one of the strongest advocates of reformed spelling, and speaking of the opposition against it he said : "There is no culture or intelligence involved; it is simply a nervous reaction against following the stimulus of the unfamiliar."[8] Whether or not Professor Thomas was wholly right in his views, his attitude reflected much of the public opinion of his day. The spelling reform got almost nowhere in the public schools; only a few teachers and school authorities accepted it or gave any evidence of a desire to give it a trial. One or two "reformed spelling" books were compiled, but they met with little or no response.

---

[8] Thomas, *Scholarship and Other Essays* (New York : Holt, 1924), p. 173.

XII

Literature Texts

THE STUDY OF LITERATURE as a separate subject was begun in American schools during the nineteenth century. The innovation had its inception chiefly in the readers of Murray, Cobb, Bingham, Darby, and others. Shortly before and after the Civil War two or three readers appeared which, as already mentioned, were composed almost entirely of literature-study material, but they were published ostensibly as texts for teaching oral reading, and were never considered seriously in any other light. With three or four minor exceptions, fully oriented "literature" texts did not come into general use until after mid-century.

A good while prior to 1850 a few volumes which might be called literature texts were printed but were not used a great deal, perhaps because literature as a separate subject had not become a part of the specified curriculum. One of the earliest books of this class was *Miscellanies, Moral and Instructive in Prose and Verse,* "for the use of schools," issued in Philadelphia in 1793, "printed for Joseph Cruikshanks." This text had a preface by Benjamin Franklin, who wrote that "a book containing so many well-chosen sentiments and excellent instructions put into the hands of children, cannot but be highly useful to the rising generation." In the same decade Mathew Carey, who came to this country from Ireland in 1785 and who founded the Philadelphia publishing firm bearing his name, put out *The School of Wisdom or American Monitor*. This volume contained "a copious collection of Sublime and Elegant extracts from the most Eminent Writers," and Carey's own name appeared on the title page as compiler. While designated in the preface as a school reader, this book in fact stands with the two or three first special literature texts for American school use. In his preface Carey said :

> In making the selections considerable pains have been taken. Many of the works of the most celebrated writers have been carefully examined—and numerous passages are to be found from Shakespeare, Dryden, Milton, Pope, Young, Watts, Rowe, Addison, Swift, Brooke, Fielding, Hervey, Johnson, Price, Montesquieu, and others of equal reputation. To familiarize the rising generation with the perusal of such illustrious writers can hardly fail to prove salutary.

In the text, which ran to well over two hundred pages, was an extensive range of literary material—the widest coverage of any schoolbook up to its time. While the selections reprinted were not long, they were sufficient to impart to students a good idea of the work of the authors represented. *The School of Wisdom* went through a second edition in 1803, showing that it met with some approval. The noted Parson Weems was an agent for Carey around the beginning of the nineteenth century, and it is probable that one of the books he peddled about the country was Carey's little anthology. Weems published the first edition of his *History of the Life and Death, Virtues and Exploits of General George Washington* in the year 1800, and peddled it along with the other books he carried about in his wagon travels. It is possible that Parson Weems, none too conscientious in recounting the cherry tree episode, went to great length in lonely rural homes or in fine mansions, to push the sale of such books as his *Life of Washington* and *The School of Wisdom* to his personal advantage.

In 1830 Moss and Company of Philadelphia printed a small schoolbook, *Elements of Mythology,* which the anonymous compiler stated was "to inspire a taste for the luxuries and refinements of intellect—to make them [the pupils] understand prose and delight in poetry—to discipline the reason and excite the imagination." This book also can be designated as one of the early literature texts. Of the material in the text the compiler wrote :

> Too many of these fictions are unfit to meet the eye of inno-
> cence, but so far as any of them convey a moral, so long as
> they throw light on the history of mankind, so far as they
> have been incorporated into our literature, either with the
> design of instruction or ornament, they require to make a part
> of useful education.

In these words, although they have a sort of clerical bent, was the germ of an idea which was eventually to take hold firmly. By degrees the study of literature came to be given an allotment of time in schools as a separate subject, and naturally, because of its inherent worth, after a while achieved the status of a fully accepted part of the curriculum.

Truman Ricard and Hiram Orcutt, the latter principal of the Thetford, Vermont, Academy and grandfather of the well-known book-designer and writer of our own time William Dana Orcutt,[1] in 1847 published a *Class Book of Prose and Poetry* : "Consisting of Selections From The Best English and American Authors." It was "Revised and Enlarged" in 1851 and re-printed a number of times afterward. This book was "designed

---

[1] William D. Orcutt was long associated with the Plimpton Press and had much to do with designing present-day school texts. From 1926 until his recent death he published several volumes on books, among them *The Quest of the Perfect Book, The Kingdom of the Book* and *The Magic of the Book,* all charming works in a delightful format.

as exercises in Parsing," the title page signified, but this quali-
fication must have been a blind that was several times resorted
to in connection with nineteenth-century textbooks for which
the time was not ripe. Rickard and Orcutt's book had a few
introductory pages on syntax and parsing, but the rest was
purely a literature text. The material consisted of forty-three
selections from Chateaubriand and Washington Irving to
Byron's "Battle of Waterloo" and Bryant's "Thanatopsis," and
were presented without any page notes or comments whatever.
The selections were set apart in the text in such a way as to
indicate that they were intended as literature material and
nothing else. The time would soon be at hand when a literature
text could be put forward as just that, but even when the last
printings of the Rickard and Orcutt book were issued that era
had not yet arrived.

After literature began to receive acceptance as a branch of
school study it still had to be defended. Herbert Spencer, in his
famous *Education,* placed science study above that of mere
literature in his evaluation of the various branches, and this had
more than a little influence in causing the study of literature to
be neglected. In addition, Andrew Lang, who was something
of a creator of literature himself, brought forth the argument
at about Spencer's time that literature was a thing of the spirit,
something intangible, naturally illusive, and in the end could
not be taught, and that it was useless to attempt to teach it in
schools.[2] It took a long time to counteract such reasoning as that
that hedged the study of literature during the last half of the
nineteenth century, and time was required in which to develop
suitable texts.

---

[2] The idea was first advanced in "Can Literature Be Taught," in the
London Illustrated News, April, 1892, and many comments on it were
printed elsewhere.

The first manuals to give literature a definite status as a school subject were the histories of literature — books that covered the subject in a comprehensive way. After the Civil War a number of these histories appeared, and they proved to be practical vehicles in bringing recognition to literature as a special study. One of the earliest was Thomas Budd Shaw's *Outline of English Literature,* a collection of lectures originally delivered in the Imperial Alexander Lyceum in St. Petersburg, Russia. Shaw, a native of London, went to Russia in 1840 to teach and remained there until he died in 1862. His *Outline of English Literature* was a product of his Russian teaching. His text was readied for the press in 1846 and printed by Murray in London. It was later reprinted in Philadelphia and was gradually introduced into American schools. Today, as well as a century ago, one could get a splendid introduction to all the basic English writers from the Shaw text. His lessons on Chaucer, Bacon, Shakespeare and a number of others were broad in scope and helpfully illuminating. The one criticism that comes to mind today is that it could have profited from a slight condensation.

Naturally competition to the Shaw book was not long in following. In 1852 Charles Dexter Cleveland's *English Literature of the Nineteenth Century* was published and later went through several editions. This was not a literature history but an anthology of selections from writers living in the century. The compiler gave a brief biographical sketch of each writer, followed by from one to a dozen selections, the importance of the author governing the space allotted. A number of other texts, covering special branches of literature and called "Compendiums," were compiled by Cleveland and were widely used. An advertisement of 1873 stated that more than 125,000 copies of these texts had been sold.

William Swinton's *Studies in English Literature* was first

printed in 1880 and, as with most of his other books, was well
received. It was divided into forty sections, each devoted to a
well-known English or American author. The sectional divisions
had a "characterization" of the author by what Swinton called
a "distinguished critic." These sketches followed the selections,
all of which were documented with copious footnotes. In his
preface the compiler stated that the studies were intended "to
bring the pupil into close friendly contact with minds . . . . so
that he will no longer be reading merely *about* the masters, but
reading the masters themselves."

In 1876 Stopford Brooke's *Primer of English Literature* was
published in England and reprinted in this country. A few years
later it was revised and enlarged into *English Literature,* a book
that represented something of a new trend. Several later American histories of literature showed Brooke's influence. In 1896
Brander Matthews, who wrote much on books in general, turned
out a small school text, *Introduction to American Literature,*
which reflected Brooke's thinking.

After the turn of the twentieth century a number of well-
constructed literature histories that held the stage for about
three decades were published. Chief among them were those
of Edwin L. Miller, William Allan Neilson and Ashley Horace
Thorndike jointly, and William J. Long, besides the widely-used
and very popular *History of English Literature,* by Ruben Post
Halleck, and *English Literature,* by John Calvin Metcalf. The
last two were comprehensive texts written from different view-
points although each was in the main historical and biographical — a sort of miniature *Chamber's Cyclopedia of Literature.*[3]

Halleck's text carried a number of facsimiles of manuscripts,
specimens of the printing of Caxton, famous title pages, and the

---

[3] This well-known British Encyclopedia covers everything of value in
British and American literature.

like. There were portraits of writers and cuts from the first edition of *Robinson Crusoe* and from early editions of *Morte d' Arthur,* the *Miracle Plays,* and other books. These illustrations, combined with the clear cut textual material on literary movements and ideals, could hardly have failed to develop an interest in the written word among students and convince them that the great body of literature that has come down to us from the past is a precious heritage to all mankind. Halleck spent some of his early years in educational administration, but his later life was taken up with industrial work, writing, and lecturing, since he was a man of broad interests.

The period around 1890 marked the first publication of small literature texts scarcely more than pocket-size. This innovation resulted in the beginnings of thorough study of individual authors. Half of a school period, or longer, was often given over to the study of one small volume. Among the first of these series were the "English Classics," edited by William J. Rolfe, the Boston educator, now known chiefly for his *Life of Shakespeare* and his "Friendly Edition" of The Bard. Rolfe's "English Classics" within a few years from their inception included texts on Gray, Goldsmith, Browning, Macaulay, and Wordsworth. In addition there were *Tales of English History, Tales of Chivalry* and Shakespeare's plays. As a result of Rolfe's recognition as a Shakespearian scholar his volumes on Shakespeare, in the "English Classics" were standard school texts over a long period. The first book issued by the well-known Ginn firm was Craik's *The English of Shakespeare,* edited by Rolfe, which was published in 1867.

During the last decade of the nineteenth century and first half of the twentieth, half a dozen substantial literature "series" of the small size were printed for school use. Outstanding among them were the "Riverside Literature Series," "Canterbury Classics," Macmillan Pocket Classics," and the "Laurel English Classics." These were all used in great numbers.

A new phase in the evolution of literature texts began with the appearance of large volumes of several hundred pages, such as the "Higher English Literature High School Series," issued by Houghton Miffin, the "Literature and Life Series," by Scott, Foresman and Company (in various editions since 1922), and the large texts published by Macmillan and a number of other firms. These books were primarily anthologies, not histories of literature; but they contain sufficient introductory and supplementary matter to give pupils a comprehension of the nature and history of literature. Despite some deficiencies these books have satisfied a pronounced need.

Some have considered these extra-large literature texts entirely too extensive and cumbersome for school use; but they have a merit all their own; their copious material forces a student to do a great deal of selective searching from time to time — a process that in itself is part of the education process. These books, in fact, possess qualities as school material that texts of lesser dimensions cannot achieve, and impart an over-all impression of literature that cannot be derived from any other medium.

XIII

Elocution Manuals

ALMOST EVERYONE IS AWARE that oratory and declamation in general once had a more conscicuous place in the life of the American people than at present. Throughout most of the nineteenth century these attainments were looked upon with such approbation that education was in part patterned after that of the Roman world of the time of Quintillian. This celebrated Roman teacher and authority on education taught that success in life depended largely on one's ability to speak well in public; the most important part of education, as he saw it, was forensic training. In our own country throughout most of the nineteenth century the interest in speaking and dramatic reading resulted in the appearance of a considerable body of elocution texts, the study of which was considered a particularly important part of the education of every boy and girl.

The elocution texts, as a class, stood apart from the readers, although they were akin to the latter and their respective functions to some degree were the same. The elocutions, as they came to be called, differed from many of the early readers only in carrying a larger proportion of material lending itself to what was believed to be dramatic expression and the technical side of speech delivery as opposed to ordinary reading. The regular school readers were for the use of children in learning

to read, while the elocution books were intended to enable the
student, as the preface to one of them stated, to become "an
effective reader and speaker." The elocution manuals emphasized the point that the clearest expression of thought was
achieved by combining the spoken word with physical action
and by using the voice to express mood and emotion.

In a foreword, Frank H. Fenno stated :

> The human voice is to be considered as a musical instru-
> ment—an organ, constructed by the hand of the Great
> Master of all Harmony. It has its bellows, its pipes, its mouth-
> piece; and, when we know the 'stops,' it will discourse most
> eloquent music. It has its *gamut,* or scale of ascent or descent;
> it has its keys, or pitch, its tones, its semi-tones, its bass, its
> tenor, its alto, its melody, its cadence. It can speak as gentle
> as the lute, 'like the sweet south upon a bed of violets,' or as
> shrill as the trumpet; it can tune the 'silver sweet' note of
> love, and the 'iron throat of war'; in fine it may be modulated
> by art to say any sound of softness or strength, of gentleness
> or harshness, of harmony or discord.[1]

This passage sums up the idea in the back of the minds of most
of the early and middle nineteenth century elocution text
compilers. These conclusions are also in accord to some extent
with the ideals of the reader compilers, as expressed by the
latter from time to time. For example, William McGuffey once
said, "The voice of song is not sweeter than the voice of speech."

Joseph Dana's *A New Selection of Lessons in Reading,* published in 1795, and Caleb Bingham's *Columbian Orator,* 1797,
rank among the first completely American school elocution
texts. The full title of Dana's book was *A New Selection of
Lessons in Reading and Speaking to Which Are Added the
Elements of Gesture.* This title is sufficient to mark the book

---

[1] Fenno, *Science and Art of Elocution* (Philadelphia: John E. Potter
and Co., 1878).

as an elocution text : furthermore Dana had taught the technique of elocution for a number of years and brought the benefits of his experience in this line into his manual. Bingham concentrated primarily on the "art of speaking" and, as his title indicates, he did not forget the oratorical side of speech. Six pages were given over to gesture, and eight pages to rules on using the voice in connection with gesticulation.

William Scott's *Lessons in Elocution,* published in New York after being originally printed in England, was reprinted in this country a number of times — perhaps more often than either of the two books mentioned above. It was one of the most popular of the early elocution texts. Scott's book was also one of the most profusely illustrated of the early elocution texts, which may have accounted for much of its popularity.

The compiler of *Lessons in Elocution* was an ardent advocate of gesticulation and the woodcuts illustrating various gestures would alone have saved his book from dullness, regardless of its textual material.

Passages pertaining to gesture indicate that Scott possessed a Latin flair in that direction and that he had a great deal of the natural actor in him. In dwelling on the standing position and arm movements, he said :

> A boy will never be embarrassed for want of knowing what to do with his legs and arms; nor will he bestow that attention on his action, which ought to be directed to his pronunciation; he will always be in a position which will not disgrace his figure, and when gesture is easy to him, it may serve as a ground work to something more perfect : He may either by his own genius or his master's instructions, build some other action upon it, which may, in time, give it additional force and variety.

With William Scott there were no half measures — perhaps

one reason his *Lessons* were so popular. In describing the expression of anger he stated :

> Rage expresses itself with rapidity, interruption, noise, harshness and trepidation. The neck stretched out; the head forward, often nodding and shaking in a menacing manner, against the object of the passion. The eyes staring, rolling and sparkling; the eyebrows drawn down over them; and the forehead wrinkled into clouds. The nostrils stretched wide; every vein swelled; every muscle strained; the breast heaving and the breath fetched hard. The mouth open, and drawn on each side toward the ears, showing the teeth, in a gnashing posture.

On the other hand, to express love the pupil was to

> Light up the countenance with smiles. The forehead is smoothed and enlarged; the eyebrows are arched; the mouth a little opened and smiling; the eyes languishing and half shut, doat upon the beloved object. The countenance assumes the eager and wistful look of desire; (see *Desire*) but mixed with an air of satisfaction and repose. The accents are soft and winning; the tone of the voice persuasive, flattering, pathetic, various, musical, rapturous.

Scott's *Lessons* were wholly addressed to the boy; when his book came out in the latter part of the eighteenth century girls had little chance to study such a subject as elocution in school classes. Not until 1789 were girls admitted to public schools in Massachusetts, and it was very much the same everywhere. In England the education of women was almost totally neglected at the time. Holland was the only country in which girls were educated as were boys.[2]

In 1787, Benjamin Rush, signer of the Declaration of Independence and otherwise a conspicuous man of his era, wrote an essay, on the education of women, and although he did not

---

[2] See Campbell, *The Puritan in Holland, England and America* (New York: Harper, 1902), II, 355–356.

speak of elocution, he had this to say about voice culture by women :

> Vocal music should never be neglected in the education of a young lady in this country. Besides preparing her to join in that part of public worship which consists of psalmody, it will enable her to soothe the cares of domestic life. The distress and vexations of a husband — the noise of a nursery, and even the sorrows that will sometimes intrude into her own bosom, may all be relieved by a song, where sound and sentiment unite to act upon the mind. I hope it will not be thought foreign to this part of our subject to introduce a fact here which has been suggested to me by my profession, and that is, that the exercise of the organs of the breast, by singing, contributes very much to defend them from those diseases of which our climate and other causes, have of late exposed them.[3]

Benjamin Rush's son James, himself a medical doctor, in 1827 published *Philosophy of the Human Voice,* an elocution text which went through a number of editions, six during its first ten years. It had a mixed reputation; some thought parts of it were "incomprehensible," while others regarded it as a superb treatise on the use of the voice. For half a century after the appearance of Rush's text a number of other compilers of elocution texts copied his "tonal system" and in general borrowed his ideas. As late as 1884 James Murdock admitted that his *Analytic Elocution* was based on Rush's work and attested that he considered Rush's text "the most complete system ever offered to the student of Elocution."

---

[3] Benjamin Rush, "Thoughts Upon Female Education," *American Lady's Preceptor* (Baltimore: Coale, 1811), pp. 66–76. This was originally delivered as an address before the Young Ladies' Academy in Philadelphia, on July 28, 1787. This particular essay was not reproduced in *The Selected Writings of Benjamin Rush,* published by the Philosophical Library in 1947, where five other pieces of Rush's writings on education are found.

In the middle of the nineteenth century a number of elocution texts of varying merit appeared. Comstock's *System of Elocution,* Joshua Leavitt's *American Lessons in Reading and Speaking,* and Sargent's *Original Dialogs* had a considerable success, Comstock's perhaps more than the others due to the fact that he had written a number of other texts, three or four of which were exceedingly popular. Moses Severance's *The American Manual or New English Reader,* primarily an elocution text, appeared during this era. Although the object of much critical approval and going through a number of editions, it seems not to have been a financial success.

Elocution Made Easy, by R. Claggett, issued in 1845, was an unusual publication that might be considered a text on the gymnastics of elocution. It was one of the quaintest of all the elocution texts, with numerous remarkable illustrations portraying the gestures and body positions that elocutionists widely agreed lent emphasis to speech. There were figures that showed the various positions in which to place the arms to indicate grief, appeal to the conscience, horror, and melancholy. By that time both men and women were pictured. One illustration demonstrated how to place the feet for ordinary delivery; there were positions for turning and for stepping from one position to another—all this as part of "the dramatics of speech." The author claimed that "a graceful and impressive action is of the highest accomplishments of the orator," and by *orator* he meant the elocution student. Claggett's book was more compact than most of the elocution texts of his time, and its brevity saved it from some of the complications that beset the longer texts.

About the middle of the century and shortly thereafter there appeared Edward Brook's *Manual of Elocution and Reading,* Philip Lawrence's *Model Speaker* (all the "speakers" used in schools were elocutions), Charles W. Sanders' *Choice Speaker*

(Sanders also issued an *Elocutionary Chart*), J. W. Shoemaker's *Practical Elocution,* Robert Kidd's *New Elocution and Voice Culture,* Alexander M. Bell's *Standard Elocutionist* and *The Fundamentals of Elocution.*[4] Of the texts named Shoemaker's *Practical Elocution* was perhaps the most widely used. It was still studied in schools in 1903 and 1904, about a quarter of a century after its initial appearance. The compiler of this text in the latter part of the nineteenth century issued a series of twenty-six small volumes, both in paper and cloth bindings, known as *Best Selections.* They contained from seventy-five to one hundred pieces each, usually brief, and all the material was practicable in the study of elocution.[5]

James E. Murdock's *Analytic Elocution,* already touched upon, was issued in 1884, and was one of the last of the texts to exalt the "tonal system" handed down from Dr. Rush's day through a number of compilers. Murdock's book was a complete revamping of Rush's early "system," with some added features culled elsewhere. While Murdock overemphasized breathing and "tones," and included some questionable rules, his work material was better and more varied than that in most of the texts used at the time. His book contained numerous pieces which must have caught the interest of the general run of school students, among them Lytle's "Antony and Cleo-

---

[4] Alexander Melville Bell was the father of Alexander Graham Bell, inventor of the telephone; both were born in Edinburgh, Scotland, and taught elocution in this country. The two wrote a dozen books on speech, sound, elocution, and training along these lines, becoming well-known authorities on the physiology of phonetics and especially the training of the deaf. This work led Alexander Graham Bell to the perfection of the telephone.

[5] One of the rarest of Edward Fitzgerald's books, his first-published *Translations into Verse,* issued in Paris in 1829 by the Gulignani firm, carries some "school exercises" evidently intended for school elocution study.

patra," beginning "I am dying, Egypt, dying," and Sir Walter Scott's poem beginning :

Breathes there a man, with soul so dead,
Who never to himself has said,
This is my own, my native land !

Conducting a school of oratory in Boston and having had experience as an actor, Murdock had a preference for material of solid dramatic value. He toured the country off and on with stage troupes, playing various parts, but never reached eminence in the theater. During the Civil War he received an officer's commission and aroused fervor in Union soldiers by his declamations in camps and other places, and after the war lectured in many parts of the country.

A one-time French opera singer, François Delsarte, during the last half of the nineteenth century had some influence on the compilers of elocution texts. Although many think Delsarte was original in his teachings, he was actually following tenets already current before his time. But he was more thorough than his predecessors. From singing in opera he turned to teaching, first singing, then declamation, through his "method" in the latter presenting what he called "a complete science." His "system" was much publicized and, althouh Delsarte himself wrote little, two or three texts using his name were printed in America, among them *An Hour with Delsarte, A Study of Expression,* by Ann Morgan, published both in Boston and New York in the 1880's, and used in some schools in elocution class work.

Early in the present century, when declamation was becoming less important, "talk" was supplanting oration and recitational exercises; and with this change, elocution, both as a school subject and otherwise, began to disappear.⁶ It was about

---

⁶A most instructive evaluation of "talk" as opposed to oratory at the

this time that Walter Hines Page said that the two great curses
of the South were oratory and fried food. Elocution exercises
were gone through more and more mechanically in schools. The
set style of gesturing and the numerous mannerisms had become
such a handicap that the "elocution" structure finally collapsed
under its own weight. Even the word *elocution* had been so
overworked that it began to take on an unpleasant connotation.
Eventually elocution became known as "spouting" and the
textbooks as "spouters." It is possible that such derision
hastened the consignment of school forensics to near oblivion.

Of course the study of elocution and the production of textbooks for the purpose never entirely ceased, and both have
increased in very recent times because of the large number of
people employed in radio, television, and the theater. Text books
with such titles as *Speech Delivery, Voice Development, Public
Speaking, Basic Principles of Speech, Oral Expression,* are used
today. Titles of texts never include the word "elocution" and
the subject has more of an institution-of-higher-education
status than it had in the nineteenth century save in the theological schools. Some of the texts used in the public speaking
courses again dwell at length on gestures, breathing exercises,
and other aids so long used in the teaching of oratory and
elocution.

---

turn of the century is to be found in Williamson, *Readings in American
Democracy* (Boston: Heath, 1922), pp. 519–520.

XIV

Handwriting and Copybooks

OUR AMERICAN PIONEERS, not too plentifully laden with the luxuries of life, must have given handwriting very meager attention except from the standpoint of utility. Chances are they looked upon penmanship somewhat as they viewed their food, their clothing, and the ordinary necessities of their hour-to-hour existence. It was not until the necessity to educate children became a public problem that the matter became something to ponder. Handwriting did not take on enough importance to achieve the "copybook" stage until about a century after the first colonists arrived.

The printing house of Benjamin Franklin and David Hall in Philadelphia, in 1748, produced some "copy" examples in *The American Instructor or Young Man's Best Companion,* by George Fisher, already described. As far as is known, this was the first printing of handwriting material in Colonial America. Before that what writing study undertaken seems to have consisted of copying from the English-produced lettering models or from individual examples set down by writing teachers. Christopher Dock, the early Pennsylvania schoolmaster, according to reports that have come down to us, exchanged holograph writing examples between schools for the use of pupils, and there must have been other exchanges of which no record is known.

In 1756 Christopher Sower, in Pennsylvania, printed three pages of writing copy in the *Hoch Deutsch Americanisch Calendur,* along with a page of "brief instructions for those who wish to learn writing." This, as far as we know, was the second American "copybook" material. Sower was an intelligent man; and he no doubt realized that there was a need for the material he was printing on handwriting, an art seriously neglected at the time. The script of Sower was large and round but very legible — the heavy writing we today consider characteristic of a man of action, which Christopher Sower no doubt was.[1]

The first American copybook as a separate text of which we know was *The Writing Scholar's Assistant,* issued in Worcester, Massachusetts, by Isaiah Thomas in 1785. The script examples in this little book seem to have been impressions from the plates used in earlier printings of Fisher's *American Instructor;* the similarity is so close that one can scarcely believe otherwise. The script is a formal lettering, hardly a cursive but rather something nearer a "print" — a form perhaps chosen for its practical aspects. One year later Miles Beach and Isaac Sanford's *New Set of Round Hand Writing Copies* was published in Hartford, Connecticut, and this is considered the second American copybook. This publication consisted of seven pages of a script which followed fairly closely certain examples in

---

[1] Since there seems to be a ready demand for them, many books have been published on the interpretation of character through handwriting. This study, generally designated *graphology,* although formulated earlier, seems to have taken hold in the days of Johann Kaspar Lavater, the father of *physiognomy,* and was practiced by his followers. The study of handwriting may throw light on the nervous structure of a person, as ontogenetic research has shown, but the chances are poor that it in any way reveals a person's mental qualities.

George Bickham's *Universal Penman,* leaning more to curls and swings than the writing in the publications already mentioned. Joseph Callender's *Round Text Copies,* the next known American copybook, was issued, also in Worcester, by Isaiah Thomas in 1787. Callender, too, apparently followed the previously published Bickham handwritings.

It is necessary to go a little into Bickham's *Universal Penman* in order to grasp fully what has been said and what will be mentioned further on. An ambitious handwriting treatise, Bickham's book was first published in London, in parts, from 1733 to 1741, and since then was reprinted in single volumes a number of times — once recently in our own country.[2] This is the most famous book on the handwriting of English-speaking peoples, chiefly because it was a true recording of the best in handwriting over a long era, and an influence that has extended into our own time. Some of the penmanship samples written by scribes included in Bickham's treatise, especially those of Willington Clark, Joseph Champion,[3] Gabriel Brooks, Nathaniel Doves, and one or two others, look as though they might have been set down by our nineteenth-century teachers of penmanship. All the Bickham scripts were easy to read, and still are. It is quite logical that the early American copybook makers made free use of the most suitable examples in the well-known book as models. It is known that copies were brought to America. Records are extant that a Pennsylvania school purchased a copy as early as 1762,[4] and that a Boston writing master owned an early issue; and it is most likely that other copies of which we

---

[2] Bickman, *Universal Penman,* a facsimile edition ed. Philip Hofer, Curator, Department of Printing and Graphic Arts, Harvard College Library (New York: Dover Publications, 1941).

[3] Champion, who wrote forty-seven of the script examples used by Bickham, turned out a number of books on the art of handwriting and was considered one of the foremost penmanship teachers of his day.

[4] *Pennsylvania Charter School Minutes,* No. 105, 1920, p. 195.

have no record must have found their way to America. In
fact, aside from Bickham's work there was but little material
which designers of copybooks could turn to before the beginning
of the nineteenth century.[5]

In 1791, John Jenkins, a New England school teacher, published a manual that was both a treatise on the technical points
of writing and an assortment of script examples. This publication is considered an important "cradle book" and it is of
importance in studying our early handwriting. The book was
published under the title of *Art of Writing* and went through
three printings — how large we have no way of knowing. Jenkins' script was the English roundhand, evidently deriving from

---

[5] Not too much has been written on the progress of penmanship in
America. In 1943, Professor Ray Nash, of Dartmouth College, published
a brochure entitled *Some Early American Writing Books and Masters,*
and in 1959 his *American Writing Masters,* a "history and Bibliography
through colonial times," appeared. These two publications, issued in
limited numbers are the only thorough studies of our early handwriting.
There have been a few general periodical and newspaper articles, but
these are astonishingly rare. Charles K. Bolton's "Colonial Handwriting"
was printed in the *Essex Antiquarian,* November 1897, and a couple of
brief papers on the lineage of our handwriting have appeared in *The
New York Times* and other widely circulated newspapers, but these
have been of a restricted nature. Paul Standard has published two or
three brief papers on the subject, but they are more technical than
historical. The *Harvard Library Bulletin,* VII, No. 1, 1953, contains an
article by Professor Nash on the early New England writing teacher
Abiah Holbrook, and here and there in histories and other volumes we
find passing mention of early American writing masters but nothing
more. Platt R. Spencer, C. L. Ricketts, and one or two other writing
teachers of the nineteenth century wrote comments on the historical side
of writing, but they went back mostly into early times and are of no
practical value in the study of handwriting as an American development.
None of these penmanship teachers looked at handwriting as practiced in
this country as separate from penmanship as an abstract art. The present
writer here acknowledges with thanks the help he has derived from
Professor Nash's writings.

the ordinary writing of the day, and using chiefly only easily executed swings and shadings. Jenkins was hardly a true follower of the Bickham types of script. He seemed to have believed that the handwriting of the general run of mankind ought not to be as fancy as the accepted Bickham examples — this even though Jenkins, speaking in the third person in his preface to the last edition of his text, said that "from early youth he had been highly gratified by examining beautiful specimens of penmanship."

John Jenkins was a native of Boston, born twenty years before the Revolution. He lived at various times in a number of other states and is believed to have died at Wilmington, Delaware, in 1822. Like other writing teachers, he was strong for garnering and citing recommendations of his work. In the first printing of his *Art of Writing* there were five pages of commendations, mostly from well-known persons; and in a later printing these were increased to twenty-eight pages. Few schoolbook compilers of the time surpassed Jenkins in obtaining public approvals of his publications. He approached many prominent citizens for endorsements, including John Hancock (certainly a bold penman), and John Adams.

Most of the writing masters of the day did not go along with Jenkins in the special "stroke" system he devised. Jenkins thought the six primary strokes in writing covered all the letter constructions of the alphabet, but others did not agree that this was true, and a little offhand experimentation in this direction shows that his objectors were probably right. One of the strong objectors to Jenkins' "method" was Caleb Bingham, the Boston school conductor whom we have already met and who is said to have been a personal friend of Jenkins. Bingham, refusing to use Jenkins' work in his classes, wrote two small copybooks of his own, *Round Text Copies* and *Ladies' Copies,* for such use, these being printed in 1796. These two books were not intended by Bingham for use outside his own schools and they were seemingly not utilized elsewhere. Calligraphic compilations were a sort of out-of-bounds work for Bingham.

Another New Englander, Henry Dean, long a resident of Salem, Massachusetts, published *The Analytical Guide to Penmanship* in 1805. Only a few copies of the first issue were printed, and the 1808 second edition, "Reissued, improved and enlarged," was announced as an even smaller edition, a note on the back page indicating that but seven copies were printed. This could have been a typographical error as it seems improbable that so few copies of a book of its sort would have been turned out. Dean's treatise was both a writing study and copy models text, containing both scripts and sets of rules. Like a number of his successors Dean thought the theoretical side of writing was of importance and went in heavily for rules and directives. His script examples were taken from various sources, the bulk of them coming from Thomas Astle's *Origin and Progress of Writing,* published in England in 1784 and reprinted in 1803 just before Dean's *Guide* came out. While Dean did not acknowledge the source of all his material, he did give credit for that taken from Astle. It is probable that Henry Dean had some influence on American handwriting progress, as his publications were primarily for writing masters rather than school pupils.

In 1809 James Carver's *A New and Easy Introduction to the Art of Analytical Penmanship* was printed in Philadelphia, and is a very rare publication today. Carver taught writing in England, and then for twelve years in Calcutta, India, "under the patronage of Sir William Jones," the well-known Indian government official who founded the Calcutta Asiatic Society and published the first volume of that Society's *Asiatic Researches* and other important oriental writings. After coming to America Carver taught penmanship in New Haven, Utica and Albany, New York, Philadelphia, and other places in this country. He, too, obtained many recommendations from those he taught, among them prominent personages. In his penmanship text he listed in an advertisement thirty-four Yale students whom he taught writing at New Haven and the enumeration of "subscribers" for his book showed fifty-three prominent Philadelphians, first among these being Dr. Benjamin Rush, then at the crest of his career. Carver's handwriting was something like that of John Jenkins, and his manual was much on the order of Jenkins' *Art of Writing*. Carver had script examples on only sixteen of his ninety-eight pages, and there was one long folded-in script page with the one word "Mammouth" on it, a term used to designate one of his script forms.

Wholly a set of models, Joseph Perkins' *Practical Penmanship,* was published some years after Carver's text, the first printing coming out in 1830 and a later issue in 1836. This was one of the first copy-model books of considerable size issued in this country that was wholly a drill manual, with the rules being left to the instructor. Perkins stated in his brief introductory remarks that "Directions for making and holding the pen, sitting at the desk, position of the paper &C &C . . . belong to the province of the teacher."[6] He further specified that it was left to the instructor to "point out the proper manner of forming the hair lines, bulbs and knots" of letters. Three scripts were presented, the "Round Text," the "Smaller and Running Hands," and "Ornamental Writing." Perkins treated ornamental lettering in a limited way, explaining that "Ornamental Penmanship, in general, is so little used in business

---

[6] One of the questions in a circular sent out in 1839 to the schools of Connecticut, was: "Do you instruct your pupils in the art of making a pen?" *Journal of Education,* I, 1856, p. 693.

writing that it is not deemed necessary to enter a systematic exemplification of the elements of but one — the Italian hand." He stated that "as this hand may be written with such facility and ease, it may with propriety be considered really a practical as well as an ornamental hand." Only one page of "Italian" models, consisting merely of the capital and small letters of the alphabet, was presented.

A conductor of a writing school in New York and later writing teacher in the Albany Academy, Benjamin Franklin Foster, used a script in his copybooks which followed that of the English writing master Joseph Carstairs. Carstairs was an advocate of rapidity and unity in script formation, and these were Foster's main points. Some of the swing that gave nine-teenth-century writing in this country its mechanical unison and continuity came from Carstairs, through Foster's influence. The script that Foster developed, with the tracing of letters patterned after Carstairs, for a period but not permanently, gave something of a new angle to the teaching of handwriting in American schools.

There was some competition between Foster and Allison Wrifford, another penmanship teacher. Wrifford's *Chirography,* first printed in Concord, New Hampshire, in 1833, showed a leaning toward the no-pen-lift writing. More stroke-saving forms were present in Wrifford's models as compared to previous writing copy examples; but these can scarcely be considered important. Practically all the "rapid hand" advocates of the era were proponents of not lifting the pen in forming the written word, and some went so far as to advise joining words, pre-senting examples for practice. This system was evidently faulty, inasmuch as not lifting the pen between words would sometimes cause a delay rather than an acceleration. Furthermore, the lifting of the pen added legibility to a written page.

In the 1830's George J. Becker, professor of writing in the

Philadelphia Central High School, compiled a series of ten copybooks which were put out by Uriah Hunt, the schoolbook publisher, of that city. These texts were known as *The American System of Penmanship* and formed one of the first extensive "series." The compiler stated that his texts were a steady progression "from the first rudiments of writing to perfect specimens of penmanship," which "made better writers in half the time usually taken" — the latter perhaps a slightly over-enthusiastic personal claim.

Between 1830 and 1840 numerous penmanship teachers were wandering about the country, and they seemingly increased public interest in handwriting. The roaming instructors were generally men who had an unusual gift for writing and for advertising their ability. A few of them compiled script books of their own. In 1842 H. H. Baker's *Self-Taught Penmanship* was published, and a number of other books of this type were sold by roaming teachers. A few such manuals were utilized in schools.

Some copybook compilers during the second quarter of the nineteenth century brought complicating novelties into their copy forms. For instance, C. C. Badlam's *Common School Writing Books,* a series first issued in the 1840's, offered multiple line copy forms for the height spacing of letters, with dots to measure the width spacing, and slanted lines to indicate the slope. These artificial and somewhat cumbersome controls evidently did not catch on too well for the "skeleton" forms in the Badlam copybooks failed to encourage any lasting imitation. It is possible that Badlam patterned his "system" after the "Mulhauser" writing, designed by M. Mulhauser of Geneva, Switzerland, and later copied in France and England — a system considerably used in Europe until our Civil War period. A suggestion of the space-slant system had appeared in Jenkins' *Art of Writing* and one or two other writing texts after Jenkins' time, but Badlam was the first to stress the guide lines—so heavily, in fact, that he attached too much importance to them.

Platt Roger Spencer, of "Spencerian" fame, based his script and handwriting publications on those of most of the copybook compilers who went before him. The coming of the steel pen, it is true, had much to do with the "method" he developed and his great success with it. Handwriting in every era has been conditioned by the instruments of writing, and such was unquestionably the case during the first half of the nineteenth century, when Spencer's star arose. The thin lines and heavy shading that were used so widely during his time were largely the fruit of the new steel pen. The quill pen, more often than otherwise cut out of the feather by the user and which had been utilized for centuries, lent itself to shading and thin line lettering, but it never equalled in efficiency the springy steel pen especially designed either for delicate lettering or for heavy work.[7]

The steel pen was invented early in the nineteenth century, but was not manufactured in large quantities and did not find acceptance by all literate mankind until later. The new pens were used in small quantities in England around 1810, but did not really take hold until a number of years later; at first they were so expensive that ordinary persons could not afford to use them. In England, in 1820, they sold for seven shillings and six pence each—more than a dollar in our money.[8] When they came to be manufactured in large quantities about 1825, after the first

---

[7] The quill pens were made from the long feathers of geese, chickens, crows, and other fowls with a small pocket knife. Of the many thousands of boys who know what a "penknife" is, not many are aware that the little piece of cutlery got its name from its use in making quill pens.

[8] Daniel W. Kittle, *Pen, Ink and Paper, A Discourse on Calligraphy* (London: "Sette Of Odd Volumes," No. 10, 1885), p. 55.

difficulties were overcome, they quickly displaced the quill pen for general use.[9] Without a knowledge of the part played by the steel pen we could not understand the progress of Spencerian writing, which could not have developed had the quill pen not been superceded.

If any one writing master's work were picked out as a likely forebear of that of Spencer it would be that of E. T. Martin. The copybooks of Martin were printed in Worcester, Massachusetts in 1847 and 1848; and the script that Martin wrote was in alignment not much different from Spencer's penmanship, especially his earliest models. In some other early copybooks besides Martin's there are examples that Spencer must have adopted as part of his set form, but there were not many such. Some likelihood exists that Spencer leaned toward a few

---

[9] Good accounts of the early history of the steel pen are to be found in *Harper's Magazine* of June, 1850, and in *Notes and Queries,* 2nd Series, XII, August 9, 1873. For a more extensive history, see A. M. Smith, *Printing and Writing Materials: Their Evolution* (Philadelphia: Privately printed, 1901). This volume's account of the fountain pen, however, is slightly misleading inasmuch as it is intimated (p. 167) that the first experiments on fountain pens were not made until the nineteenth century. The fact is fountain pens of a kind were made as far back as the middle of the sixteenth century, the first known picture of one appearing in Daniel Schwenter's *Deliciae Physico-Mathematicae,* published at Nurnberg in 1751. This, a reprint of a book first issued in 1636, an extremely rare volume today, containing much information on early scientific inventions. The illustration in question shows the component mechanical parts of the early conception of the fountain pen. D. E. Smith, *History of Mathematics* (New York: Dover, 1958), I, 421, speaks of the Nurnberg book but makes no mention of the fountain pen. One of the best brief historical sketches on the steel pen's progress in America, aside from its general history, is to be found in Johnson's *New Universal Cyclopedia* (New York: 1877), in the article "Pen," by L. P. Brockett, in which almost every phase of the early steel pen is covered, insofar as it concerns America.

of the letter forms of Henry Dean, whose examples and tenets were current prior to Martin's books.

Spencer's first products were in the form of copy cards. Then came a series of copybooks, the first of which was issued in 1848. These copybooks were followed by a number of volumes on the technical "art of writing." Eventually Spencer began to produce pen points and holders—old magazine advertisements tell of the merits of Spencer's "nibs" (pen points) and his other writing implements. In 1873 an advertisement indicated that fourteen types of Spencer pen points were available.

Like most successful men, Spencer went along with his time. He made many addresses all over the country and like the ladies' hats and the Victorian architecture and *decor*, he was ornate in his choice of words. In one of his lectures, some of which, according to reports, were attended by large throngs, he said, "Many of the ancient heathen writers considered writing as a gift vouchsafed to man by the gods themselves; and many enlightened Christians suppose that it was first revealed to man from the summit of Mount Sinai, amid the thunders of the giving of the law and testimony." He asserted at another time that his handwriting was inspired by the "graceful form of the feathered grass, the vine and the undulatory waves of Lake Erie." This geographical reference was due to the fact that his family had moved from East Fishkill, New York, where he was born, to near Ashtabula, Ohio, and the youthful Spencer spent his late-boyhood days on the shores of Lake Erie. Here in his second home Platt Roger Spencer perhaps found much of the inspiration for his unusual eloquence as well as for the "undulating-wave" qualities of his ornate, "steelengraving" penmanship.

When others took up the metronome around mid-century[10] to

---

[10] E. G. Folson, a teacher of penmanship in the Albany Commercial College, was the first advocate of the use of the metronome in timing

regulate the time consumed in forming letters in handwriting Spencer advocated its use, declaring that "In writing by the metronome, every downward motion is associated with the beat of the instrument, while the upward motions are made in the intervals. It will be seen that all the letters, long and short, requiring the same number of motions, are thus executed in precisely the same time." Seemingly actually to believe in the merits of the instrument, he further stated : "This exercise is a powerful incentive to improvement, each pupil feeling that every other one is executing the same form that he is, at precisely the same moment of time."

In Spencer's day children must have spent hours watching metronomes swinging back and forth as they laboriously and half-hypnotically inscribed their writing lessons. The mental efforts that were required to attempt to synchronize the movements with the monotonous swing of the timing contrivance and to strive to form every letter just as every other pupil did must have added an almost unendurable wearisomeness to writing exercises. That such a thing as a swinging metronome was *ever* used in connection with teaching children to write constitutes perhaps one of the most anomalous practices that can be found anywhere in the history of American education.

After his sons grew up Spencer brought them into his publishing, manufacturing, and distributing business. They were R. C., H. C., L. P., P. R. Jr., and H. A. Spencer, and the later publications carried all their names. Sons-in-law were also taken into the firm when the organization was at the height of its prosperity. So many Spencerian copybooks were issued that no one ever made an effort to estimate their number. W. W. Livengood, vice-president of the American Book Company, said

---

writing in this country. He introduced the time-regulating system after the Civil War and called it "Chirythmography," coining the term from the three Greek words meaning *time, hand,* and *writing.*

that Lyman Spencer, one of the sons, told him that he could make no more accurate guess of the number of Spencerian copybooks put out than an ambiguous "millions upon millions."[11]

Following the Civil War a number of copybook series came out as "systems," gradually making inroads into Spencer's near monopoly. Prominent among these latter was the "Eclectic System," a manual and series of copybooks compiled by L. S. Thompson, O. H. Bowler, and N. E. D. Anler, and published by Van Antwerp and Bragg. The script used by Thompson and his associates was the ordinary cursive of the day, which had become generally known as Spencerian, with a little of the twirl taken out. The Eclectic Series consisted of a primary book "for lead pencil," eight copybooks accompanied by writing cards, and a ninth copybook of "offhand writing, German Text, Old English, and Marching Letters."

The day was approaching when large schoolbook-publishing houses were to take over writing-book publication, which for some time in most cases had been free lance ventures. A number of the leading textbook publishers in the country, along with Van Antwerp and Bragg, during the post-Civil War period produced large editions of copybooks in series. In some instances publishers claimed superiority of their products over the texts of competitors, when actually there was no such difference. Between the Civil War and 1875 there were half a dozen well-known series.

The big publishers introduced a few innovations now and then — in most cases efforts to make it appear that something "new" was being brought into handwriting. One of these artificially evolved changes was increased letter slant for a period

---

[11] Livengood, *Our Heritage* (New York: American Book Company, 1947), p. 19.

after the Civil War, and one or two efforts were made to introduce a backhand script. These attempts at novelty more often than not were worthless or a detriment, and after a time each was given up.

During the 1880's copybook production to a certain degree began to scatter over the country again. The production of the texts had found such a wide market that many supposed that such publishing offered bright prospects of large profits. Teachers of penmanship in several cases formed small firms devoted solely to copybooks manufacture, two or three such organizations springing up in the South and as many west of the Mississippi River. As an example, A. and A. Allen, teachers of Nashville, Tennessee, started the "Allen System of Penmanship," issuing publications containing many rules and with a script that was nothing but the generally accepted writing of the day. These mushroom firms evidently in most cases met with financial losses rather than the easy profits expected, and with one or two exceptions were soon liquidated.

From 1885 to 1895 a noticeable change came into school copybooks. For a long time no considerable evolution in handwriting in general had taken place. Outside of dropping the long *s*, which occurred about mid-century,[12] the average American school penmanship looked much as it had for a century. Then a quick change took place. It was at this period that "vertical" writing appeared. In copybooks this at first was a straightening up of the old slanting letters, and the result became a cross between roundhand and "print." Some time elapsed

---

[12] The first book in which the long s was abandoned in printing was Ames, *Typographical Antiquities,* issued in London in 1749. It was half a century later before other publishers saw the light and followed. Many older persons used the long s in their handwriting until the Civil War period, particularly in the South. It originally came into our handwriting from Germany.

before copybook makers fully agreed on what the *standard* vertical would be.

A number of well-known copybook compilers around the turn of the century had a part in promoting the vertical hand, but they did not originate it. The vertical script had been evolving for two or three decades, and it is hardly possible to say where or just when it had its beginnings. It may have resulted from more and more people gradually and unconsciously adopting the new form, both in the United States and Great Britain. Copybook makers in the early 1890's may have seen individual handwriting that appealed to them and may have worked similar samples into their copybooks, thinking that in this way they were introducing a new and worthwhile element. In this way, it seems, "vertical" writing actually evolved and took hold. The first book to give an extensive exposition of the handwriting was John Jackson's *The Theory and Practice of Handwriting,* printed in England and later in New York, in 1894. We can find old records dating back to the middle of the century with scripts that were "vertical" or something very similar to it, and it stands to reason that such a fresh form must have caught the eye of those seeking for a new writing style or improvement in the old."

By 1900 the elaborate Spencerian, with its too many flourishes and embellishments, had vanished from the schools. The time-worn scripts (still much used into our own day in advertising) did not disappear suddenly from school publications, but after a time they were all gone. The copybooks of the last decade of the nineteenth century quite plainly betray the fact that their compilers labored under an uncertainty as to what script to use. A copybook maker would put out a text

---

" Richard Daniels, *Copy-Book or a Compendium of the Most Useful Hands of England, France, Spain and Italia, Etc.,* published in London in 1664, has some script examples which show suggestions of vertical.

harking back to the old script, and soon afterward an entirely different one from his hand would appear in the "new" writing style.

At about this time A. N. Palmer, editing *The Western Penman* and connected with the Western Penman Publishing Company, a Midwestern firm, began putting out copybooks. Contemporary with Palmer, two other compilers working together, C. P. Zaner and E. W. Blosser, started issuing similar texts. The copybooks of these three practically took over the school-writing field for a period. The beginning of the "Zanerian System" and the "Blosser System," as the publications of the pair became known, coincided with the appearance of the "Palmer System." Blosser at one time had worked with the Spencers and he used the ordinary Spencerian script at first, later changing over to the newly developed hand, and Palmer pursued the same course. There were at times slight variations in the scripts used by compilers, but eventually the "new" hand came to be utilized exclusively.

In the later issues of the Zaner-Blosser copybooks the method of beginning children with "print" and gradually leading to cursive script was adopted, and before long this had become the general procedure in teaching. Some educators disapproved of this method, and it is not universally advocated today. Years before Zaner's and Blosser's time the great Russian novelist Leo Tolstoy, in his early peasant school at Yasna Polyana, taught his youngest pupils to "print" words and later to write regular script as they progressed—a system that Tolstoy himself is said to have thought out. This may have been the first use of this method of teaching handwriting to beginners.[14]

---

[14] Ernest J. Simmons, *Leo Tolstoy* (Boston: Little Brown, 1946), p. 196. Tolstoy published a spelling book and a series of four readers which were printed in the hundreds of thousands. Not many writers on Tolstoy (including Simmons, who wrote so thoroughly on the Yasna Polyana

Near the turn of the nineteenth century Mrs. M. M. Bridges, in England, formulated a script that was one of the first used in schools that went back to the old Italian cursive.[15] The "Bridges Script" has been a disturbing factor in the evolution of recent school handwriting even in America. The American proponents of such writing were at first somewhat inclined to mix it with vertical, but in the end a script was brought out that could not be accounted for in that way. Some handwriting, notably examples by William Morris and others, in a minor way anticipated this new form, but Mrs. Bridges was the first to develop it to a definite schoolbook status.

In regard to future handwriting, despite the merits or faults of particular letter designs, it would appear that too much uniformity in form or in methods of execution should not be taught. Handwriting is as pre-eminently individualistic as one's facial features. It is possible that in future teachers of writing will drill pupils in a variety of hands, then let the pupil settle on the script that suits him individually. This might do away with some of the aversion to the task of handwriting.

Mankind has an inherent dislike of the act of setting thoughts down in handwriting — which perhaps accounts for the neglect of handwriting. The use of the typewriter, as many people believe, has nothing to do with this neglect. This prevalent half-conscious aversion is not anything new; John R. Green

---

school) have made mention of these schoolbooks on which the famous Russian spent many months at the time his genius was at its highest — just after publication of *War and Peace*. An account of the readers, however, does appear in Maude's *Life of Tolstoy* (London: Oxford Press, 1953), I, 350.

[15] E. M. Thompson in his splendid article "Palaeography," in the *Encyclopedia Britannica, 13th Edition,* says that modern English cursive owes its origin to the sixteenth-century Italian cursive.

quotes the King of England of two centuries ago as saying, "Of all things I do not like writing."[16]

Handwriting most certainly deserves more respect than we give it at the present time. The thirteenth-century Mohammedan scholar, as-Zarnuji, in a very quaint book on education said "O Hilal [student], do not separate yourself from ink for it is good in itself and it is good for those who have it in their possession."[17]

---

[16] Green, *History of the English People* (New York: Belford Clarke, 1884), IV, 83.

[17] az-Zarnuji, *Tarlim Al-Muta 'Allim — Tariq At-ta 'Allum, (Instruction of the Student: The Method of Learning)* (New York: King's Crown Press, Columbia University, 1947), p. 62. This unusual book of less than one hundred pages was not translated from the Arabic into English until the 1940's, and then was printed under a subsidy.

XV

School Histories

UNTIL THE NINETEENTH CENTURY history was little valued as a school subject. More often than not it was left to the teacher to decide whether the subject was even to be taken notice of. Prior to the first two decades of the century but two or three true school histories had been published in America. A number of other texts had a few supplementary pages on "history" as apart from other subject matter. But aside from this meager body of material there was no printed textual matter for use in the study of the past in schools. There have also been periods since that time when the evaluation of history study in schools has been low. About the time science began to achieve a strong position in our educational program history was neglected, both in this country and in England. Augustus Jessop, in his *Coming of the Friars and Other Historical Essays,* published in 1889, speaking of that period in England, said (p. 259):

> In our elementary schools History is almost entirely ignored. A whole people is rapidly breaking with the past from sheer ignorance that there is any past worth knowing.

The well-known sociologist, Albert Galloway Keller, wrote, "The past is not dead, but only foolishly forgotten or light mindedly ignored; it is present in all that is today or will be tomorrow."[1]

---

[1] Keller, *Man's Rough Road,* (New Haven: Yale University Press, 1932), Foreword.

196

Other writers with a philosophical turn of mind have similar observations on the relationship between the past and the present. We can remember from our school days that Patrick Henry said in his immortal freedom speech, "I know of no way of judging of the future, but by the past." Authors in considerable numbers could be quoted on the attitude that finally brought the study of history into the schools and that keeps it there today.

Noah Webster's revision of the *Grammatical Institute, Part Three,* printed under the title *American Selections,* a reading text printed in 1787, carried *A History of the United States,* the first appearance in any schoolbook of authentic American historical material. It was, as Harry W. Warfel says in his life of Webster, "the first time in the United States a schoolbook recorded the history of the events which led to the formation of the nation."[2] In 1823 Webster's *Letters to a Young Gentleman Concerning His Education* was printed in New Haven, and·this had subjoined, to use a term of the author, "A Brief History Of The United States."

Morse's *Geography Made Easy* incorporated a chronology at the end of the volume; and by the time of his 1789 *American Geography* the compiler thought it was time to use some American history material, and "A Brief History" of thirty-six pages, by Noah Webster, was printed along with the geographical material. Morse's original chronology in *Geography Made Easy* was headed "An Improved Chronological Table of Remarkable Events, Discoveries and Inventions; Comprehending in one View The Analysis, or Outlines of General History, from the Creation to the Present Time." The first entry, of the year 4004 B.C., marked "The Creation Of The World and of Adam

---

[2] Warfel, *Noah Webster, Schoolmaster to America* (New York: Macmillan, 1936), p. 89.

and Eve." Almost a thousand years intervened between this item and the next, which carried the date 3017 B.C. and which recorded an episode laconically entitled "Enoch translated into heaven." Dated almost seven hundred years later, the next item proclaimed "the old world destroyed by a deluge which continued 377 days." There may be some question as to the accuracy of the 377 days, since the Bible says, "And the water prevailed upon the earth an hundred and fifty days." This difference is explained by the fact that several versions have come down to us as to the duration of the flood.

The date given for the creation of the world, 4004 B.C. is of course the one set by the Irish Archbishop James Ussher, long a widely accepted item of chronology. A great deal has been written about Ussher's *Annales Veteris et Novi Testamenti,* published in two volumes in 1650–54 in which his historical chronology was set down; but his dates are naturally no longer credited. Most present-day writing in regard to Ussher's dating of the creation of the world is derisive in character, but not all. Sir William Cecil Dampier, in his highly esteemed *History of Science,* treated Ussher's date of the creation in a way quite different from that of most other writers. He said :

> Geological study must have suggested doubts about the chronology of Archbishop Ussher, who put the date of creation in the year 4004 B.C., but even a well-informed man seriously contended in 1857 that God had put misleading fossils into the rocks to test the faith of mankind. It may be impossible to refute this argument; indeed the world may have been created last week, with fossils, records and memories all complete; nevertheless the hypothesis seems improbable.[3]

---

[3] Dampier, *History of Science* (New York: Macmillan, 1949), p. 310.

Whewell followed a somewhat similar line of thought, although not referring to Ussher's chronology.[4]

Chronologies have been compiled from the time of the Middle Ages. After the invention of printing the number increased, and during the nineteenth century their study began to meet with considerable favor in schools; they must have appealed to the average student. John Fiske, the historian, as a schoolboy of eleven set down in 1853, from memory, a chronology from 1000 B.C. to 1820 A.D. that filled sixty pages of a large notebook.[5] A majority of the chronologies began with the creation of the world, as did Morse's, and for a long time most general histories followed this pattern. Even H. G. Wells, considered intellectually a modern of moderns, in his *Outline of History*, went back to the time of creation. He did not use the regular biblical chronology, however, but used the now-generally-accepted evolutionary approach.

In 1820 Joseph Emerson Worcester's *Element of History*, with a separate *Historical Atlas*, appeared. This was the first really comprehensive and ably written American school history — a practicable school text. It was Worcester's second publication; his first having been a small geography. In 1828 Worcester edited Johnson's *Dictionary*, the next year made an abridgement of Webster's *American Dictionary*, and a year afterward brought out his own *Comprehensive Pronouncing and Explanatory English Dictionary*. In 1846 he issued his *Universal English Dictionary*, which he subsequently enlarged a number of times. It was natural that such a man — an established lexi-

---

[4] Whewell, *Bridgewater Treatise on Astronomy* (London: Bohn, 1852), pp. 19 and 243.

[5] Perry, *John Fiske* (Boston: Beacon Biographies, Small Maynard, 1906), p. 6.

cographer, constantly adding to his material and bettering it—
should revise his school history, which Worcester did.

The *Elements of History* went through several revisions, and
the 1830 revised edition was exceptionally popular and went
through extensive printings. In 1833 the compiler revised his
history again, this time omitting the atlas so that the text could
be sold for school use at a lower price. With this issue the
Worcester history became the most popular book of its class.
The volume covered in clearly written prose ancient, medieval,
and modern history, extending well into the factual story of
the United States and its founding.

About the time the Worcester history was coming into its
own, Pinnock's *Goldsmith's Abridgement of the History of
Rome* was issued in Philadelphia by Kay and Biddle, the first
edition of which was dated 1835. Kay and Biddle was an
enterprising publisher of schoolbooks, and evidently they
wanted to try out histories of other countries and for this reason
took over American publication of the Pinnock books, originally
English publications. The man from whom these worth-while
texts took their name was William Pinnock, born in Alton,
Hampshire, England. He taught school for a period, then
turned to book selling. At the age of thirty-five he began writing
and publishing a number of small educational texts, almost
pamphlets, known as "Catechisms." These were highly successful, and he then turned out the "abridged" (although not too
much reduced) Goldsmith histories under such titles as Pinnock's *Goldsmith History of England*, Pinnock's *Goldsmith
History of France*, and Pinnock's *Goldsmith History of Rome*.
Some of the Pinnock books in the American editions were
sufficiently popular to remain in print for a quarter of a
century.

The Goodrich "Peter Parley" histories, along with the Joseph
Emerson Worcester text, were the first school histories to became

nationally popular. The Peter Parley books were used by younger students everywhere. These texts had characteristics not too strongly represented in competitor volumes, dwelling especially on destructive snowslides, earthquakes, and any sort of disaster. Striking illustrations portrayed the crumbling of buildings in the Lisbon, Caracas, and other earthquakes. In schoolbooks of the first half of the nineteenth century such disaster pictures were somewhat common — those of the Lisbon earthquake in particular. This terrible holocaust had a pro found effect upon the whole of civilization, and unquestionably Goodrich and his Peter Parley books did their part in keeping alive interest in the Lisbon disaster.

Much of the material in the Peter Parley histories was pure fiction, even in some of the texts intended for higher students. In the *Parley Pictorial History of the World,* issued over a period of thirty years, there are flowery passages more fitting for a fiction magazine than for a text from which school children were supposed to obtain a knowledge of history. The *Pictorial History,* published under the name of Samuel G. Goodrich himself, describing the supposed ancient kingdom of El Dorado in South America, said :

[The king every day was] covered with powdered gold, so that he looked like a golden image. The palace of this glittering monarch was built of brilliant marble as white as snow. The pillars of the palace were porphyry and alabaster. Its entrance was guarded by two lions, who were fastened to a tall column by chains of massive gold. After passing the lions a fountain was seen, from which gushed a continual shower of liquid silver, through four large pipes of gold. The interior of the palace was too splendid to be described. It contained an altar of solid silver, on which was an immense golden sun. Lamps were continually burning, and their dazzling radiance was reflected from innumerable objects of silver and gold.

Nathaniel Hawthorne, then a young man, was doing work for Goodrich at the time the *Pictorial History of the World* came out and one can almost believe that the noted novelist wrote the words quoted above on El Dorado. While it is not easy to imagine that such a writer as Hawthorne would have written "chains of massive gold" instead of "massive chains of gold," anyone engaged in hack writing—which this passage was— might have let such a phrase slip by. It is well known that Samuel Goodrich was the first to recognize the ability of Hawthorne, and the latter's biographers have been liberal in their praise of Goodrich's early help at a time when others were giving the future author of *The Scarlet Letter* no notice at all.[6]

The first of the outstanding Goodrich histories from a text standpoint, and one of real value, was the *History of the United States of America,* initially issued in 1822, which stood above the other Peter Parley books in merit. This history was not written by Samuel Goodrich (Peter Parley) but by his brother Charles Augustus. It was that author's first of several books. Samuel and Charles A. Goodrich were first cousins of Chauncey A., who became the well-known Yale professor and who edited the 1847 edition of Webster's *Dictionary.* All three of them wrote industriously. Samuel G. Goodrich, who originally published his brother Charles's *History of the United States of America,* sold the publishing rights and it was in this later period that the book enjoyed an immense popularity. Samuel Goodrich, speaking of the history in 1856, said: "Several hundred thousand copies of it have been sold."[7] Charles Goodrich wrote other school histories, among them a *Child's History of the United States,* which was still being printed as late as 1878.

---

[6] Newton Arvin, *Hawthorne* (Boston: Little, Brown, 1929), pp. 46–53, gives a full account of the Goodrich-Hawthorne relationship.

[7] Goodrich, *Recollections of a Lifetime* (New York: The Arundel Press, *ca.* 1856), p. 570.

Before the middle of the nineteenth century there were published a few school histories that do not often appear in bibliographies and are not much known of today. Among them was Emma Willard's *History of the United States for Schools,* issued in New York in 1831, which forty years later was being advertised as in its "30th Edition." Mrs. Willard's history is of special interest because of the fame of the compiler, who was elected to the American Hall of Fame in 1905 and was well known before that. A pioneer in higher education for women, Mrs. Willard was the author of a number of books on various subjects, among them *A Treatise on the Motive Powers Which Produce the Circulation of the Blood,* issued in 1846. Despite her other achievements, Emma Willard's chief fame rests on the authorship of the poem "Rocked in the Cradle of the Deep," which appeared in 1830 and was soon afterward set to music, and which still maintains a perennial popularity.

A fairly large *History of the United States* was published by John Frost in the middle 1830's, and the book was later condensed into a smaller text under the same title, "for use in common schools." In this latter form the book was popular and remained in print as late as 1852. The text, small in size but not so in verbosity, was among the last of several pocket-size histories of the first half of the century. It was also one of the last of the ill-adapted school histories that contained so much irrelevant material.

About the time Frost's diminutive book was losing its hold a new form of school history, concise and with carefully selected material, came into vogue and marked a forward movement in the study of history in schools. These new texts, with their numerous improvements, soon displaced the older and more clumsily assembled texts.

The histories of these new compilers — with the aid of fresh-thinking printing designers, it might be added — had quite a different appearance from those which had been previously used. Instead of the accustomed closely set and crowded pages, those set in the new type-face were designed for easier reading and study. The text was more concise and pithy than school history writers twenty years previously would have imagined feasible.

The *Condensed School History of the United States,* by William Swinton, compiler of the Swinton readers, was one of the first of the school histories of the new class. Swinton numbered each paragraph in his text in heavy figures and the name of each important person or place was printed in bold-face type the first time it appeared on a page. As Swinton obviously calculated, this practice was intended to emphasize the high spots of the lesson material. After a careful examination of one of these texts, however, one can scarcely escape the conclusion that the compiler overstepped himself in changing so radically the appearance of the pages, which resembled type-face displays more than the pages of a schoolbook. The bold-face words averaged from ten to a dozen a page, and the pupil must have experienced a feeling of gliding over the whole page too rapidly — a sensation not conducive to a proper concentration on the subject matter. In some of the later editions of Swinton's text the use of the bold-face type was curtailed, but not to a sufficient degree.

It is only natural that a man with Swinton's teaching and journalistic background should strike out on new paths, even though the results might go somewhat awry. In any event, school history compilers for the next generation followed his lead or took advantage of his more practical innovations. The texts of J. B. Blackburn, W. N. McDonald, and L. J. Campbell; the Barnes histories written by Joel Dorman Steele; the Catholic histories of the Benzigen brothers; the eclectic history texts of W. E. Thalameimer—all these and others were patterned after Swinton's plan.

A few compilers of the last half of the century did not adhere too strictly to the new system of presentation, which had been gradually becoming "telegraphic" and more like a catalog in style, but instead evolved methods of their own, generally straight-forward narration. Edward Everett Hale's *History of the United States,* (1887), was in ordinary readable narrative. It is not likely that a writer who penned "The Man without a Country" would have been satisfied to write even a school history in any other way. Horace H. Scudder, who wrote charming essays on *The Rubaiyat of Omar Khayyam* and other engaging subjects, put out a school history in 1884, and his, too, was readable.

Edward Sylvester Ellis's *Primary History of the United States* did not tend toward a syllabus-like arrangement—this because the compiler had much preparatory experience in writing. Ellis penned historical works of massive proportions; *The People's Standard History of the United States,* issued in 1895 in six large volumes illustrated with hundreds of engravings, some in color, by well-known artists, was one of his works. These huge *de luxe* sets show copyrights from 1895 to 1900 and many copies were sold at a high price through the traveling agent system, a form of distribution at its height at this period. Ellis also wrote novels, including a number of those commonly termed "ten centers"; in fact he was long known as the "Dime Novel King."[8] *Seth Jones,* one of Ellis's "ten centers" issued in 1860, sold 450,000 copies in six months—no mean record. Much of the Ellis's fiction appeared under pen names, and only a skilled bibliographer can trace many of them.

---

[8] William Targ, *Bibliophile in the Nursery* (Cleveland and New York: World, 1957), p. 20.

A number of historians who turned out high-class work in the regular trade-book line also compiled school histories, some of which won wide approval during the latter days of the nine-teenth century and the first two or three decades of the twentieth. Chief among the historians in this category were John Bach MacMaster, Benson J. Lossing, and John Fiske, all well known in their time. The school histories of all three may be described as a cross between the "catalog" and the straight-forward narrative type—although it must be admitted that everyone might not agree with this description.

John Fiske's *History of the United States for Schools* was a volume of more than five hundred pages, and, despite its size, was widely used. In his preface Fiske told why he wrote his history:

> I was solicited by half a dozen publishing houses to write a school-book for the study of American history, and in all these requests the same reason was alleged. The desire was expressed for a book from a professional hand instead of the mere compilations formerly in use.

Fiske's text was first issued in 1894 and, although it was as much a compilation as other school histories of the day, it went through many printings within a decade of its publication. It is only natural that John Fiske's school-history efforts were crowned with success, because he was the top history writer of his time, and his text, with its explanatory maps, notes, lesson-questions, collateral reading lists, and so on, was one that could be effectively used. While Lossing's and MacMaster's texts were met with much approval they were not used as widely as was Fiske's.

Around the end of the nineteenth century many of the widely accepted texts were keeping close, in a general way, to the catalog form, among them being the outstanding books of D. H. Montgomery and Philip Van Ness Myers, the last long a professor of history and political economy at the University of Cincinnati. Both these authors' texts were astonishingly popular. Thomas B. Lawler, relating how the Montgomery histories became widely popular almost overnight, states that Montgomery's *Leading Facts of American History,* appearing in the early 1890's, "changed almost in the twinkling of an eye, the position of the house [Ginn and Company] in the elementary schools and gave it a position which two years before was undreamed of."[9] In the same history of his publishing firm (p. 73) Lawler further says that the Myers histories "were another milestone in the development of the house of Ginn."

Philip Van Ness Myers' *General History,* one of his most successful volumes, in its final editions appeared in a splendid format, which no doubt increased its popularity. One of the first schoolbooks that Ginn put out in the fine format, it was a superb example of a school text. Numerous such specimens have appeared since, especially in the history class, not only from Ginn but from other firms as well. Myers was a lucid writer with a widely informed mind and a vivid imagination. The last chapter of the 1906 edition of the *General History* was headed with the lyrical lines from Alfred Tennyson's "Locksley Hall":

> For I dipt into the future, far as human eye could see,
> Saw the Vision of the world, and all the wonder that would
> be;
> ....
> Till the war drum throbbed no longer, and the battle flags
> were furled
> In the Parliament of Man, the Federation of the World.

This chapter, entitled "The World State," was the only one in the history with a poetry quotation as a heading. Myers appar-

---

[9] Thomas B. Lawler, *Seventy Years of Textbook Publishing: A History of Ginn and Company* (Boston: Ginn, 1938), p. 156.

ently believed, much in unison with the thought of the time,[10] that an era of universal peace was at hand; but he lived through the First World War and until 1937 when Hitler, the modern Attila, had reached the height of his power. Had Professor Myers revised his *General History* in his last years it is not at all probable that he would have retained Tennyson's words as the heading of his last chapter.

It is somewhat difficult to understand today how books such as Montgomery's, each one of which was scarcely more than a syllabus in style and stood greatly in need of adjustment to the currents of history, could have been as successful as they were. It may be that their popularity rested in their completely unimaginative adherence to unadorned statement, the direct diction, the omission of any word not required to convey the bare thought. Myers' texts were unquestionably of a higher order, and it is not difficult to see how they met with approval and remained in favor.

Numerous local and regional school histories have been published, among them various state histories and those of the Pacific Coast, New England, and other sections. As early as 1779 Hannah Adams, the first American woman to earn a livelihood from writing, published a *History of New England*. Jedidiah Morse and Elijah Parish, in 1804, issued a *History of New England* (Charlestown : Printed and Sold by Samuel Etheridge), "for schools and private families"; and since their time other school histories with the same title have appeared.

---

[10] The idea of a perfect political world originated in the mind of the French philosopher and mathematician Marie Jean de Caritat, Marquis de Condorcet, late in the eighteenth century and was a dream of the nineteenth century. Tennyson was expressing in his lines what de Caritat maintained was an inherent possibility to be achieved by man. With the international contentions since Tennyson's day the hope for such a world has been shattered, although the vision perished slowly.

All the western states, as young as they are historically, have had their individual texts. The state of Nevada, whose total population is less than that of hundreds of cities in the country, has its school history, *Our State Nevada*. There have been a "Confederate" and other Southern histories for school use, and in 1911 *A School History of the Negro Race in America* was published.

Some of the Southern histories were not too impartial in their presentations. *The Southern History of the United States*, by W. N. McDonald and J. S. Blackburn, issued in Baltimore in 1869, four years after the war, although published as a general United States history, was in its last pages wholly a Confederate text — one that would, as the authors said in the preface, "meet the demands of the present occasion" and "more fully supply the wants of education in the South." The two authors lived on the borderline of the Southern states, McDonald being superintendent of the Louisville, Kentucky, high school, and Blackburn principal of the Alexandria, Virginia, high school. With their geographical backgrounds, one might have expected from them a more conciliatory turn of mind. The book in its latter pages was a sort of Southern hero-worship story of the Civil War. One has to read but a few passages about the battles to see how restricted the vision of the authors was, and it is only necessary to quote one passage to prove the strength of the hero worship. In their story of the death of Stonewall Jackson, the great soldier was thus extolled (p. 448):

He was so pure, so noble, so untiring and so brave, that all heads bowed down to him. His splendid victories had excited the admiration of the world, but the fame of his warlike deeds was even obscured by the brightness of his virtues. Even his enemies praised him, and admitted that his angelic goodness almost consecrated the cause for which he fought.

The last chapter of the text was captioned "Congress Abolishes the State Governments." Obviously the South in which this schoolbook was penned is not the South of today.

Mary Tucker McGill's *History of Virginia,* was used for perhaps as long a period as any other state history; but during its two or three decades of usage John Eston Cooke's *Stories of The Old Dominion,* which was primarily a book of stories, encroached on the McGill text as a school history in lower grades. Cooke's stories of Captain John Smith, Pocahontas, Washington in the wilderness, Point Pleasant and the death of Cornstalk, Elizabeth Zane, and John Marshall was almost purely a history in itself. So popular was this book that the author was selected to write the first volume of the American Commonwealth series of histories edited by Horace E. Scudder, and Cooke gave it the title *Virginia, The History of a People.*

The suspicions engendered by our time have wrought changes in the writing of school histories. Propaganda elements, indecisive national attitudes, artificial coercions and restrictions enter into the task today as they did not before our time. Perhaps at no other period has the planning and writing of school history been so singularily burdensome — much more so than any other form of composition. This is particularly true concerning our relations with other nations during the present century.

George Sarton says that it is not always easy to draw "the line between the 'old' and the 'new' when it comes to certain books;" and it is today definitely not easy to discern where to draw the line between the "old" and "new" way of writing history for school study — to say what ought to be included and what should be left out.

---

[11] George Sarton, *The Appreciation of Ancient and Medieval Science during the Renaissance* (Philadelphia: University of Pennsylvania Press, 1955), p. 95.

The study of civics in our schools has all along been pretty well considered a part of history study. Many of the large history texts have carried the Declaration of Independence, the Constitution, and other notable civic documents, with lesson arrangements for their study. Numerous separate elementary civic texts were being printed in the first quarter of the present century. Today, however, the subject is merging more or less into others as far as the lower schools are concerned.

For a long time the civic texts were in most cases penned by history compilers, but within the past three decades or so they have been assembled by people who have made a special study of politics, legislation, and sociology. The whole range of civics has been raised, and this has necessitated enlargement of the texts in this field. During the last quarter-century we have had texts with such titles as *Development of European Cities, Forms and Functions of American Government, American State Government,* and *Your Country and Mine*—all books of considerable size. One of the above, W. Brooke Graves' *American State Government,* recently issued by Heath without a date, has more than a thousand pages.

XVI

General Science Texts

IN 1798 BENJAMIN RUSH stated that chemistry had become "a necessary branch of a gentleman's education,"[1] and not long afterward chemistry texts in considerable number began to appear in this country. In 1770 Dr. Rush had himself already published a *Syllabus of a Course of Lectures on Chemistry*, made up of lectures delivered at the College of Philadelphia, later to become the University of Pennsylvania. Because of the interest of the volume as a cradle book it was reprinted in facsimile by the University of Pennsylvania Press in an edition of five hundred copies in 1954. But two copies of the original edition are known to exist — one in the University of Pennsylvania Library, the other in the library of the Historical Society of Pennsylvania. Berthollet's *Laws of Chemical Affinity* was printed in Baltimore in 1809, at a time when general chemical textbooks were beginning to appear. Berthollet was associated with Lavoisier and others in formulating the system of chemical nomenclature which, with a few changes, has now achieved worldwide acceptance.

Benjamin Silliman, graduated from Yale in 1796 and some time later appointed professor of natural science there, in 1808

---

[1]*The Selected Writings of Benjamin Rush* (New York: Philosophical Library, 1948), p. 94.

edited and published an edition of William Henry's *Epitome of Experimental Chemistry,* the first thoroughly comprehensive chemistry treatise printed in this country. Every chemistry student knows "Henry's Law" pertaining to gases—namely that the weight of gas when dissolved is proportional to the pressure. Henry's book appeared in England in 1799 and went through eleven editions in thirty years. Later Silliman added seventy-five pages of useful notes to his work. The book was reprinted in Boston in 1810 with copperplate illustrations of the instruments commonly used in chemical work at the time. Silliman's own *Elements of Chemistry* was published in 1830, and this text met with much success, chiefly because the compiler was well known as a teacher and as a lecturer able to hold the attention of an audience on any scientific subject he chose to discuss.

Sir Humphrey Davy's *Elements of Agricultural Chemistry* was first printed in the United States in 1820, and the next year it was reprinted in different sections of the country. This volume, which became a classic of science, was made up of lectures delivered by Davy before the Board of Agriculture in England in 1812 and later. These published lectures made up the first well-known text on agriculture and its chemical relations, and formed the basis of several later American school-books pertaining to the chemical side of plant growth. In the beginning of his lectures Davy stated that "agricultural chemistry has not yet received a regular and systematic form," and his text was a notable fulfillment of this need. At the end of the 1820 American edition of Davy's book was a ninety-two page "Treatise on Soils and Manures," by "A Practical Agriculturist," and every American agricultural text which closely followed its appearance profited appreciably from this supplement.

A text of more than six hundred pages, Brande's *Manual of Chemistry,* was first printed in this country in 1821 by George

Long, a New York publisher who issued a number of school-books, some of them higher school science texts. The Long edition of Brande's book had "notes and emandations" by William James MacHeven, M.D., "Professor of Chemistry in the College of Physicians and Surgeons of the University of the State of New York." Brande's manual was originally printed in England in 1819, two years before its appearance here, and was rightly considered one of the excellent texts of its day in its field. William Thomas Brande, born in England in 1788, studied medicine and became an assistant to Sir Humphry Davy. For twenty years he and Davy were editors of the *Quarterly Journal of Science, Literature and Art,* a periodical which did a great deal to advance science, and the two worked together on many important experiments.

In 1826 John W. Webster published a *Manual of Chemistry,* which was primarily for use at Harvard, the lessons being "arranged in the order in which they are discussed and illustrated in the lectures at Harvard University." This book, like the others already mentioned, was suitable for use in ordinary higher school classes, and they were so used in a limited way. John W. Webster's *Manual* was, as the author stated, "on the basis of Professor Brande's," and contained the "principal facts of chemical science." The historian of American chemistry, C. A. Browne, especially commented upon the fact that Webster's text gave "a full representation of the elements," and he pronounced the book one that "marked an important advance in our system of chemical education."[2]

The chemical texts mentioned constituted the foundation upon which the great structure of chemical science in America was raised, but prior to the publication of most of these books

---

[2] *Journal of Chemical Education,* IX, 1932, 705–706.

a small chemical text had been published for use by school children — Mrs. Jane Marcet's *Conversations on Chemistry.* This tiny schoolbook, originally published in England and later the first American chemical text for the lower grades, was printed in New Haven, Connecticut, in 1809. The book had good engravings by Amos Dolittle and a brief supplementary chapter on "Fixed Alkalies, by H. Davy." Mrs. Marcet's *Conversations* went through a number of printings in this country. After the book was well established, an edition, "with additions by J. L. Comstock," was printed in Hartford, Connecticut, with Mrs. Marcet's name omitted. The only mention that Comstock, who put the book out, made of the real compiler was in his preface where he referred to "the author, herself a woman." The *Conversations on Chemistry* achieved its extensive popularity primarily because it was simply written; in addition, it was in the question-and-answer form approved at that time for such a subject.

The noted scientist Michael Faraday gave Mrs. Marcet's *Conversations on Chemistry* credit for starting him upon the study of chemistry, which led to accomplishments that made his name known everywhere. In 1804, at the age of thirteen, Faraday was apprenticed to a London bookbinder, with whom he remained for eight years. During this time after work hours he read many of the volumes he bound and thus coming upon Mrs. Marcet's *Conversations* was deeply interested. Late in life he wrote a letter to a friend telling of how he happened upon the book, and related the story of the part it played in his life.

Within a few years after the issuing of the Marcet *Conversations on Chemistry,* Comstock's own *Elements of Chemistry* was published and it reached a fourth revised edition by 1846. At this time a large proportion of the school chemistry texts were beginning to be turned out by the professional textbook writers, one copying a good deal from another; and Comstock's text was of this sort. While Comstock's chemical text met with some success, it was not printed as frequently as most of his other popular volumes.

A well-known professor of chemistry in the University of New York, John W. Draper, published his *Textbook of Chemistry* in 1846; backed by a name standing high in chemistry at the time, the book quickly took hold. Draper stated that his book was the product of his own teaching and that it was not "an untried work." "It is intended," he said, "as a manual arranged in such divisions as practice has shown to be suitable for daily instructions." The text contained about three hundred illustrations, most of them small cuts but all pertinent to the subject matter. Draper was a professional chemist aside from teaching the subject, and his important research work in photography made portrait photography possible. He was the first president of the American Chemical Society and one of the founders of the New York University Medical School. Notwithstanding all this, he is best remembered at present as the author of the *History of the Intellectual Development of Europe,* a two-volume treatise published in 1862, in which the methods of physical science are applied to the delineation of the events of history.

In 1869 another limited-sized chemical manual, a *Handbook of Chemistry,* by W. J. Rolfe and J. A. Gillet, for the lower grades, was printed in Boston. This was one of the most compact of the nineteenth-century chemical texts. The title showed the compilers to be teachers in the high school at Cambridge, Massachusetts; and at the time of the issuance of this little chemical text no one knew that one of its compilers, William James Rolfe, was destined for fame as a Shakespearian scholar. The *Handbook of Chemistry* was Rolfe's second book; in 1866 he had published a *Handbook of Latin Poetry,* a small schoolbook.

Ira Remsen's *Organic Chemistry,* chiefly a translation, and James H. Shepard's *Elements of Inorganic Chemistry,* both appearing in 1880, were among the first school texts dividing the subject. All advanced study of chemistry today is broken down into organic and inorganic. A specialist in one branch is not necessarily expected to have a thorough knowledge of the other, but this was not the case prior to 1880. Within a few years after the appearance of Remsen's and Shepard's books, separate texts on organic and inorganic chemistry were becoming somewhat common. Because of the advance of chemical knowledge a noticeable change was taking place in methods of instruction in the subject, and Remsen, in particular, had much to do with this change through his textbooks. Speaking of Remsen, Professor F. J. Moore said, "He had much to do in shaping chemical thought during the last half of the nineteenth century."[3] From 1901 to 1912 Dr. Remsen served as president of Johns Hopkins University, adding a great deal to the prestige of the institution.

The first book by Edward L. Youmans, *Classbook of Chemistry,* a superb text for its day, was written while the author was almost blind, and published in 1851. The volume was an immediate success, eventually selling to the extent of one hundred and fifty thousand copies — unusual for a chemical text a century ago. Youmans presented his material in an easy-to-understand style, and in his pages, as John Fiske said, "the chemical elements were alive."[4] The Youmans text was used over a long period; one reason for its popularity, besides its straightforward treatment of chemistry, theoretical and prac-

---

[3] F. J. Moore, *A History of Chemistry* (New York: McGraw-Hill, 1931), p. 305.

[4] Fiske, *Edward Livingston Youmans, Interpreter of Science for the People* (New York: D. Appleton, 1894), p. 69.

tical, was the fact that it treated from a chemical standpoint, processes close to the people's daily lives, such as the production of butter, properties of the blood, the working of the digestion, and the whys and wherefores of plant cultivation.

Youmans perhaps stands at the top of our schoolbook compilers in one respect—general influence during the nineteenth century in popularizing science. This man stood unique in his time as a spreader of the written word of science. It was through his efforts with writers and publishers that the works of Herbert Spencer and several other noted foreign scientists were introduced in the United States. In 1872 he founded the *Scientific Monthly,* which still survives and which, along with the *Scientific American,* has evoked an enormous output of scientific writing of the highest order. All his life Youmans was afflicted with eye trouble, but despite this serious handicap he performed an almost unbelievable amount of productive work. The story of his life, one crowded with achievement, is well told by John Fiske, his long-time friend, in *Edward Livingston Youmans.*

When Joel Dorman Steele became a school teacher in south-central New York state in the mid-nineteenth century he at once saw the need for more elemental science texts than were available. He set out to produce three limited-sized treatises, writing first a *Chemistry,* published in 1867, then an *Astronomy* and a *Natural Philosophy,* issued a year and two years later. A year later he turned out a *Geology.* All the early Steele science school texts were put into a "Fourteen Weeks Series," and soon they were the most widely used schoolbooks in the country aside from certain readers and arithmetics. Steele patterned his system of presenting material after the one that William Swinton had used a few years before, and this method well suited Steele's subject matter.

While Steele did not introduce such homey topics as butter,

digestion processes, and plant growth into his chemistry text, as did Youmans, he spiced his pages here and there with items of interest that added an element almost entirely absent from other such texts. In more than one place he quoted Shakespeare, sometimes tellingly, though not always. On one occasion he wrote :

> Hamlet must have been somewhat more of a chemist than a madman when he gravely assured the king that "man may fish with the worm that hath eat of a king, and eat of the fish that hath fed of the worm."[5]

He brought a religious tinge in here and there. The preamble to the Introduction of the same text read :

> "Dead mineral matter," as we call it, is instinct with form. Each tiny stem is attracted here, repelled there, holds and is held by bands of iron. No particle is left to itself, but, watched by the Eternal Eye and guided by the Eternal Hand, all obey immutable law. When Christ declared the very hairs of our head to be numbered, he intimated a chemical truth, which we can now know in full to be, that the very atoms of which each hair is composed are numbered by that same watchful Providence.

Although this preamble might be criticized as being too ornate for a chemical text it reveals Steele's way of thinking.

In the first part of the nineteenth century Professor Peck, of Harvard, defined "natural philosophy" as chemistry, but the subject so designated some time later became physics. A good tracing of the lineage of "natural philosophy" is to be found in W. F. G. Swann's "Three Centuries of Natural Philosophy," an address delivered at Swarthmore College on October 29, 1927, and reprinted in the *Journal of The Franklin Institute,* January, 1928.

---

[5] Steele, *Fourteen Weeks in Chemistry* (New York: Barnes, 1873), p. 239.

Comstock's *Natural Philosophy,* which came out in 1830, was one of the most successful of the early books of its class. The text discussed hydraulics, acoustics, optics, electricity, and pneumatics, and dwelt on topics the thought of the period was just awakening to—the working of the lately improved microscope, for instance.[*] As a novelty, seven pages of Comstock's text was devoted to time, practically ignored by other natural philosophy compilers. Even today little is found in schoolbooks on this subject.

Early "natural history," or at least as the term was first used, had an affinity with "natural philosophy," and often books under these respective titles were closely akin. The term "natural history" as used in our time perhaps had its inception in our early botany books. One can scarcely reach any other conclusion after a thorough examination of the early issues of these texts.

Many of the earliest American botanical books originated in eastern Pennsylvania. William Bartram whose *Travels,* published in the late eighteenth century, was considered a classic from the time of its appearance, lived in Philadelphia. William Young, Jr., whose *Herbacées d'Amerique* was published in Paris in 1783, also lived in Philadelphia. In 1818 Benjamin Smith Barton's *Compendium Florae* was also issued in Philadelphia—a description of plants found within ten miles of the city. In 1802 Constantine Rafinesque, Turkish-born and the greatest name in American botany, moved to Philadelphia and

---

[*] Microscopes of a sort had been known on this side of the Atlantic for a long while, but little had been written about them. Cotton Mather possessed one, seemingly the first in this country. Cohen, *Some Early Tools of American Science* (Cambridge: 1950), p. 111. Thomas Brattle of Boston had one but a short time later. The Reverend Joseph Green, visiting him in 1711, recorded in his diary on May 29th: "I was at Thomas Brattle's heard ye organ and saw strange things in the microscope."

lived there seventy years, except for periods of travel, until his death. In nearby Lancaster an early *Child's Botany* was printed in 1828. By 1831 it had gone through four editions, the last printed in Boston. This was a small manual of one hundred pages.

Almira Hart Lincoln's *Familiar Lectures on Botany,* "including practical and elementary botany, with generic and specific descriptions of the most common native and foreign plants, and a vocabulary of botanical terms," printed in Hartford, Connecticut, in 1831, was frequently reprinted. Some issues appeared under the title *Botany for Beginners.* The compiler, who afterward married Judge John Phelps (her later texts were written under the name of Mrs. Lincoln Phelps), wrote several schoolbooks on science — a geology, a chemistry, and a natural philosophy, besides the *Lectures on Botany.* Her books were fairly extensively used and she was one of the early popularizers of botany through schoolbooks. Mrs. Lincoln seems to have had an extraordinary love for plant life, judging from some of her pages. Like her sister, Emma Willard, Mrs. Phelps had a strong mind, and took part in organizing and conducting a number of well-known schools over the country. For fifteen years she was connected with the Patapsco Female Institute, at Ellicott Mills, Maryland, near Baltimore, and while there wrote much that was worthwhile. She lived to the age of ninety-one and was active to the end. Like her sister, she turned out books which had nothing to do with education, one or two of them being unusual studies.

John L. Comstock's *Introduction to Botany* was published in 1832 and continued to be printed for more than a quarter of a century, going through more than one revision. This was a text of encyclopedic scope, but, notwithstanding its bulk, it was widely utilized; by 1856 it was in its thirty-third edition. In an advertisement of the first edition, essentially a preface, the compiler stated :

> It is hoped the compiler has not sacrificed science to popularity, but while the first has been kept constantly in view, as much facility has been afforded the student, both in respect to arrangement, figures and explanations as could reasonably be desired.

Comstock sacrificed nothing in the way of material in order to save space. Along the line of several of the school botanies of the time, his text had a dozen pages given over to the "Language Of Flowers," based on folklore of the day of which the following are samples :

Pansy : Think on me while I'm away.

Burdock : Don't come near me !

Violet : I must be sought to be found.

After the line on the violet this verse appeared :

> A woman's love, deep in the heart,
>   Is like the violet flower,
> That lifts its modest head apart,
>   In some sequestered bower.

And then, after a break, these lines followed :

> That strain again ! It had a dying fall.
>   Oh ! It came o'er my ear like the sweet south
> That breathes upon a bank of violets,
>   Stealing and giving odor.

The "sweet south" reference was used by several nineteenth century schoolbook compilers, but no source was ever given. The lines, of course, are from the opening passage of *Twelfth Night,* the editions of Pope and those who followed him. Most modern editions of Shakespeare have the wording "sweet sound," as in the First Folio.

While Comstock's *Botany* was still popular the books of Dr. W. S. W. Ruschenberger began to appear, his *Elements of Botany* being No. 7 of "The Ruschenberger Series of First

Books of Natural History." This botany was completed while the compiler was a surgeon in the United States Navy Hospital in New York, and was first published in 1844. The title page indicated that the manual was "from the text of Milne Edwards and Achille Conte, Professors of Natural History in the College of Henry IV and Charlemagne." Dr. Ruschenberger qualified that information by saying in his preface :

> Besides the work of Messrs. Edwards and Conte, which forms the skeleton of this, I have freely consulted the writings of Lindly, Loudon, Smith, Gray, Reed, and others, and as freely appropriated whatever seemed useful to us in carrying out the design of forming an accurate, brief, and simple treatise on the Elements of Botany suitable for beginners, whether young or old.

The Ruschenberger texts, although a side line and evidently a hobby, were good workable manuals. Dr. Ruschenberger was a man of broad mental interests. Matthew F. Maury points out that the doctor when on one of his voyages around Cape Horn and to India, made observations on the specific gravity of sea waters in various places and on trade winds, sending him the results of his studies.[7]

The Fisher Professor of Natural History at Harvard, Asa Gray, finished his *Manual of the Botany of the Northern United States* in the year 1848. This great compilation at once became the standard work on the subject, and Gray's name was the outstanding one in American botany next to that of Rafinesque. Within the next few years Gray put out a number of small school botanies, which gained immediate favor. His *How Plants Grow* was published in 1858, and while he devoted a good many pages to plant growth, it was, like all his volumes, a botany. Shortly afterward his *Lessons in Botany,* a small text,

---

[7] Maury, *Physical Geography of the Sea* (New York: Harper, 1857), p. 90.

appeared. This latter book came out in a revised edition in 1887 — a text that went into plant growth more heavily than did the one titled *How Plants Grow.*

Gray's texts in which plant growth and plant nature were discussed opened the path to the agriculture texts which appeared during the last part of the nineteenth century and later. These were distinct from the earlier chemistry-agriculture books, and put the study of farming and agricultural pursuits on a new basis. They brought the study to a practical, down-to-earth viewpoint. One of the first of the useful agriculture texts of this class was J. I. Campbell's *Manual of Scientific and Practical Agriculture,* issued in 1859, during the early days of Gray's books. The first hundred or so pages were given over to the old treatment of the subject, stressing chemistry and so on; but the rest was devoted to plant development, rotation of crops, soil, tillage, pasturage — matters that came home to those who earned their living from the earth. Campbell was professor of physical science in Washington College in Virginia, and his book must have been of considerable assistance to later agriculture text compilers.

When W. S. Goff, professor of agriculture in the University of Wisconsin, died in 1902, he had an agriculture text, *First Principles of Agriculture,* almost ready for publication. D. D. Mayne, principal of an agricultural school, completed the manuscript and prepared it for the press. Published in 1904, it was an outstanding example of the new type of text in its category — brief in subject matter, the cobwebs of pedantry swept away, easy of comprehension, and well illustrated with photographs. Such publications showed that the old prolix texts with impractical subject matter were on the way out. In addition to its many good black-and-white illustrations Goff's *First Principles of Agriculture* had a number of color plates of fruits, fowls, and different kind of cattle. (Color plates were just beginning to be used in schoolbooks.)

In 1907 Arden M. Soule and Edna Turpin's *Agriculture, Its Fundamental Principles* was published. An excellent practical treatise, it was one of the first to include a comprehensive treatment of the insect enemies of plant life—knowledge that was eventually to become of great importance. Later on agricultural manuals began to emphasize soil, dealing with bacterial action and so on. Any number of texts appeared with the word *soil* in their titles. In 1915 Charles L. Quear's *Soils and Fertilizers for Schools* was published—a title with a little conscious or unconscious humor in it.

The physical sciences of geology and astronomy never gained the full acceptance in schools that the biological sciences did—perhaps rightly so. A few well-known geologists and astronomers compiled school texts for these studies, but they were not very widely used. James Dwight Dana, the best-known mineralogist and geologist of the mid-nineteenth century, turned out the first popular school geology text. Dana's first writing was in the form of government reports. He was appointed geologist for the Wilkes Expedition sent to the Southern Pacific region in the late 1830's by the United States government, and for a number of years was in government service.[*] In the 1840's

---

[*] The Wilkes expedition was one of the most unusual in our maritime history inasmuch as it was organized chiefly on the recommendation of Jeremiah N. Reynolds, who, along with Captain John Symmes, advanced the theory that there were vast openings at the North and South Poles into the center of a hollow earth. The expedition was primarily to find out as much as possible about the southern portion of the globe, and several scientists were taken along. The publications about the voyage into the Antarctic region furnished the plot material for some of Poe's early stories, and from the same source Herman Melville developed much of his *Moby Dick*. The odd history of Reynolds is told in an article in the Winter, 1937, *Colophon,* "J. N. Reynolds: A Brief Biography," by Robert

Dana became associated with his father-in-law, Professor Benjamin Silliman of Yale, in editing and writing for the *American Journal of Science*. Later he was made professor of natural history and geology at Yale. His *System of Geology* and well-known *Manual of Mineralogy* had been published previously, but it was in his Yale years that he compiled his several school texts. The study of mineralogy in our country was enlivened early in the century by the gift of a large collection of mineral specimens to Harvard University by Dr. I. Lettsom, of London.[9] Dr. Lettsom is best remembered for his verse:

When any sick to me apply,
I physics, bleeds and sweats 'em,
If after that they die,
I can't help it.
                    I Lettsom.[10]

Dana's *Textbook of Geology,* perhaps his most widely used volume aside from his noted *Manual of Mineralogy,* was published during the Civil War and was based on the bulky *Manual*. The *Textbook of Geology* explained all the essential points of the subject and told a great deal about our country that had not before been recorded in a schoolbook. It was popular for a long period. *The Geology Story Briefly Told,* "an introduction to geology for beginners in the science," a smaller text, was issued in 1875, but evidently was never much utilized. One prominent feature of Dana's text is open to criticism — he overemphasized the historical side of geology, emphasizing

E. Almay; and much comment on Melville's derivation of his material from Wilkes' *Narrative* and other writings on the expedition is to be found in Howard P. Vincent, *The Trying-Out of Moby Dick* (Boston: Houghton Mifflin, 1949).

[9] Cohen, *Some Early Tools of American Science* (Cambridge: Harvard Press, 1950), p. 115.

[10] Dr. Cohen quotes another version of the rhyme, of which there are several.

the importance of fossils. These must be studied before the successive ages of the earth can be comprehended, but it can be correctly charged that Dana covered the subject of fossils at too great length in his volumes, which were for school study and not for specialists. Inclusion of such material was shaped by the thought of his time; it was the day of the introduction of ideas on evolution and the thought of mankind was being influenced by revelations of the age of the earth, the descent of living things, and the nature of animal life of the past.

The first edition of Joseph Le Conte's *Elements of Geology,* "for colleges and for the general reader," published in 1877, was an exhaustive study of geology that at once found a deserved place in the academic world. La Conte said he had not tried to produce a manual "such as has been penned by Dana," meaning the *Manual of Mineralogy,* but that he had "endeavored only to present clearly to the thoroughly cultured and intelligent student and reader whatever is best and most interesting in Geologic science" — which he did admirably. In 1884 Le Conte's much smaller *Compend of Geology,* his first lower school text, appeared and also became popular, continuing to go through printings until after the turn of the century.

In the *Compend of Geology* Le Conte stated that he had tried "to awaken the faculty and cultivate the habit of observation, by directing the attention of the pupil to geological phenomena occurring and geological agencies at work *now* on every side, and in the *most familiar things.*" The emphasis on individual observation in school geology study is in great measure to be credited to Le Conte; after his time field work had a distinct place in the study, both in schools and in colleges. According to his own statement Le Conte himself found out much of what he knew of geology in this manner. The *Compend of Geology* went into the natural structure of American terrain in a way no other school geology had done and contained much material of that kind not found elsewhere. The structural history of rivers was extensively covered and the geysers and odd formations found in the West were described more fully than they ever had been, from a geological point of view.

Joseph Le Conte, born on a plantation in Liberty County, South Carolina, not far from Savannah, came of a family that produced a number of scientists." Joseph's father was a learned naturalist and his brother John became well known for his technical and scientific publications. Both John and Joseph first taught in small Southern colleges, but later became professors in the University of California. Joseph, aside from being one of our most eminent geologists, wrote on psychology, the relation of religion and science, binocular vision, evolution and philosophy, and was the author of a number of books on these subjects. A trip with Agassiz into the mountains of New York State while still a student drew Le Conte's attention to geology and led him to make it his lifework. It appears that Louis Agassiz had such a diversified training and could expound his ideas so clearly that he was instrumental in guiding a number of young men into various channels of work, in which, in most cases, they became outstandingly accomplished."

An *Elementary Geology,* by E. B. Andrews, an Ohio geologist and at one time a teacher of geology in Marietta College, was published in 1878. This text contained a full treatment of coal, which had previously been practically ignored in school

---

" Only recently an absorbingly interesting diary kept by a member of the Le Conte family, seventeen-year-old Emma Le Conte, during the Civil War when Sherman was raiding the South, has come to light. The diary was published in 1957 by the Oxford Press under the title *When the World Ended, The Diary of Emma Le Conte.*

"James Teller, "Louis Agassiz and Men Of Letters," *The Scientific Monthly,* Nov., 1947, gives much information on Agassiz's influence over others.

texts. Andrews discussed coal and fuel supplies from an econ-omic as well as a geological viewpoint. His little text, perhaps somewhat too fully, went into local geology—that of the Great Lakes section and the surrounding Ohio homeland, and was among the first school science texts to be so substantially adapted to local environs.

Several astronomy manuals that met with a measure of approval for a time were issued. But, like geology, astronomy has never been completely accepted as a part of the common school curriculum. After making some progress in the early part of the nineteenth century it lost ground as widespread interest in other subjects became pronounced. The first popular school text in astronomy was Elijah H. Burritt's *Geography of the Heavens,* which was published in 1834 and passed through a number of editions. Its unusual popularity is attested by the fact that it sold over a quarter of a million copies before its final edition in 1856.

The *Geography of the Heavens* had a sixteen-page introduc-tion by Thomas Dick, the English writer on astronomy, and the volume was surprisingly erudite, although its material was not always applicable to the subject at hand. It is somewhat puzzling to visualize how the manual was effectively handled as a school text, notwithstanding the fact that it went through a quarter of a century of publication. Much mythology was interspersed through the text matter and a great deal of astron-omy history was included but was so scattered that it could hardly have been thoroughly utilized. The 1856 edition was revised by H. Mattisun, who improved the text materially, but by this time the book had outlived its usefulness and was soon to pass altogether from notice as far as schools were con-cerned. The author, Elijah Burritt, now known as "The Forgotten Astronomer," was the father of the noted "Learned Blacksmith," Elihu Burritt.

About the same time that Burritt's text was issued (1834), a *Compendium of Astronomy,* from the pen of John Vose, a New Hampshire school teacher and at one time principal of Pembroke Academy, was first printed in Boston. Vose's *Compendium* was far more suitable for teaching the rudiments of astronomy than was Burritt's *Geography of the Heavens.* The compiler stated that it had been his aim "to render the principles of the science so simple that they may be understood, not only by the scholar who spends a few weeks at the academy [a reference to the academy he conducted], but by him whose means and views do not carry him beyond the common school." The little *Compendium,* evidently intended only for use at Pembroke Academy, was all that the writer claimed, and one today cannot comprehend why a text such as Burritt's coming out at the same time, so amazingly outdistanced it in popularity.

The World, or First Lessons in Astronomy and Geology, by Hamilton L. Smith, A. M., printed at Cleveland, Ohio, by M. C. Youngglove and Company in 1848, was an excellent text for its era — especially so considering the place of its origin. The volume, mostly given over to astronomy, was well printed, and assembled, and its illustrations, numbering around a hundred, were most unusual. The illustrations were by an early resident of Cleveland, and the author stated in his preface:

> It is but right to say that the engravings have all been executed in this city by J. Brainerd; and when we add that they are not from transfers, but from pencil drawings, they will be acknowledged as very creditable specimens of the artist's skill.

The illustrations were more than "creditable specimens." The preface of the book was dated Cleveland, August, 1848 — before a railroad had reached the place. Andrew Logan, Cleveland's first printer, had arrived and started a newspaper only thirty years earlier — a paper that suspended publication before it was a year old because of lack of paper.[13]

Prior to the Civil War, when quarto-size geographies were beginning to come into vogue, a large-size astronomy appeared, and there was at least one imitation of it. This first large text was *Smith's Illustrated Astronomy,* a quaint volume nine and a half by eleven and a half inches in size. It was compiled by Asa Smith, "Principal of Public School No. 12, City of New York," and first appeared in 1848, the year in which the Cleveland book, just discussed, was issued. The outstanding feature of the Asa Smith text was the superb illustrations in black and white, most of them in white lines with a heavy black background. These fine drawings took up almost every second page of the eighty-page volume. The four concluding "sidereal maps" were by the compiler, but no mention was made of the name of the artist who drew the other pictures.

Much of the text of *Smith's Illustrated Astronomy* was in the form of questions and answers, but one column of many of the large two-column pages was devoted to straight astronomical information, graphically illustrated, on such topics as "Eclipses," "Origin of the Universe," "Phases of the Moon," "Comets," "Spots on the Sun," "Centripetal and Centrifugal Forces," and notes on the various planets. Some of the questions, although the answers were given, were not ones that many of the pupils are likely to have understood. It is revealing to glance at some of the questions and the answers set down. On page 11 of the 1855 edition the lesson began :

Q. In what points of a planet's orbit do its mean and true places coincide?

A. At the aphelion.

---

[13] Oswald, *Printing in the Americas* (New York: Gregg, 1937), p. 332.

Q. What straight line connect these points and passes through the sun?

A. The apais line.

Q. When is the true place of the earth or planet behind its mean place?

A. While it is moving from the aphelion to the perihelion.

The lesson continued with progressively more difficult questions.

Dorman Steele's *Astronomy* was published in 1868, taking a place among the "Fourteen Weeks Series." It was as lucid as a text of its sort could be — much more so than the Smith text just discussed — and achieved as widespread usage as a book of its class could expect at the time of its appearance. Charles A. Young's *Lessons in Astronomy*, issued in 1890, was one of the last of the nineteenth-century texts of this category. Like Burritt's *Geography of the Heavens*, it contained legends and mythology, and was not assembled too efficiently. But by Steele's and Young's day astronomy had declined in esteem as a common school study, and was soon to be replaced by other sciences.

XVII

Physiologies and Mental Science Texts

ONE OF THE EARLIEST physiology texts used in America was R. C. Faust's *Catechism of Health for the Use of Schools,* an adaptation from the German, printed in Boston in 1795. Copies are very rarely found today. Less than half a century before the issuance of Faust's *Catechism* what is considered the first genuine modern textbook of physiology was printed. This publication was Haller's *Prima Linae Physiologiae,* of the year 1747. A second treatise on physiology by Haller was his *Elementa Physiologiar Corporis Numani,* issued in parts from 1757 to 1760.[1]

William Mavor's *Catechism of Health,* a school text similar to Faust's, was published in New York in 1805 and in a Baltimore edition twenty-four years later. This book was originally from the pen of an English writer who compiled a number of

---

[1] For an account of Albrecht von Haller, whose books were all European products, see Norenskiold, *History of Biology* (New York: Tudor, 1946), pp. 234–238, and Hemmeter, *Master Minds of Medicine* (New York: Medical Life Press, 1927), pp. 276–296. Hemmeter says on p. 285, "When we turn from any writers of physiology preceding his time and open the pages of Haller's *Elementa,* we feel that we have passed into modern times."

school texts. Mavor's *British Nepos,* "consisting of the lives of illustrious Britons," a book for school use, was published in 1829. His English Grammar, first printed in 1820 and going through a number of editions, was his most popular book.

Comstock's *Physiology,* issued in 1836, was the first widely used American school physiology. In the preface the compiler states that Thomas Dick had expressed the need of "a treatise on Comparative and Human Physiology for the instruction of youth," and it was Comstock's belief that he had filled that need. He thus quoted Dick:

> It is somewhat unaccountable and not a little inconsistent that while we direct the young to look abroad over the surface of the earth, and survey its mountains, rivers, seas, and continents, and guide their views to the regimen of the firmament . . . that we should never teach them *to look into themselves,* to consider their own corporal structures, the numerous parts of which they are composed; the admirable functions which they perform; the wisdom and goodness displayed in their mechanism, and the lessons of practical instructions which may be derived from such contemplation.[2]

Almost the entire first half of Comstock's *Physiology* was devoted to topics other than human anatomy, such as the "mechanical functions" of Polypifera, Hydra, Infusoria, the forms of insects, vertebrate animals, the stomach of the sheep, and the relations of an animal's horns and its stomach. The few random remarks included in the front section of the text on the bones of the "human trunk and arms" and on "the human stomach" are couched in medical-course terms.

---

[2] Thomas Dick, mentioned a number of times previously, was a Scotsman and once a school teacher, who wrote much on education and who perhaps had some influence on early nineteenth-century schoolbook development. He is best known for his astronomical works, but wrote on many subjects. In 1847 his writings were published in Hartford, Connecticut, in nine volumes, and Harpers later issued his astronomical works in three volumes.

Comstock included subject matter that had little to do with the everyday life of school pupils. In the section on "muscular exercise," turning abruptly away from topics applying to people in general, he said :

> With respect to clergymen it is well known that there exists an artificial difficulty in their indulging in that kind of exercise which is most congenial to mental and muscular vigor, owing to the habits and opinions of society.

Three pages were devoted to the philosophical side of clergymen's lives and their "muscular exercise."

Five pages were devoted to archery, in the course of which the author said :

> This exercise is peculiarily advantageous and proper for females, on account of the reasons given why they ought to employ every means for invigorating the chest in early life, and were these recreations generally adopted, we have no doubt but many a slender one who would occupy an untimely grave, might be preserved to herself and society.

There were many similar passages in Comstock's *Physiology* on phases of daily existence.

Even in defining physiology, the compiler was, as in many other instances, behind his time. He stated that physiology was "a discourse on nature, and hence is applicable to an explanation of the laws which govern the growth of vegetables, and the crystalization of minerals," and that it was, as well, "a discourse on the functions of animal life." Comstock was going back to an earlier and totally archaic conception of the word. It is true that at one time the term was understood to cover much more ground than it does today. When William Gilbert's noted book *De magnete,* printed in Latin in 1600, was translated into English the title became *The Magnet: New Physiology Explained, With Many Arguments and Experiments* because the translation appeared during a period when the word physiology had the meaning of "natural philosophy" in general. With such an antiquated conception of the subject Comstock naturally was susceptible to floundering.

Mrs. Jane Taylor's *Primary Lessons in Physiology for Children* was first printed in 1839 and a revised edition came out a decade later. This text was in the form of questions and answers and had a vocabulary at the end. It treated of the anatomical side of physiology, and was evidently copied from medical works, old and new. It was probably intended as a substitute for Comstock's much more cumbersome text but must not have succeeded in that direction. The compiler of this little *Primary Physiology* was not the English Jane Taylor who wrote children's books and was the author of familiar "Twinkle, Twinkle, Little Star," which has appeared in numerous schoolbooks.[3]

The *Primary Physiology* and the *Practical Physiology* of Edward Jarvis were stepping stones from the old type of physiologies to the new. His *Practical Physiology* came out in 1847 and was printed until after the Civil War, showing that it possessed merits. This text treated of foods, exercises, and the nervous system, and discussed rest and fatigue and such topics. There was a twenty-three page section on "mental philosophy," which dealt with daydreams, fear, and other mental states — topics practically ignored in previous physiologies and which gave an interesting touch to the work. The concluding chapter discussed "the length of life," "ways of imparing the constitution," and "the effects of education on the body" — subject matter perhaps never looked upon lightly by pupils. The Jarvis physiologies were the first to use the health motif, and it was logical that they should have some influence on later compilers.

The Cutter physiologies, by father and son, were the first

---

[3] The "Twinkle, Twinkle, Little Star" verses were first published in *Rhymes for the Nursery* (London: 1806), and soon became and still remains one of the best-known children's poems in our language.

nationally used American texts of their class. Calvin Cutter's *Treatise on Anatomy, Physiology and Hygiene* was first issued in 1845, gradually took hold and finally came out in a revised edition seven years later. A larger text, *Analytic Anatomy and Hygiene,* was issued in 1849 and twice revised. Several hundred thousand copies of this book were sold in the 1850's and 1860's. The *Comparative Anatomy, Physiology and Hygiene,* by the son, John C. Cutter, was first printed in 1884 after its completion by the younger Dr. Cutter while he was professor of physiology and anatomy in the Imperial College of Agriculture in Saporra, Japan, where the preface was dated.

The Cutters, despite their intelligence, subscribed strongly to the nineteenth-century belief in the dire effects of overstudy, especially upon children and young men and women. This was a tenet widely credited at the time, both in England and the United States. The novelist Thackeray, who himself spent much time in study and did hard mental work, mentioned the evils of overstudy in *Pendennis.* Scores and scores of references to the ill effects of overstudy are found in nineteenth-century writings. So brilliant a man as Dr. Jacob Bigelow, who filled several professorships at Harvard and turned out writings of a high order on education and science (he gave currency to the term *technology*), believed in the perils thought to lurk in too concentrated study, saying that "limits cannot be transcended without aggregate deterioration in distracting the attenion, over-loading the memory or overworking the brain, and sapping the foundations of health."[4]

Dr. Calvin Cutter wrote in one of his *Physiologies:*

In youth much mischief is done by the long period of attendance at school, and the continued application of the mind which the ordinary system of education requires . . . . In early and middle life . . . an unusual degree of cerebral dis-

---

[4] Bigelow, *Modern Enquiries* (Boston: Little, Brown, 1867), p. 7.

order is a common consequence of this excessive and continued excitement of the brain. This unhappy result is
brought on by severe study . . . . Sir Walter Scott and President Harrison afford sad examples of premature death from
overtaxed brains.[5]

Who hears nowadays of a boy or girl, or a college or university
student, overstudying? The real trouble today most often lies
in the other direction.

Around the time the popularity of the Cutter physiologies
was at its peak two texts were written by school teachers who
obtained "approval" for their writings from medical doctors,
this information being conveyed on the title pages. In contrast
to the lack of the scientifically trained writers during the first
half of the nineteenth century, two or three texts appeared
during the second half bearing names well known in the scientific and medical world. Thomas H. Huxley's *Lessons in
Elementary Physiology,* a school text first printed in 1866,
went through numerous printings in England until 1917; and
an edition of Huxley's and Youmans' *Physiology* was issued
by the Appletons in this country in the 1870's. (Edward L.
Youmans worked with Huxley in publishing the latter's works
in the United States.)

During the last half of the nineteenth century the school
physiologies turned to propaganda against the use of spirituous
liquors. Some texts of this period dwelt at great length on the
harmful effects of alcohol. Almost half of the *Child's Health
Primer,* published in 1885 by A. S. Barnes, with no compiler's
name shown, was given over to the "effects of alcoholic drinks,
stimulants, and narcotics upon the human system." This text
also registered forceful objections to the use of tobacco. The

---

[5] Cutter, *Anatomy, Physiology and Hygiene* (Boston: Mussey, 1853),
pp. 366–7.

book had an official endorsement on the verso of the title page signed by Mary H. Hart, National and International Superintendent of the Scientific Department of the Woman's Christian Temperance Union. The *Young Temperance Manual, An Elementary Physiology,* by Eli F. Brown, M.D., issued in 1888, and a number of other texts had similar endorsements.

A popular physiology over a period of twenty-five years, Alfred F. Blaisdell's *Our Bodies and How We Live,* first printed in 1884 and revised in 1892, carried as a subtitle, "An elementary text-book of physiology and hygiene for use in schools with special reference to the effects of alcoholic drinks, to tobacco and other narcotics on the bodily life." It is to be noted from Blaisdell's wording that he evidently considered tobacco as belonging among the narcotics. At that time there were few places where a physiology not containing a strong protest against the use of liquor and tobacco would have been received with favor. Several states had laws requiring physiologies and kindred texts to carry antiliquor lessons. In the preface of Dulany's *Physiology,* Baltimore, 1896, the act passed by the general assembly of Maryland was quoted in full, and a number of texts used in other states printed such state or local laws.

In 1901 William Thompson Sedgwick published his classic *Principles of Sanitary Science and Public Health,* a book which brought marked changes into the subject matter of school physiologies. Within a few years they were all to become more oriented towards the relationship of sanitation to the maintenance of health and well being.[6] Books with such titles as *Physiology, Hygiene and Sanitation; Healthy Living; The Healthy Community; Cleanliness and Health; Hygiene and*

---

[6] Max von Pettenkofen, born in Germany in 1818, was a forerunner of Sedgwick in researches in sanitation, the effects of bad water, improper clothing, and so on. See Henry E. Segrist, *The Great Doctors* (New York: Doubleday, 1958), p. 378.

Sanitation were soon to appear. In 1906 Sedgwick, who was professor of biology and public health at the Massachusetts Institute of Technology, along with Theodore Hough, dean of the department of medicine in the University of Virginia, issued a school text, *Elements of Physiology,* but strange to say it contained no material on the sanitation ideas which Professor Sedgwick had already advanced. This suggests that the Sedgwick and Hough physiology might have been written before the classic "sanitation" text was published.

Physiologies in our own time are very different from what they were even during the first years of the present century. Titles of present-day books for beginners which have supplanted old physiologies indicate their nature : *Keeping Well, Active and Alert, Everyday Health, Helping the Body in Its Work, Health through the Year,* and *Healthy and Happy.* The cheerfulness and carefree approach to everyday life and the simplicity and gay directness of these books make them practical on every page. One of the most important features of these later-day physiologies are the many illustrations, which are so appropriate for books to be used by young people.

The mental sciences found a place in the schools before the biological sciences did so. Before the nineteenth century several texts on "mental philosophy" were available—treatises on the mind and its manifold workings and on "morals," or "moral science" as it was then designated. Many of the early mental study books used in the schools had a theological bent, more often than not due to the fact that they came from the pens of writers theologically trained.

One of the earliest of the mental science texts used in this country was *Improvement of the Mind,* by Isaac Watts, a noted divine. Printed in England during the lifetime of Samuel Johnson, it was one of the Doctor's favorites. Dr. Johnson said that

"Whoever has the care of instructing others may be charged with deficiency in his duty if this book is not recommended." On another occasion Johnson was asked by a young friend to list the most important books for the latter to study, and among them was Watts' *Improvement of the Mind.*' The book covered fairly well the subject as it was known in the last part of the eighteenth century. Such items as attention, memory, prejudice, and writing, were intelligently discussed. This volume was printed at a number of places in the country. One edition appeared in Washington in 1813 — one of the early books printed in the national capital. Soon after the printing of Watt's book in Washington other school texts were printed there; already such books had been turned out in considerable number in near-by Alexandria.

In 1830, John Abercrombie, a Scottish physician, published his *Intellictual Powers of Man,* an extraordinarily readable volume which enjoyed an unusual popularity. While it was still practically a new publication Jacob Abbott revised it, omitting a chapter on "The history of intellectual philosophy," and including "additions and explanations to adopt the work to the use of American schools." This book, of approximately three hundred pages in Abbott's edition and other American issues, was used in school classes for a third of a century and met with more favor than any single volume of its class. Dr. Abercrombie had a gift for introducing intriguing material and presenting it in an appealing style. He dwelt upon thinking, confidence, dreams, caution, and melancholia, covering these and many other equally interesting topics in logical study outlines.

In the beginning Abercrombie stated that success in the use of his text depended upon willingness to give it patient, persevering study, and throughout his book he emphasized the

---

' Boswell, *Life of Johnson,* George Berbeck Hill, ed. (New York: n. d.), IV, 360.

value of application in all intellectual pursuits. In this he was
of course following a good line of reasoning. However, there
were a few spots in his text which required the application
of one of his own lessons—that on "Credulity." In a section on
the influence of sickness and accidents the compiler cited the
very unusual case of a man who:

> suffered such an injury of the head that a large portion of
> the bone was removed on the right side; and extensive sup-
> puration having taken place, there was discharged at each
> dressing, through the opening, an immense quantity of
> matter mixed with large masses of the substance of the brain.
> This went on for seventeen days, and it appears that nearly
> one half of the brain was thrown out mixed with this matter;
> yet the man retained all his intellectual faculties to the very
> moment of his dissolution; and through the whole course of
> the disease his mind maintained uniform tranquility.[8]

Dugald Stewart's *Elements of the Philosophy of the Human
Mind* was first put out in England in 1792; in revised and
abridged editions it was later reprinted a number of times in
the United States, appearing as late as 1864, when an edition
revised by Francis Brown, professor of Moral and Intellectual
Philosophy at Harvard, was issued. The philosophical conclusion of Dugald Stewart were of such import that William
Whewell, who was credited with being one of the great thinkers
of his time and who became Master of Trinity College,
Cambridge, and later vice-chancellor of the university, in the
Bridgewater Treatise on Astronomy, made some comments on
them. Stewart's thinking not only appealed to the academic
minds of the time but also to those we call "the man on the
street." Excerpts from his writings found their way into such
periodicals as the *Penny Magazine* and other contemporary
publications of a popular nature.

---

[8] Abercrombie, *Intellectual Powers of Man* (New York: Collins, 1860),
pp. 119–120.

Francis Wayland's *Moral Science* and *Intellectual Philosophy,* both published around the Civil War period, were the first books of their category by an American to achieve any considerable popularity and widespread use in schools—both were reprinted a number of times. Wayland is noted as one of the outstanding college presidents of the nineteenth century, taking hold of Brown University in 1828, when it was a small dental school and in a quarter of a century bringing it to the stature of one of the important American universities. President Wayland's work at Brown brought him into a position of leadership in which he had much influence on higher education.

Strange though it may now seem and unlike most school texts, portions of the forgotten books on the mental sciences used in our nineteenth-century schools are in a marked degree interesting to read; here and there are nuggets which, except for the infrequent scholar, have been washed away by the river of time into the sea of oblivion.

Despite the interest inherent in the subject, during the mid-nineteenth century there was opposition to it and an occasional belittling of its worth. A writer in *Putnam's Magazine* in 1854 (IV, 667) said, "The greater part of these metaphysical speculations are utterly empty and worthless abstractions, and have no other effect than to waste the interest of those who are engaged in them . . . . The sooner they are removed out of the domain of study, the better for the world." But at that very time a number of well-known scholars were issuing volumes of considerable stature on "the science of the mind" which the *Putnam* writer was so vigorously berating.

In the 1880's psychology texts began to put in an appearance.[9]

---

[9] The German Wilhelm Wundt, sometimes referred to as "The Father Of Psychology," and Francis Galton, who might almost equally well be so designated because of his *Inquiries into Human Faculty,* issued in 1883, did much of their important psychological work in the 1880's.

Among the early ones for school use was David J. Hill's *Elements of Psychology,* initially printed in 1886. It treated of mental science from the newly developed viewpoint. Within a decade and a half perhaps a dozen psychology texts something on the order of Hill's were in print—an old subject under a new guise. Daniel Putnam's *Elementary Psychology,* issued in 1889, reverted somewhat toward the "moral" side of the subject, touching upon "The Moral Nature" and "Origin and Nature of the Moral Law." It appropriated some material from Jevon's *Logic,* the latter a book which was printed in several editions in this country for school use. A blank page was bound in Putnam's text following each chapter, "for making notes and in taking the means of reference, etc.," making it one of the forerunners of the workbook form of text so common today.

Since the beginning of the twentieth century the mental sciences have not been too strongly pushed as separate and independent subjects in American schools. The subject of psychology as it stands today has become too complicated for ordinary school study, and is reserved for college and university courses. Under its present status it has passed entirely beyond the reach of common school students.

XVIII

Geographies

THE SOMEWHAT MASSIVE *Cosmography* of Peter Heylyn, the
first book of its class in our language, was printed in England
in 1621 and later reissued in successively enlarged editions.
This folio-size publication, justly famous in its own right, in
its first issue can be spoken of accurately as the direct ancestor
of our school geography and the beginning of this genre of
books as far as the English language is concerned. The Heylyn
Cosmography, following in the wake of Latin books of its sort
previously printed, was written by a man of varied experiences
and accomplishments who lived through the turbulent times
of Oliver Cromwell and, being a royalist, fared shabbily,
losing his home, a vast library, and all else he possessed.
Although published when the author was not yet twenty-one,
the *Cosmography* of Heylyn was described over three centuries
later by the *Encyclopaedia Britannica,* which is not usually
too liberal with praise, as "a useful book."

Four years after the Heylyn *Cosmography* came out and
while Heylyn was still a young man, Nathanael Carpenter's
Geography was printed at Oxford in 1625; it was the first
geography in the English language. The full title of Carpenter's book was *Geography delineated forth in Two Books,
containing Spherical and Topicall points thereof.* Since Hey-

lyn's work had appeared but a few years before, it stands to reason that Nathanael Carpenter, an Oxford teacher and interested as he was, would have turned to the Heylyn's *Cosmography* for the pattern for his *Geography,* even though the *Geography* was to be much smaller in size. The *Encyclopaedia Britannica* says of Carpenter's *Geography* that it is "a little-known book." Only a few copies of it, in fact, are in existence today; an old copy may be seen in the Library of Congress and one or two others are to be found in large institutional libraries. Upon examination, the copy in the Library of Congress proves to be a small volume, hardly more than a pamphlet in dimensions, but pretty much like one might expect a first geography printed in English, "for students," to be.

Between Nathanael Carpenter's time and that of our own countryman Jedidiah Morse, numerous "geographies," "grammars of geography,"[1] small volumes of "cosmography and geography," and such publications appeared in England, and the geography took on gradually the status of a schoolbook. By the time of the appearance of Morse's *Geography Made Easy,* in 1784 — the first American school geography — the form of this class of text had become well established as that of the old cosmographies on a smaller scale.

Jedidiah Morse's *Geography Made Easy* was printed while the compiler was still a student. To help pay his way through Yale, Morse taught school in New Haven, and it was the

---

[1] Pat Gordon, *Geography Anatomatized or the Geographical Grammar,* first issued in England in the early eighteenth century and one of the most popular of the early geographies, went through edition after edition, being in the 18th, "Corrected and ſomewhat Enlarged, and a set of new maps," in 1744. This book was used in England and in this country and in it were items not included in other geographies; for instance, it tells of the cave near Hamelin, in Germany, where 130 children "were swallowed up alive in that very Place above 400 years ago." California is described as an island.

lectures he delivered to his classes that made up his first text. In his prefatory "advertisement" in the first edition he relates in the third person how he came to publish the text :

He at first intended it as a manuscript only, for the use of schools under his immediate instructions, but from various considerations and more particular from the advice of several worthy gentlemen, he has been induced to enlarge and improve his former plans, to bestow more particular attention to the execution of it, and then to exhibit it to the public view.

All down through the years many of us, especially those with a political turn of mind, have been urged on to do things by our "worthy gentleman friends," and it must be observed that Morse was in a way something of a politician.

The Morse text was a small book of just over two hundred pages in its first issue, but by its eleventh revised edition it had grown to more than four hundred pages, and was cut down again in a corrected edition of 1814. The early editions were not good examples of printings but later ones were fair in this respect. There were two maps in the first few issues by the well-known engraver Amos Doolittle, but in later editions the maps, still restricted to two, were by a lesser-known engraver.

The Morse *Geography* continued a great deal of material that scarcely merited a place in a school text. In the section on the United States in the first revised edition (1809), there was a long inventory of the animals, birds, snakes, and fishes reported to be indigenous to the American land. The black snake, it was said, "will destroy the rattlesnake by twisting around it and whipping it to death." It was stated that it had "been reported that they have sometimes twined themselves around the bodies of children, squeezing them until they die" — a delectable story for small children, almost all of whom had to pass along paths where a black snake might at any moment appear! Or did such information, imparted as fact, prepare pioneer children for the difficulties they were bound to encounter and would have to overcome?

The fishes were described very minutely and divided into classes, according to the compiler, after the writings of "Mr. Pennant, in the *British Zoologist*."[2] The piscatorial world, as Morse described it, was made up of the Catacoeus, Cartilaginous, and Bony classes — the last being catalogued under sixty-nine names. In this list were the skipjack, sucker, dab, shiner, hardhead, and mummychog. In a footnote Morse tactfully admitted: "Probably some that are placed under this division belong to one or the other of the preceding." There is but little likelihood that anyone ever worried about the probable inaccuracies of the classification with the exception of Morse himself.

Morse described his own New England in these words:

New-England is a hilly, and in some parts a mountainous country, formed by nature to be a home for a hardy race of free, independent Republicans. The mountains are comparatively small, running nearly north and south in ridges parallel to each other. Between these ridges, flow the great rivers in majestic meanders receiving the innumerable rivulets and larger streams which proceed from the mountains on each side. To a spectator on top of a neighboring mountain, the vales between the ridges, while in a state of nature exhibit a romantick appearance.

Several of the early geography compilers, as well as the writers of other texts, paid friendly tributes to their native heaths. At

---

[2] Thomas Pennant (1726–1798) was the author of such noted volumes on natural history as *History of Quadrupeds, British Zoology, Indian Zoology,* and *Genera of Birds.* At the age of sixty-seven he planned a work that was to embrace every country, describing their products and animal life. He lived only four years afterward — long enough, however, to complete two volumes, and his son finished two more volumes that had been left incomplete.

the ends of several sections descriptive of a country or state Morse added a bibliographical paragraph enumerating publications pertaining to the geographical and historical aspects of the territory. These notes appeared only in certain issues of the geography. Morse's seems to have been the first American school text provided with bibliographical lists, which were later to become a conspicuous feature of certain classes of texts.

Morse is best known for his geography, but he did much besides schoolbook compiling. In his early career a clergyman, he gave up this profession in middle life to work at other pursuits. He did considerable writing, edited two periodicals, and later went into government work. When almost sixty Morse made a trip into the Illinois Indian country to report on the state of that territory and of the Indians for the War Department. Journeying into such a region at the time was no easy task even for a young man. In 1882 a volume by Morse was printed in New Haven under the title *A Report to the Secretary of War on Indian Affairs, comprising a Narrative of a Tour performed in the Summer of 1820*. This was the first comprehensive and accurate written description of certain sections of the Illinois country.

Through some source of error Nathaniel Dwight's *Short System of Geography* has a number of times been credited with being the first school geography issued in America. A well-known encyclopedia of our era carries this information, and two or three times elsewhere the book has been mistakingly so described. Nathaniel Dwight, a brother of Timothy, one time president of Yale College, published his *Geography* in 1795. At that time Morse's geography was at the height of its popularity, but Dwight's text prospered nevertheless. Within twenty years it had gone through seven editions, the seventh carrying commendations by John Trumbell, Chauncey Goodrich, and other influential New Englanders. The geography had the advantage of being briefer than Morse's, and was in the question-and-answer form in favor at the time.

While Dwight dealt somewhat violently with peoples outside his own land, he did not always write in too friendly a vein of his fellow Americans, including, now and then, his New England neighbours. For example, answering his own question about New England diversions, he wrote :

Dancing is a favorite one of both sexes. Sleigh-riding in winter, and skating, and playing ball (of which there are several different games), gunning and fishing are the principal; gambling and horse-jockeying are practiced by none but worthless people, who are despised by all persons of respectability.

This latter segment of the population he in one place designated as "nuisances in society." He thought well of the state of science and general knowledge among New Englanders, whom he considered well educated. "Science," he stated, "is greatly cultivated and more generally diffused among the inhabitants than in any part of the world." He ended the paragraph in which this statement occurs with the words : "Almost every individual is well informed." He accused the Virginians of being "attached strongly to pleasure and dissipation," a pronouncement originally from the fertile brain of Noah Webster.[3]

[3] Many prominent New Englanders of the nineteenth century were not too liberal in their estimates of people in different sections of the country. Charles A. Goodrich, in his *Universal Traveller,* a book on "arts, customs and manners," (Hartford: Canfield and Robins, 1837), while not too strong in praise of women elsewhere, has the following (p. 22) on the character of women in New England: "Their minds often possessing a fine share of intelligence, are remarkably distinguished by amiable dispositions. A gentle and affectionate temper, ornamented with sprightliness and gilded with serenity, may be fairly considered as being extensively their proper character. Their manners are in entire symmetry with their

Although Dwight came from one of the prominent families of New England and was a descendant of Johnathan Edwards, he was not above including scores of obvious errors in his *Geography*. His low regard for such a large proportion of mankind must have been the result of a feeling which seems to have run in the Dwight family. A writer has said of Timothy, the brother of Nathaniel, that he thoroughly possessed a "conviction of the general depravity of man."[4]

In 1812 Elijah Parish's *New System of Geography* came from the press in Newburyport, Massachusetts. The text immediately caught on because of the fact that Parish was a well-known and active New England divine. In two years the geography had gone through three editions, and was displacing those of Morse and Dwight. The compiler was a minister of Byfield, Massachusetts, and his text was highly recommended by clergymen, other professional men, and by various school authorities. Among the endorsers were two of the best-known school text compilers, Noah Webster and Lindley Murray.

In his *Geography* Parish divided the inhabitants of the United States into categories not previously listed in any American schoolbook :

> Though there is no distinction acknowledged by law in the United States, fortune and the nature of professions form different classes. Merchants, lawyers, physicians and clergymen form the first class; farmers and artisians, the second; workmen who let themselves by the day, the third. In public amusements these classes do not commonly intermix.

---

minds and faces. A universal sweetness and gentleness, blended with sprightly energy, is their most predominant characteristic. There is nothing languid in their deportment, and rarely anything affected. They are affable, obliging and cheerful; while they are at the same time grave, discreet, and very rarely betrayed into impropriety."

[4] Samuel Lee Wolfe, *The Cambridge History of American Literature* (New York: Macmillan, 1933), II, 205.

This line of tought now seems remote, but it has been but little more than a century and a half since it had considerable acceptance, many still holding, as did John Cotton and others of the early New England governing class, that the people had no right to strive to govern themselves. Cotton even once said that democracy is "the meanest and worst of all forms of government,"[5] and he believed that a privileged few should govern — a way of thought that Elijah Parish evidently shared. Parish himself was a native of Lebanon, Connecticut, coming from an ordinary family, and he apparently had no connections that could exalt him very much socially.

The compiler included in his text paragraphs that could have had but local interest. Speaking of his home town, Byfield, he said :

> Dumner academy in Byfield has a good library and a handsome fund. The buildings are convenient, pleasantly situated between the tidewater of Parker and Mill rivers, on the turnpike, four miles from Newburyport, and twenty-eight miles from Boston.

In describing the city of Washington, Parish mentioned some of the hotels, their street addresses, how many stories tall they were, and even their dimensions. He stated that "the gaol is 100 feet by 26, and two stories high." Today it seems astonishing that so much material of such limited interest should have found its way into the pages of a widely used American geography.

The text contained one innovation — the inclusion of footnotes giving the source of much of the data presented, especially items gathered from old and little-known books. Almost every page had its footnotes, and they must have added to Parish's prestige as an author of broad range and erudition. Although

---

[5] Hart, *National Ideals Historically Traced* (New York: Harper, 1907), p. 70.

the Parish geography came from a writer more widely read than other geography compilers of the day, his text did not compare in general worth with its poorest competitors. The sound material was more than counterbalanced by the trifling and worthless. The geography was a product of its time; and apparently the duration of its use in schools was similarly limited.

In 1818 Jacob A. Cummings' *First Lessons in Geography and Astronomy* was printed in Boston. This was the first miniature geography. It was just a little over five inches square, and had only eighty-three pages, bound in stiff paper. The subject matter was as compact as was the diminutive volume itself. Cummings was a printer and publisher and at various periods had connections with prominent Boston publishers. He was always interested in putting out school texts, and the little geography must have been designed to sell at a low price; Cummings very well recognized the commercial demands of the day. It was perhaps mainly because of its low cost that *First Lessons* was widely used and went through a number of editions, selling well even after the compiler and original publisher died in 1824.

Cummings published an *Ancient and Modern Geography* of larger size, but it was the small *First Lessons* that stood out as a trail blazer. The *Ancient and Modern Geography* was printed for a number of years, but evidently never won anything like the popularity the small geography did—it was not the kind of text to achieve extensive usage. The larger geography of Cummings was accompanied by a folio atlas containing nine maps in black and white, engraved by Nathaniel Morse, son of Jedidiah. The map of the western part of the United States showed a large blank space between the Rocky Mountains and the Pacific Coast range marked "unexplored

country."[6] No boundary line between the United States and
Canada was shown west of the Rockies, as there was none fixed
at the time. The western side of Great Salt Lake was not charted;
instead the map bore the words : "The western limits of this lake
are unknown." On the other hand the eastern portion of the
United States was shown with remarkable accuracy.

Worcester's *Elements of Geography* appeared in 1819, and
went through a number of impressions before it was revised in
1830; after which the revision itself was printed many times.
This was a well-assembled text, and was a guide for several
that followed. The 1830 edition, published by a Boston firm
descended in part from the Jacob Cummings establishment,
appeared at a time when a new format was being evolved in
many schoolbooks. A decided improvement was noticeable in
this edition over previous issues, and the material was limited
to that that really belonged in a school geography. Nowhere in
Worcester's text did there seem to be any of the useless matter
which had cluttered many pages of nearly all such works with
the exception of that of Cummings.

Pronunciation of all the place names in Worcester's book
was either shown in parenthesis or indicated by breaking the

---

[6]A map of the United States in the atlas of Gutherie's *Geography,*
printed in Philadelphia in 1820, traced the "supposed course of a river
between the Bonaventure [imaginative river south of Great Salt Lake] and
the Bay of Francisco." Tanner's *New American Atlas,* published in 1823
with a number of excellent maps, showed several imaginary rivers flow-
ing from the Rocky Mountain region into the Pacific, including the
mythical Bonaventure. The only rivers approximating actuality in
Tanner's book in the Pacific territory were the Colorado and Columbia.
In the corner of the map of the western region was a note saying that
some of the rivers shown were "of doubtful validity." The so-called Bonaventure, now the Green River, was designated by the early Spaniards Rio
de San Buenaventura and was much misplayed on maps. Information on
the absurdities of early maps is to be found in H. H. Bancroft, *History
of the Northwest Coast,* 2 vols. (San Francisco: 1892).

word down into syllables in the body of the text. One of the pronunciations possibly a product of the folk-speech of the time was Indiana, given as *In-je-an'-na.*[7] This pronunciation appeared in the lesson on the "Western States"—these being Tennessee, Kentucky, Illinois, Missouri, "together with the territories." Numerous small but well-executed woodcuts were incorporated. These engravings were the work of Alexander Anderson, and among them were "Indians Taking Buffalos," "Catching Whales," "Silver Mining," "Bull Fighting," and others equally picturesque, all in the catchy Anderson manner. Both the first and revised editions of the text had an accompanying large-size atlas.

A number of atlases were issued as separate and independent publications, unconnected with any special geography, for use in schools. Among them was the *Atlas of the United States* by Sidney Morse, son of the geography compiler and brother of Nathaniel, already mentioned. Another was Carey's *American Atlas,* which was published before Sidney Morse's and which went through numerous printings. Amos Doolittle engraved some of the maps of the Carey atlas. Sidney E. Morse was an expert map maker and developed the process of wax engraving, which to a certain extent changed cartography. Morse kept the process a secret for a number of years, but the method eventually became generally known. The first atlas printed by this process was titled *The Geographic Atlas* and was issued in 1841. In 1844 and 1851 Sidney Morse's quarto-size *School Geography,* "with one hundred and fifty elegant engravings and over fifty beautiful maps," was issued by Harper and Brothers, but was not successful. It was too late for the once-

---

[7] Baldwin, *Universal Pronouncing Gazeteer,* a dependable work printed in 1845, gave the pronunciation that we use today.

eminent name of Morse in the field of geography to add prestige to such a text.°

The little Peter Parley geographies, patterned somewhat on Cummings' *First Lessons* and covering a considerable range of titles, were published in large numbers. They bore such titles as *Tales about Europe, Tales about America,* and *Tales about South America.* These texts were obviously for children in the lowest grades — those just beginning the study of geography. Although widely used in schools, they were much like regular trade books and much of their sale was through trade book channels. Goodrich made arrangements for an English publisher to print his texts, and they were sold in Great Britain by the thousands just as they were in this country.

One of the Peter Parley books was the *Malte-Brun Geography,* first issued in 1831. Goodrich drew the material for this text from Conrad Malte-Brun's huge *Universal Geography.* Conrad Malte-Brun, born in France, was considered one of the world's greatest geographers at about the beginning of the nineteenth century. His *Universal Geography,* the first volume of which was published in 1810, was gradually added to until his death in 1826; and one volume was printed after his death. In 1827 a six-volume edition was printed in Philadelphia, and in 1834, a three-volume set in Boston. There is no indication, in Goodrich's autobiography or elsewhere, that he made any arrangement with the Malte-Brun family for the use of the material or the Malte-Brun name.

The same type of illustrations was used in this Goodrich geography as in the other Peter Parley texts, and the general

---

°An account of the introduction of Sidney Morse's development of his cartographic processes and of his map making is to be found in Erwin Raisz, *General Cartography* (New York: McGraw Hill, 1948), a valuable treatise on its subject. A flair for invention was apparently a trait of the Morses. Samuel F.B., the inventor of the electric telegraph, was Sidney's brother.

makeup of the book was similar. In the *Malte-Brun Geography* illustrations of human interest and interesting action were striven for, as in all the books Goodrich issued.

Olney's *Introduction to Geography,* for "the youngest classes in schools," and his more advanced *Practical System of Modern Geography,* stood out as important texts of the first half of the nineteenth century. *Modern Geography* was first published in 1829 and within twelve years had reached its thirty-fourth edition. This geography captured the feeling of the time as well as any other schoolbook. The text abounded in statistics and information on items of contemporary national importance. Olney had the best and most complete description of the territory west of the Mississippi that had appeared in a geography up to his day, and this was not material set forth in a dry manner.[9] He included material of special interest to boys, such as this account of game indigenious to the western country:

Perhaps no other country in the world furnishes so great a variety of wild game as this territory; and on this account it has been termed the paradise of hunters. Countless numbers of buffaloes, elk, deer, and other wild animals, traverse the vast prairies. In some instances, ten thousand buffaloes are in one herd. As the grass fails in one place, they travel in a body to another; and when moving, the ground trembles to a great distance—their bellowings and noise may be heard for miles.

Olney seems to have had an extraordinary knack of selecting dependable information on matters almost wholly ignored in other geographies. In the 1841 issue of the *Modern Geography,* for instance, was a list of railroads "finished or in progress in the United States," showing their routes, connections, and mileage. Although the first geography to present such data, it was not the first to make mention of railroads — Curtis and Brook's

---

[9] Williams, *Life of Washington Irving* (New York: Oxford Press, 1935), II, 79, says: "In the 'thirties almost any volume on the trans-Mississippi frontier, on the Indians, or the new lands would command attention."

Geography of Massachusetts, printed in Boston in 1830, had that distinction.[10]

The illustrations of Olney's geographies were unusually good, and in most cases would have reached a special excellence had they not been so small. They were technically well done and displayed discrimination in the choice of subjects. Such pictures as "Selling A Circassian Female," "Travelling in Kamchatka," "A Choctaw Village," and "William Penn Framing a Treaty with the Indians," together with early railroad and street views and various scenic reproductions, set off the text in a fitting manner, and the illustrations must have been of unusual interest to the students.

A ferment of innovations in geography designing occurred at about the middle of the nineteenth century and resulted in an extraordinary new look. It was one of the most decided and rapid changes that had yet involved any one class of schoolbooks, and the geography text arrived at its golden age almost overnight, so to speak. The little text that barely filled a coat pocket was on its way out, and in its stead there was beginning to appear the large "folio-page" book, with its scientifically arranged maps in color—a class of book that henceforth was to be familiar to American school children. The era of good, accurate maps was at hand, and there were to be no more geographies issued without such reliable charts of land and sea, and no further use for the separate geographic atlas. Maps were to be part and parcel of the geography itself.

Arnold Guyot was the earliest geography teacher and compiler to advocate a wider use of maps. In his teaching in the College of New Jersey, which in 1896 was to become Princeton

---

[10]John L. Blake, *A Geographical, Chronological and Historical Atlas,* published in 1826, had four pages on "Canals and Rail-ways," but this book was issued "for subscribers" and was not a schoolbook.

University, he emphasized the necessity of a thorough study of topography. This study, he said, was necessary to a full comprehension of a region or a country. It is believed today that the modern method of teaching geography in schools was to a large extent brought about through the insistence of Guyot on this one point. Arnold Guyot was the first scientist-scholar to participate in teaching geography and in writing about it in this country.

Arnold Henry Guyot was born in Switzerland in 1807, and studied at the College of Neuchatel where he became acquainted with Louis Agassiz. They developed a lifelong friendship and the streams of their lives flowed closely for years. The young Guyot was a student of Karl Ritter, the top German geographer of his day, who believed that geography should be a sort of comparative-anatomy study of the globe upon which we live. Ritter's *Comparative Geography* was first issued in this country by J. B. Lippincott in 1865, and was later reprinted by the American Book Company. The book was a reissue of Ritter's *Geographical Studies,* printed earlier in Germany, and was not an ordinary geography but a treatise on the science of geography. Ritter thought of rivers, plains, and mountains as so many distinct physiological organs of the earth, each with its special functions in relation to mankind. Guyot early fell into line with the teaching of Ritter and was so influenced that his lifework was wholly shaped by it.

In 1848 Guyot came to the United States at the suggestion of Agassiz, his friend. One of his first American activities was a course of lectures delivered at Lowell Institute. Later he was employed by the Massachusetts State Board of Education in a lecturing capacity. He went wherever he was needed and delivered addresses on the subjects he was familiar with: meteorology, physical geography, glaciers and their movements, and the ice age. In 1850 he prepared and published an exhaustive series of directions for meteorological observations," and the United States Weather Bureau was founded on the basis of the developments worked out in these papers. In 1854 Guyot went to the College of New Jersey, now Princeton University, as professor of geology and physical geography, remaining there until his death. The well-known Guyot Hall, the Biology and Geology Building at Princeton, rich in many natural history exhibits and collections, was named in his honor.

After Professor Guyot's geographies were all out they bore the titles *Introduction to the Study of Geography, Elementary Geography for Primary Classes, Intermediate Geography, Common School Geography,* and a *Grammar and High School Geography*—all comprising a series of progressive difficulty. The *Physical Geography,* intended to stand alone as a separate text, became one of the best-known books that Guyot wrote. It was an excellent text on the subject and generally acknowledged as the best up to its time. Many later texts were patterned after it.

Guyot's books were the first folio size geographies to be widely used. His geographies were all so printed, some of them being among the largest school geographies ever issued. Guyot's were not the first geographies in the folio format, however. Credit for the first text of this class belongs to a man we have already heard much of — Samuel G. Goodrich; his Peter Parley *National Geography,* issued in 1845, was the earliest of the folio geographies.[12] Goodrich, like Noah Webster, also ranked first in a number of spheres.

The life of another American geographer, Matthew Fontaine

[11] See Annual Report, Smithsonian Institution 1897, vol. 2 (1901), p. 301.

[12] See William E. Pulsifer, *Brief Account of Education Publishing in the United States* (Atlantic City, 1921), p. 10.

Maury, paralleled that of Arnold Guyot in more ways than one. He was born in Virginia one year earlier than Guyot and died nine years sooner. In work and accomplishment, more than in time, the lives of these two eminent men coincided. Both were teachers and writers, by nature as well as by circumstances. Maury, because of the fact that he wrote *The Physical Geography of the Sea,* the classic American book on geography, may possibly be known after Guyot is forgotten; but certainly the Princeton teacher will be remembered for many decades to come.

Maury's *The Physical Geography of the Sea,* first issued in London in 1855, was reprinted in New York some time later. After that, suddenly becoming famous, it went through numerous editions and was translated into many of the languages of the world. Probably no other American book has ever been translated and printed in so many tongues in so short a time — high acclaim for any writer. Perhaps no American author has ever received more world-wide honors that were conferred upon Maury.

Two splendid prose works of the nineteenth century were marked by striking opening paragraphs. One is Charles Doughty's *Travels in Arabia Deserta,* which unfortunately only too few have ever taken the trouble to read. In a few words in his opening passage Doughty revealed that he was a poet writing prose. The opening paragraph of Maury's *Physical Geography of the Sea* is equal to that of Doughty and creates in the reader a mood of expectancy which is fulfilled by a marvelous book.

At many places in the book Maury treated the most technical subjects in poetic terms. In a chapter on the winds he said :

When the pump-maker came to Galileo to explain how it was that his pump would not lift water higher than thirty-two feet the philosopher thought, but was afraid to say, it was owing to "weight of the winds," and though the fact that air has weight is here so distinctly announced, philosophers never recognized the fact until within a comparatively recent period, and then it was proclaimed by them as a great discovery. Nevertheless, the fact set forth so distinctly in the book of natue as it is in the book of revelation; for the infant, in availing itself of atmospherical pressure to draw milk from its mother's breast, unconsciously proclaimed it.

Baron Humboldt was right in pronouncing this book of Maury one of the most charming in the English language.

The school geographies of Guyot and Maury were different in one respect. Guyot's were spontaneous and self-conceived, while Maury's were written to order as the result of an offer in 1866 by Richardson and Company of New York, a firm which a few years later became the University Publishing Company. In arranging for the school geographies the publisher figured on profiting from the great renown of the author of *Physical Geography of the Sea*. Otherwise Maury's school texts might never have seen the light of day.

Maury's *First Lessons in Geography* originally appeared in 1868. The *Elementary Geography* and *Manual of Geography* appeared two years later, and the *Physical Geography* in 1873. More than five thousand schools were using the *First Lessons*, the *Elementary Geography*, and *Manual of Geography* in 1871, and the compiler's income from them for one year was thirty thousand dollars.[13] The year before Maury died he sold his copyrights to the publisher, but an arrangement was made by which he retained certain rights that insured himself, and his family in case of his demise, a fair share of the earnings from the books. In 1880 the *Manual of Geography* was revised by Mytton Maury, and this book, as well as the *Elementary Geog-*

---

[13] Wayland, *The Pathfinder of the Seas* (Richmond: Garret and Massie, 1930), p. 147.

raphy and the *First Lessons,* were used into the twentieth century. Maury's *New Elements of Geography,* a revision of the elementary text, was being issued under a changed copyright as late as 1931.

Much in the writings as in the life of Mathew Maury had a flair of the romantic. No one can read the great *Physical Geography of the Sea* without feeling the consummate power of the poet in almost every page. The same quality can be seen in a smaller measure in Maury's first little school texts and in his other geographies. It is true that the poetic touch in Maury's geographies were given added weight by the illustrations, some of which were admirably done even if at times touched by the exaggerated romanticism of the time.

The geographies of Samuel Augustus Mitchell lapped over from the first half of the nineteenth century into the second, the early editions belonging to the old class of geographies, and those appearing after the middle of the century, to the newer folio-page genre. The Mitchell geographies became an institution because they were used so long and because they evolved from a one-man production into a family industry, with two full generations of Mitchells making a vocation of producing them.

The first of these well-known texts was the *School Geography* issued as far back as 1839 and supplemented by a separate atlas of sixteen pages. The geography was an immediate success, and within a year Samuel Augustus Mitchell was putting out additional geographies. In 1840 his *Geographic Reader* and *Primary Geography* were published, both going through numerous printings. The next year *A Key to the Study of the Maps in Mitchell's School Atlas* appeared, a small geographical text that saw little use, although it was reprinted once. In the preface of this small text it was said that it "forms an easy introduction to the study of maps—the foundation of all geographical knowledge"—an assertion predating by a number of years Guyot's similar pronouncement, already commented upon.

In 1845 the *Ancient Geography* was printed, and this for a period was one of the popular Mitchell texts, which was remarkable considering its special category. In 1850 the *Intermediate or Secondary Geography*, which was a step up from the primary geography, was first issued. According to an advertisement it was to be called *High School Geography*, but before publication the title was changed. The early Mitchell geographies were in good format and most of the maps were made by J. H. Young, the foremost American map maker of the time. Young's work has been compared to, and seems to have been based on, that of John Arrowsmith, the younger— the Englishman who turned out beautiful and accurate maps. The maps of both John Arrowsmith and Young are still, despite all subsequent progress in engraving and the art of printing, a treat to the eye.

Augustus Mitchell—he often dropped the first name Samuel —bought a printing establishment in Philadelphia in the 1830's, and it was here he started his geography publication after a period devoted to printing an atlas, not for school use, which sold well, and a *Travellers Guide*. Around the middle of the century Mitchell took over the Henry Schenck Tanner mapmaking business in New York. Tanner was a well-known cartographer and turned out a popular atlas and other publications. Tanner published one of the earliest descriptive and statistical accounts of American railroads, *A Description of the Canals and Railroads of the United States*, in 1840, and Mitchell used a certain amount of the data in this book in his geographical texts.

Within a few years of the publication of Mitchell's first

geography he had two hundred and fifty employees in his Philadelphia establishment, all engaged primarily in the production of geographies. He made every effort to obtain the latest data on discoveries for inclusion in his texts. He kept in correspondence with some of the explorers of his day, sparing no expense to obtain the most suitable illustrations. Many of the pictures in the early issues of his geographies had the exaggerated portrayal common to the era, but the latter texts were all illustrated in a realistic way. The excellent engravings no doubt had a great deal to do with the widespread success of the later Mitchell geographies.

In the late 1850's Mitchell brought out a complete new series but also continued to publish his old series "revised and with some material added." The titles of the new series were : *New First Lessons in Geography, New Primary Geography, New Intermediate Geography, New Geography and Atlas, New Physical Geography* and *New Ancient Geography.* The new atlas volume had forty-four well-arranged maps. The Mitchell *Physical Geography,* written by John Brocklesly, professor of mathematics and natural philosophy in Trinity College in Connecticut, plainly revealed the influence of Guyot, both in text matter and maps. The maps of the *Physical Geography,* drawn and engraved by J. M. Atwood of Philadelphia, were of a high order. Their few errors were the result of misinformation generally accepted as true at the time.

The new series of Mitchell's geographies were issued in a small format, as were the earlier books. But in the 1870's the Mitchells saw the handwriting on the wall and realized that the large-size texts like Guyot's were completely superseding the smaller books. They then brought out their quarto texts. Augustus Mitchell had died in 1868, and his wife and children published the series of larger texts. They used the name of S. Augustus Mitchell as author, but some of the copyrights were in the names of Mrs. S. Augustus Mitchell and S. Augustus Mitchell, Jr. These later texts were as great a success over a long period as were the early Mitchell geographies.

No other geographies were used so extensively over a long period as were Mitchell's. Fry's and Atwood's texts, issued later, surpassed them in production for relatively short periods, but in overall production the Mitchell texts far surpassed all others.

During the period following the Civil War, when geography was of great interest, a number of texts from various pens were widely used. Among them were Colton's *New Intermediate Geography, Common School Geography,* and *Outlines of Physical Geography;* Cornell's little *First Steps in Geography;* the Sadlier Excelsior Series; Warren's three geographies; and a number of others, all of which achieved wide popularity. The Colton texts were first issued in 1872 and went through many printings during the next two decades. These geographies were well adapted for school use, containing dependable subject matter and put up attractively — just the sort of books that appeal to children.

S. S. Cornell was a producer of maps, and his one little text, *First Steps in Geography,* initially issued in 1858, met with extraordinary success considering that it was just a small text that stood by itself. It was in catechism form, all concisely worded, and the illustrations, not too many of them, were of an especially delightful nature. The maps were somewhat over-colored as compared to later standards, but their simplicity must have endeared them to school children of the time.

D. M. Warren's *Primary Geography, Common School Geography,* and *Physical Geography,* which appeared in the 1870's, were of a high class. The maps in this large *Common School Geography* were among the first to show railroad routes. The text introduced some other novelties. At the back was an eight-page "System of Map Drawing," by E. A. and A. C. Apgar, which was not only protected by copyright but by patent as well. E. A. Apgar, who was at one time superintendent of schools of New Jersey, had previously published a treatise on map making. A number of map-drawing manuals was published around this time but, like the regular drawing books which have been printed for a century and a half, never took hold too strongly in the schools."

During the last three decades of the nineteenth century small-size local geographies came into vogue. There had been a few such texts printed previously, but they had never become popular. As early as 1827, Samuel R. Hall, author of *Lectures on School Keeping,* the first book by a native American for guidance in conducting schools, published a *Geography and History of Vermont,* which was used to a limited extent in the schools of Vermont. In the last part of the century any number of state geographies appeared, along with New England, Southern, Western, and other regional geography texts. A state with so little a population as West Virginia had two — Knote's *Geography of West Virginia,* written by a school teacher and published in 1883; and Kinney's text of the same name, written by a lawyer and issued in 1895. Some states had three such texts before 1900. Shortly after the turn of the century the large geographies began to add supplements of from thirty to forty

---

" Carl W. Drepperd, *American Drawing Books, A Contribution toward a Bibliography* (New York: New York Public Library, 1946), constituted a splendid check list on drawing books published up to the time of the Civil War, including many of those compiled for school use. Rufus Porter, a wall painter, peddler, and tinker, wrote a drawing book early in the nineteenth century, *A Select Collection of Valuable and Curious Arts,* and peddled it himself for many years. He prospered so well from the sales that he used part of his funds to establish the famous magazine *Scientific American.* Rembrandt Peale's *Graphics: A Manual of Drawing and Writing for the Use of Schools,* was published in 1838.

pages covering the state in which the text was to be sold. These supplementary sections were generally compiled by local authorities, and bore the name of the authors. Separate state and local geographies, notwithstanding the appearance of supplements, carried over into the twentieth century, and a few are still printed. Since 1900 we have had a *Pacific Coast Geography,* a *Southern Geography,* and a number of newly-brought-up-to-date state texts. In a few cases the large geography supplements have been reprinted for separate local usage.

Since the beginning of the present century a new type of general geography compiler has appeared. E. S. Tarr, Frank M. McMurry, Richard Ellwood Dodge, Albert Perry Brigham, Alexis Everett Frye, and Wallace W. Atwood rank among the outstanding ones. These were all men of high academic standing and, like their predecessors Guyot and Maury, had a deep personal interest in the study of geography.

The trend in compiling geographies at present is toward emphasizing human development, the effect of climate upon the population, the relations between the various races, the effect of material resources on peoples and areas, population changes and migrations, and other similar topics. There have always been changes of emphasis in geographies from time to time, and there seems no reason to believe that there will not occur other such shifts in the future.

The history of the use of globes in this country and of their early manufacture stands apart in the annals of our progress in the study of geography. Near the end of the eighteenth century Thomas Keith, an instructor to Princess Charlotte of Wales, a schoolmaster, and at times a special instructor in mathematics, wrote a *Treatise on the Use of the Globes,* which was published in England and reprinted in this country. This was one of the early manuals on globe study used in American schools. In 1813 *A Treatise on Globes and Maps,* by John Lathrop, Jr., a teacher in the Salem-Street Academy of Boston, was printed in that city; the author stated on his title page that the volume was compiled from the work of a number of authors, the first named being Keith. The text was reprinted at late as 1821. In 1753 Christopher Sower printed a small sixty-page book, *Description and Use of the Globes,* by Theophilus Grew, a Philadelphia mathematics instructor; but this volume was in the main a treatise on trigonometry, the first published in America, and on surveying, and was scarcely a treatise on globes.

Most of the texts on the use of globes, strange to say, were a mixture of astronomy, geography, and astrology. They contained accounts of the solar system, information on star positions, time differences over the earth, tide movements, and even data on religion. Eclipses were described and explained, as were the flights of comets. The names of Newton, Copernicus, and other astronomers appeared frequently, but even they did not prevent the inclusion of a great deal of material from the dead past of astrology. Constellations in the Zodiac were listed, and the numbers of stars in them were enumerated. Some practical information was given on terrestial globes and maps and their uses, but there was no abundance of workable data in this line. The late-eighteenth and early-nineteenth-century texts on globes were more fanciful than practical.

The first globe produced in America was made by a Vermont farmer, James Wilson, and was dated 1811. This globe was a terrestrial sphere. The following year the same maker turned out the second globe produced in our land—this one a celestial sphere. Both of these, entirely handmade, are now in the Yale University Library. The story of the acquisition of the Wilson globes by Yale University was told in *The New York Times* of February 13, 1949, and an account of their construction is to be found in the Proceedings of the American Antiquarian Society, vol. 48, 1938.

The Wilson globes were made of wood, and covered with a plaster surface; the mapping was engraved in twelve "orange-peel-gores," pasted on. Wilson in his early manhood saw a foreign-made globe at Dartmouth College while visiting there, and conceived the idea of making one himself. He knew little geography, astronomy, or engraving. Through almost desperate sacrifice he was able to procure a Third Edition of the *Encyclopaedia Britannica,* from which he learned the rudiments of the subjects connected with globe construction; and he walked all the way from his Vermont home to New Haven in order to learn something of the art of engraving from Amos Doolittle, returning afoot to Vermont.

The ingenious Vermont farmer, no longer a young man, spent about a year making the first copper engravings for his globe, only to find that they were out of proportion and that new ones must be made. After finally completing his first globes, Wilson proceeded to make others, which readily sold. He gradually hired workmen to help him, and when about sixty years of age he established a globe-making firm in Albany, New York, and before very long he was supplying nearly all the globes used in this country.

Today almost every schoolroom has its globe, and most children's conception of the earth as it floats through space and carries us with it on its flight through time is derived from observing such globes, in the classroom and elsewhere.

XIX

Progress of Schoolbook Publishing

UNTIL WELL ALONG in the nineteenth century schoolbook output in our country was the result of individual undertakings, in regard both to composition of the subject matter and to manufacture and distribution. Practically no organization, at least in the sense in which we use the term today, was connected with creation or promotion until the beginning of the second quarter of the century. Take the matter of writing or collecting the material: a teacher, doctor, clergyman, or anybody might decide to write a text, do the necessary work, confer with the proprieter of a printing establishment, and a book appeared. Thus there was a new book for other compilers to contend with, to be forgotten within a month or so or to meet with widespread acceptance over a number of years.

In other instances a printer might need a local issue of a certain type of text, if for no other reason than that transportation from a distance was difficult and expensive; the printer consulted with a local citizen sufficiently well educated for such a task as compiling a text, and in this way a schoolbook was planned and brought into existence, to take its place in the open marts for better or worse. Or, again, a printer so inclined might set to work preparing a text himself and, after the necessary study, assemble a usable manual and print it on his own presses. Many texts were produced in this way and some of them attained wide circulation. William Smellie, editor and writer of much of the first edition of the *Encyclopedia Britannica,* it is worthy of note, was a printer, and his work in a printing establishment in Scotland led him to conceive the great reference work.[1]

Not until about the end of the first quarter of the nineteenth century did any carefully planned and reasonably well-organized method of producing schoolbooks get under way. Prior to this era there was no establishment that could produce the wide range of books needed to cover the whole field of education. Books for school use had all along been put out here and there in a scattered hit-and-miss fashion due to odd contributing circumstances. Around the beginning of the second quarter of the century a change was beginning to take place. A number of firms began issuing schoolbooks on what we today consider a planned business-like footing, chiefly the fulfillment of going printing firms and small publishers beginning to take advantage of the steadily mounting demand for school texts, which the new social and education condition was creating.

Once begun, organized production of schoolbooks in large numbers was achieved within a comparatively short period. From 1820 to 1830 any number of printing concerns of limited capacity started to issue schoolbooks in quantities as a result of the accelerated countrywide need for such publications. In cities as far south as Charleston, South Carolina; over the

---

[1] Smellie was no ordinary man. Herman Kogan in his story of the encyclopedia, *The Great E B* (Chicago: University of Chicago Press, 1958), p. 9, says Smellie at the time of the issuance of the first encyclopedia was only twenty-eight, but was "a veteran in wit, genius and . . bawdry."

Alleghenies along the Ohio River at Wheeling, Cincinnati, and Pittsburgh; as far north as Maine and New Hampshire, printers turned to the production of schoolbooks for booksellers and for individual compilers. Two or three well-known Boston firms, a like number in New York and Philadelphia, and one in Baltimore went into school-text publication on a considerable scale, and one or two of these houses before long were concentrating wholly on educational material.

The first schoolbook publishing firm that can accurately be designated as well organised was the house of Solomon King of New York. This bookseller and publisher was in business for a little over a decade, from 1821 to 1832. The concern maintained a staff of a sort and had sufficient equipment and other facilities to carry on a systematic business. During this time King turned out a number of primers, readers, calculating books, and other texts, nearly all of a small size, along with other works not classed as schoolbooks but all issued for the benefit of children. This New York book producer also sold many texts not published by him, including Daboll's arithmetics, Morse's geographies, and other widely used books. He advertised his business as devoted to "toy books," and he did specialize on books for the amusement of children. At the same time, however, he published quite a number of more serious works and good schoolbooks. King, all things considered, was our first real "publisher of children's books," an appellation widely recognized and utilized today. He can equally well, in a strict sense, be spoken of as the first "educational publisher."

The firms of Samuel Wood and Mahlon Day, both with a somewhat similar business in New York City, were contemporary with, and even predated King's establishment somewhat; but neither of these firms specialized in school texts and children's books to the extent that King's did. Because of this, the publishing firms of Wood and Day, although schoolbook producers, do not stand in exactly the same classification as does the Solomon King establishment. That Mahlon Day did a big "toy book" business is certain, however. In the 1830's he was advertising that, besides schoolbooks, he had 150 toy books of his own printing, in addition to others from Baltimore, Philadelphia, and Boston.[2] The Mahlon Day firm did not survive after the death of its founder.

In the late 1820's Samuel Goodrich began to publish school texts and later he conducted an organized staff for writing such books. His publications, most of which had "Peter Parley" somewhere on the title page, were produced through outside printing concerns or publishers. He was the first to employ on salary what became known as the "professional compiler." Goodrich's texts owed most of their success to the fact that more often than not they were put out in small size, were very simply written, and were printed in the clearest type with lesson-headings in large capitals. Practically every one of his books had attractive illustrations — at a time when the latter were not too plentifully used. Besides all this, the books were made to sell at a low price, most of them having thin cardboard bindings. While many of the Peter Parley books from the standpoint of subject matter were poor specimens of schoolbooks, the influence of Goodrich brought a measure of improvement into schoolbook publishing; and it may be mentioned, also, that many of the general run of children's books of today have some of the blood of the Peter Parley volumes in their veins.

Goodrich has told how he designed his books on the basis of his memory of those he had himself loved in his boyhood days,[3] and how he was led to put his school texts and other

---

[2] Weiss, *Catalogue of Chapbooks in the New York Public Library* (1936), p. 35.

[3] Goodrich, *Recollections of a Lifetime* (New York: Arundel Press, 1856), p. 165.

children's books into large, clear type. Referring to his reactions as a boy of ten, he wrote :

My father had a considerable library, but it consisted mostly of theology, a great deal of Latin, and in large folios. Into such a forbidding mass I never penetrated save only that I sometimes dipped into a big volume which happened to be in large print. This was in English . . . . I read whole passages of this book aloud, spelling out the large words as well as I could. I did not understand a sentence of it, but I was fascinated by the fair large type. This circumstance I have never forgotten, and it should not be overlooked by those who make books for children.

It is not necessary to go into detail about the many publishing firms that have produced the millions of schoolbooks from the time of King, Wood, Day, and Goodrich to our own era. Anyone wishing to delve into the history of such publishing should turn to J. C. Derby's *Fifty Years Among Authors, Books and Publishers* which was printed in Hartford, Connecticut, in 1886, and to Hellmut Lehmann-Haupt's *The Book in America,* published in New York in 1939. These two books are replete with schoolbook publishing history, with details about various firms and their beginnings and progress. Individual histories of several firms have been published and also will prove useful in studying schoolbook publishing. Chief among these individual histories are those of the Appleton, Macmillan, Ginn, American Book Company, and three or four other firms.

It is well known that down through the history of American education there has been an almost constant change in schoolbooks. An educational publisher has stated that any day a textbook may be produced that almost overnight will render obsolete existing texts on the subject. This assertion came from W. W. Livingood, editor-in-chief and vice-president of the American Book Company, and his statement is too accurate to be questioned. Much has been written on the readiness to adopt new school texts in opposition to those formerly used, but much that has been penned along this line has done little to explain the situation as it actually existed.

What has caused the constant discarding of schoolbooks for new ones? Is there any justifiable reason for continuously, sometimes after a surprisingly brief period rejecting existing texts in favor of others designed to take their place? There is a reason, and we may discern what it is if we go into the whys and wherefores of schoolbook usage—whether or not we consider the frequent changes desirable. Blaise Pascal has said that "all the succession of men, through the course of many centuries, must be considered as the same man who always subsists and is forever learning."[4] If nothing more, the fact that man is always learning has resulted in his discarding the books which children study and using others more adapted to the purpose for which they are designed. The high mortality among schoolbooks has been brought about more by a constant need for improvement than by any effort to increase sales.

The change in school texts after certain periods of usage is a phenomenon that the schoolbook publisher accepts as an inherent part of his business, and frequent changes, although they sometimes bring heavy losses to publishers, have resulted in improving the quality of our text books. Let us consider one point which will emphasize how the publisher has worked toward making schoolbooks better through the production of new ones—the matter of illustrations. Up to 1825 or 1830 the pictures in the few illustrated school texts were poor examples. Copper and steel engravings were almost unknown in schoolbooks because of the prohibitory cost of such reproductions. Some of the early books had a woodcut frontispiece, but no other illustrations; a number had small wood engravings per-

---

[4] Chevalier, *Pascal* (London: Sheed and Ward, 1930), p. 70.

haps on four or five pages, and these as a rule were of poor quality. Sometimes one had to scrutinize them closely before he could determine what they represented. Then, because of new developments, within a comparatively short time the use of illustrations increased sharply—a far-reaching advance.[5]

Eric Nordenskiold, speaking of pictorial illustrations in scientific books, said that it is "a means of extending human knowledge the importance of which can be appreciated only if we consider what it means in our day and what should be the consequence if modern science were to be deprived of it."[6] George Sarton, the well-known historian of science, had something similar to say on the subject.[7] What these two eminent historians have pointed out about the value of pictures in scientific works applies equally to school textbooks in general. The advent of good illustrations made practical certain classes of schoolbooks which otherwise would have been of little value and usefulness.

Schoolbook improvement along this line has come about through the efforts of publishers to improve their productions. This fact is pointed out to show what actually transpired through the initiative of publishers, whether or not it was prompted by competitive compulsion.

As most of the schoolbooks issued at the present time are published and circulated through somewhat specialized media, textbook publishing has become largely separated from that of

---

[5] This change came chiefly through the development of wood engraving by Thomas Bewick. Wood engraving dates from the Middle Ages, but the design was not cut away from the block instead of leaving it standing until Bewick did it and permitted the reproduction of illustrations with little effort and at low cost. This brought engraving to a point where it could be profitably and extensively utilized in schoolbook production.

[6] Nordenskiold, *History of Biology* (New York: Tudor, 1935), p. 92.

[7] Sarton, *Six Wings, Men of Science in the Renaissance* (Bloomington: Indiana University Press, 1957), pp. 124 and 282.

regular "trade" books, although it is true that numerous firms are engaged in both. Schoolbook writing is now more an "agreed-upon" task than is trade book production, which to a large extent is dependent upon current conditions, but the factor of unpredictable vagaries and caprices on the part of the public has a place in both. The schoolbook producer is definitely today a specialized technician with managerial ability and intimate firsthand contact with output. He must now possess a sounder judgment than that generally exercised by the producer of schoolbooks in former times.

Within our era the printed text has been supplemented here and there by inventions such as motion pictures, radio, phonograph recordings, and television, and we hear a great deal about these things. We may well ask whether these new inventions will displace the schoolbook. There seems to be but one answer — as remarkable as the inventions are, and notwithstanding their impact upon our time, they have made no such decisive headway as an accepted and integral portion of the educational system as to threaten *the displacement of the book*. Our educational system at present is still dependent upon the teacher and the printed page, and they must continue to be the chief means of imparting knowledge, just as has been the case through century after century. We, of course, should use any product of scientific genius to the extent that it is useful, but we must always remember that children are human beings and that education is a humanistic process.

Bibliography

General Accounts

Barnard, Henry, *Memoirs of Teachers and Educators* (New York : F. C. Brownell, 1859). A 524-page volume with thirty lengthy biographies, among them several of early schoolbook compilers. These biographies have been for a century the chief source of information on a number of the persons whose lives and work are traced.

Barnard, Henry, *The American Journal of Education,* founded in Hartford, Conn., by Barnard in 1856 and surviving until 1881. It is one of the greatest sources of history on schools, schoolbooks, and collateral subject matter. One of the best brief appraisals of Barnard's work is in the article in the February, 1897, *Review of Reviews,* "Henry Barnard, The Public School Pioneer." This article quotes the *Encyclopædia Britannica* as saying that *Barnard's Journal* "is by far the most valuable work in our language on the history of education." The 31 volumes of the *Journal* were reprinted by the United States Bureau of Education in 1892. The set has a 128-page analytic index.

Compayre, Gabriel, *History of Pedagogy* (Boston : Heath, 1891). A near-classic work containing much material on schoolbooks, although very scattered.

Cubberly, Elwood P., *Public Education in the United States* (Boston : Houghton Mifflin, *ca.* 1934). Has an excellent, well-illustrated chapter (9, Part 1) on early American schoolbooks and their evolution.

Dunn, Courtney, *The Natural History of the Child* (New York : John Lane Co., 1920). Contains two chapters on early schooling in England, touching on studies, Latin and English books, and arithmetics, as well as on the history of the slate, steel pen, and other educational materials. A hodge-podge book that is amusing though not too scholarly.

Encyclopedia of Religious Knowledge (Brattleboro, Vermont, 1835, printed in Boston by Shattuck and Company). A long one-volume reference work with a great number of biographical sketches of early schoolbook compilers — many of them clergymen — upon whom nothing can be found elsewhere. A remarkably good book for its time in its sphere.

Freeman, Ruth S., *Yesterday's School Books, A Looking Glass for Teachers of Today* (Watkins Glen, N. Y. : Century House, 1961). A small volume written in a simple vein, with chapters on various classes of early texts, especially those published since 1850.

Fryatt, Norma A., *Children's Literature,* catalog of an exhibition Nov. 19, 1954, to Feb. 28, 1955, in the Pierpont Morgan Library. Covers a magnificent exhibit, including a number of the rarest of early schoolbooks, both foreign and American — primers, hornbooks, battledores, and others.

Hall, G. Stanley, *Recreations of a Psychologist* (New York : Appleton, 1920). In the last chapter, "Note On Early Memories," the well-known educator discusses schoolbooks he remembers using as a boy, throwing light, in a short space, on the kind of impressions schoolbooks make on children.

Hall-Quest, Alfred L., *The Textbook* (New York : Macmillan, 1918). Has a chapter on the history of textbooks. Written by a professor of education in the University of Cincinnati, it is chiefly a treatise on the use of schoolbooks.

Hazlitt, W. Carey, *Schools, Schoolbooks and Schoolmasters* (New York : Stetchert & Co., 2nd edition, 1905). Although written by an Englishman and treating of educational development in Great Britain, this book can be read with much interest and profit in connection with the history of American schoolbooks. The horn-

book is discussed, as well as other subjects of especial bearing on
the study of our schoolbook lineage.

Johnson, Clifton, *The Country School* (New York : Appleton,
1893). This book, a forerunner and parent of the book listed
below, contains considerable material on early textbooks, and,
from love of the subject, Johnson evidently worked up to his very
worthwhile *Old Time Schools and Schoolbooks*. In all his writing
Johnson had the folk touch, which made his books very popular.

Johnson, Clifton, *Old Time Schools and Schoolbooks* (New York :
Macmillan, 1904), reprinted a number of times. A popular treatment of early school texts. Constructed as the book is, there are
necessarily many gaps. It is one of the most interesting of all the
books on American school texts.

Kiefer, Monica, *American Children through Their Books, 1700–
1835* (Philadelphia : University of Pennsylvania Press, 1948). A
scholarly and worth-while study, with generally entertaining
information on numerous schoolbooks.

Lehmann-Haupt, Hellmut, *The Book in America* (New York :
Bowker, 1939). A comparatively recent volume on the history of
the book in America which throws special light on the conditions
under which schoolbook production developed in Colonial times
and later. Specific information is presented on a number of
individual schoolbooks and series. A sort of retracing is made of
the history of firms J. C. Derby tells of in his *Fifty Years Among
Authors, Books and Publishers,* which is listed near the end of
this bibliography.

Littlefield, George Emery, *Early Schools and Schoolbooks of New
England* (Boston : The Club of Odd Volumes, 1904). By a
Boston bookdealer who had a long experience in handling many
old schoolbooks. Scarce, since it was issued in a limited edition of
only 167 copies.

Merriwether, Colyer, *Our Colonial Curriculum, 1607–1776* (Washington : 1907, Capitol Publishing Co., 1907). A fair coverage of
schoolbooks prior to the time of the Revolution. Evidently but

few copies were printed, and the book is scarce and is not even to be found in many large libraries.

Nietz, John, *Old Textbooks* (Pittsburgh : University of Pittsburgh Press, 1961). Well-illustrated recent treatment of texts issued during the eighteenth and nineteenth centuries. The evaluation of many compilers and their works, this is one of the most important studies that has been written on schoolbooks, although it was not intended as a historical-lineage treatment of the subject.

Pope, A. A., *Errors in Schoolbooks* (Boston : privately printed, 1892). Pope, a bicycle manufacturer, offered prizes to anyone pointing out errors in schoolbooks, and he accumulated something less than a hundred over a period of years. A supplementary pamphlet was issued following the first one.

Rosenbach, A. S. W., *Early American Children's Books* (Portland, Maine : Southworth Press, 1933), by America's most-written-about antiquarian book dealer. Gives bibliographical data on a number of the rarest school texts. More a catalog of Dr. Rosenbach's collection than a regular bibliography.

Stone, Wilbur Macy, *Emasculated Juveniles (American Book Collector, March, 1934)*. Information on deletions from children's books, some of them school texts, because considered pernicious, heretical, over-drawn, or otherwise objectionable.

Targ, William, Editor, *Bibliophile in the Nursery* (Cleveland and New York : World, 1957). The chapters (unnumbered) "In The Cradle," by Mrs. E. M. Field, "Geoffrey Chaucer Goes to School," Marchette Chute, "Milestones of the Nursery," Anonymous, "Mental Pabulum of Godly Children," Monica Kiefer, "The McGuffey Readers," Henry Ford and D. Kenneth Laub, and "Nineteenth Century Children's Books," Jacob Blanck, are either all entirely or primarily on schoolbooks. This interesting material is reprinted from former books or periodicals.

Weeks, S. B., *Confederate Text-Books, 1861–1865,* in Annual Report, Bureau of Education 1898–99, Washington, 1900, I, 1139 to 1155. Lists a number of schoolbooks and enumerates some of the difficulties entering into the production of books for Southern schools during the Civil War. A forerunner of the volume, *Confederate Imprints,* later put out by the Boston Athenaeum.

Wines, E. C., *Hints on a System of Popular Education* (Philadelphia : Hogan and Thompson, 1838). A splendidly written, long-overlooked book of considerable worth in frequent passages on schoolbooks of a century ago and their usage. It discusses the shortcomings of some and shows what types of texts the time demanded. The volume ends with a 34-page catalog of books for sale at the Hogan and Thomson establishment in Philadelphia (two doors below Sanderson's Hotel) — many of them school texts used by our forebears.

Book Dealers' Catalogs

There have been issued at various times book dealers' catalogs that contain information of extra importance in studying schoolbook lineage, sometimes with bibliographical data to be found nowhere else except in the works listed themselves. These catalogs are numerous and it is possible to list but a few of the outstanding ones. All those enumerated covered schoolbooks in general rather than any special division of them.

Beauchamp Bookshop, London. *Early Children's Books,* catalog 19, Summer 1954. Covers a good many A-B-C books, primers, a battledore, and a hornbook, some of them American. According to word from the dealer this whole collection was sold to the University of California.

Grafton and Co., London, *Hornbooks* (London, 1923). A catalog of fifty hornbooks, perhaps the greatest number ever listed in a dealer's catalog. Well-illustrated and the items described in detail. It will perhaps never be possible for a dealer to get so many genuine hornbooks together again.

Midland Rare Book Co., Mansfield, Ohio. Catalogs issued under the title *Midland Notes* from time to time contain excellent schoolbook bibliographies. Catalog 49, issued in 1953, under the title *Children's Books* is of particular value.

Edward Morril and Son, Boston, *American Children's Books* (Boston : about 1953), a 100-page catalog of most remarkable content as far as schoolbooks are concerned. Texts of every division of school study appear. This firm has dealt in many old schoolbooks.

Bernard Quaritch Ltd., London, *Rare and Valuable Early School-books,* 15th, 16th, and 17th centuries, (London : 1932), catalog 464. A hundred-page indexed catalog, listing in the usual perfect Quaritch manner many schoolbooks that were forerunners of and models for numerous American texts. One of the most valuable catalogs of its kind.

Isaiah Thomas, Jr., Boston, *Catalogue of Books* (Boston : 1811), published at the Boston Bookstore. A 64-page listing of many books, including textbooks printed a century and a half ago. It represented the Thomas bookstores in both Boston and Worcester.

Primers — Hornbooks

Arbuthnot, May Hill, *Children and Books* (Chicago : Scott Foresman & Co., *ca.* 1947). A most excellent book on children's books. Traces the lineage of various classes of children's books, beginning school texts, the hornbook, and so on. As in a score of other books on early children's books, one looks in vain for even a mention of A-B-C books, millions of which have been printed.

Folmsbee, Beulah, *A Little History of the Hornbook* (Boston : Horn Book Inc., 1942). A small history of the hornbook. The small size of the volume precludes a very varied treatment.

Ford, Paul Leicester, *The New England Primer* (New York : Dodd Mead & Co., 1899). A reprint, in splendid format, of the earliest-known edition of the *New England Primer,* with an introduction which is one of the best portrayals of the famous little book. Ford, who knew books well, wrote not only from the standpoint of bibliography but treated soundly the historical and social phases of the primer.

Heartman, Charles F., *The New England Primer Prior to 1830* (New York : privately printed, 1916). A splendid bibliography with a brief introductory history of the primer. Many pages of the little primer are reproduced in facsimile. A few issues not listed have been found since the bibliography was first printed, but these perhaps can be counted on the fingers of one hand.

Heartman, Charles F., *American Primers, Indian Primers, Royal Primers* (Highland Park, N. J. : privately printed for Harry B. Weiss, 1935). A dependable, well-illustrated bibliography of primers (other than the *New England Primer*) prior to 1830.

Livermore, George, *The Origin, History and Character of the New England Primer* (New York : privately printed for Charles F. Heartman, 1915). This volume originally published in 1849, contains a facsimile of the fragment of a 1764 edition of the *New England Primer*. This, in the 1849 printing, was the first book issued on the *New England Primer,* and the present 1915 issue is the only reprint. Oddly, according to the title page, only twelve copies of the 1849 edition were printed. Equally singular is the fact that the 1915 reprint was limited to thirty-five copies.

Merritt, Percival, *The Royal Primer* (Cambridge : Harvard University Press, 1925). The best study that has been made of a noted primer that came up along with the *New England Primer* and which was printed frequently in England and in the American colonies.

Plimpton, George A., *The Hornbook and Its Use in America* (Worcester, Mass. : 1916), reprinted from the Proceedings of the American Antiquarian Society, October, 1916. The most complete treatise on the hornbook ever issued in the United States. Mr. Plimpton tells of his difficulty in assembling the few hornbooks he collected from various sections of Mexico and the United States.

Scribner's Private School Primer (New York : printed for the advertising department of *Scribner's Magazine,* 1903). Contains a dozen interesting full-page facsimiles of rare primers used a century and half ago.

Vail, R. W. G., *The New England Primer Issued Prior to 1830* (American Book Collector, March, 1935). A thorough review of the first edition of Heartman's bibliography, by a man who had a good knowledge of early American schoolbooks. Contains data on collectors of the *New England Primer*.

Weiss, Harry B., *Chapbooks in the New York Public Library* (New York : N. Y. Public Library, 1936). Lists some early A-B-C books and primers with good bibliographical data.

Readers

Drake, Daniel, *Pioneer Life in Kentucky* (New York : Henry Schuman, 1948). Originally published in 1870, this is a reprint of a book showing the astonishing meagerness of training of most of those in the medical profession during the early nineteenth century. Alexander Hamilton McGuffey married Drake's daughter Elizabeth, and *Pioneer Life in Kentucky* contains almost as much material on the McGuffey family as on the medical profession in pioneer days, which was its subject. An important book on American history and of especial interest as connected with the McGuffeys. This book is referred to in Chapter 10, in connection with Joseph Ray and his arithmetics, where some history of the volume is given.

Ford, Henry, *The McGuffey Readers* (Colophon Spring : 1936). A good deal of bibliographical data and some illustrative material on the readers. It was put together by those in charge of the Ford Museum, with Mr. Ford named as author. Mr. Ford gathered one of the largest collections of McGuffey readers.

Hughes, Raymond Grove, *McGuffey and His Peerless Readers* (Charleston : *West Virginia Review,* September, 1931). Written by a man living near William McGuffey's birthplace. Contains picture of an old spring house on the farm in Washington County where the log cabin stood in which McGuffey was born.

McGinley, Phyllis, "Lessons for Today from McGuffey," *(New*

York Times Magazine, May 20, 1951). Chiefly a picturing of the contents of the readers. The article was printed in a condensed form in *Reader's Digest,* August, 1951. This type of article frequently appears in popular magazines.

Minnich, Harvey C., *Williams Holmes McGuffey and His Readers* (New York : American Book Co., 1936). The most valuable volume on the readers from a bibliographical standpoint. It has complete listing of the various issues of the readers, and many important facts on their lineage. At the end of the volume is an extended bibliography on McGuffey.

Mosier, Richard D., *Making the American Mind* (New York : Columbia University Press, 1947). A study of the social and moral ideas in the McGuffey readers, dealing at great length with the influence of the books. Perhaps in this volume, as in the writings of many other authors, the effect of McGuffey on character formation has been overestimated. Many writers fail to take into consideration the disconcerting fact that the Civil War, the most egregious fruit of all American faulty thinking, occurred during the time that McGuffey was supposed to be molding character into a noble form.

Pringle, Henry F. and Katherine, *He Scared the Devil Out of Grandpa (Saturday Evening Post,* January 22, 1955). Popular article on McGuffey and his books in the usual style of this class of paper.

Ruggles, Alice McGuffey, *The Story of the McGuffeys* (New York: American Book Company, 1930). This book, by a descendant of Alexander McGuffey, is primarily a coverage of her grand-father's family. It treats especially of the part that Alexander McGuffey played in the creation of the readers and spelling book.

Sullivan, Mark, *Our Times,* Volume 2 (New York : Scribners, 1927). A good analysis of the readers of the nineteenth century by a well-known journalist. Sullivan treats of the readers as "the backbone of instruction in Common Schools." He is especially ardent in praising McGuffey's books, helping, perhaps more strongly than anyone else, in creating the McGuffey legend of our day.

Vail, Henry H., *History of McGuffey Readers* (Cleveland : privately printed, limited to 354 copies, 1911), later reprinted. This was the first volume devoted exclusively to McGuffey and his books. Vail played a large part in the publication of the McGuffey readers over a long period, at one time being editor of the series. Although Vail had personal contacts with McGuffey and those who knew him, his biography is not as valuable from a bibliographical standpoint level as is Minnich's.

Reeder, Rudolph R., "Historical Development of School Readers," *Contributions to Philosophy, Psychology and Education,* Vol. 8, No. 2 (New York : Columbia University, 1900). (Was originally bound with No. 1, and because of this is difficult to find in some libraries). Much on *New England Primer,* hornbooks, and other early class materials. Traces early development of readers through Noah Webster's texts, and goes into religious influences in readers to some extent.

Anonymous, *Story of Mary and Her Little Lamb* (Dearborn, Mich. : privately printed for Mr. and Mrs. Henry Ford, 1928). A quaint little book of much interest to those concerned with nineteenth-century reading texts. Gives a full history of the poem. In the April 2, 1927, *Pathfinder* (Washington, D. C.) is a letter headed "Mary or Lucy?", on the "Lucy had a little Lamb" version of the poem. This called attention to the publication of the verses with the name "Lucy" throughout in *Town's Second Reader* (1848–1854). This Town version of the poem, although the *Pathfinder* item does not say so, was printed some years after the verses were originally written and published by Sarah J. Hale. Town evidently changed the name with the idea of adding novelty to the version used in his reader.

Grammars, Spelling Books, Rhetorics, Elocution Manuals,
Literature Texts

Bass, Althea, *With Benefit of Grammar (Colophon,* August, 1937).
A great deal of material on Indian educational texts not much
heard of elsewhere. Shows why, because of the Indian languages,
it has always been so difficult to prepare schoolbooks for the use
of the Indian.

Bell, Alexander Melville, *Principles of Elocution* (Salem, Mass. :
James P. Burbank, 1878). The 13-page introduction to this text
seems to be one of the best evaluations of the place held by elocution in the nineteenth century. Bell, the father of the inventor of
the telephone, wrote eleven books on the voice, speech, and
elocution, and knew a great deal about the historical as well as
the technical side of the subject. Other volumes of Bell's, par-
ticularily *Essays and Postscripts on Elocution* (New York : 1890),
contain material on the lineage of school elocution.

Brown, Gould, *Grammar of English Grammars* (New York : 1851,
William Wood and Co., 1851) and reissued several times until
1869. This school text, extraordinary for both its size and
material, as already mentioned, was one of the most complete
histories of early American grammars (and British ones, as well)
up until the time of its last publication. At the beginning of the
book there is a "Catalogue of English Grammars," and according to this list 245 separate grammars were published in America
prior to 1869, not counting reprints—a statement that seems
almost incredible.

Carpenter, George R.; Baker, T. Frank; Scott, Fred. N., *The
Teaching of English* (New York, 1903; New edition, 1913).
Contains a good deal of probing of early grammars. Has extensive bibliographies on phases of grammar study and on other
matters pertaining to grammar lineage.

De Quincey, Thomas, "Rhetoric," in De Quincey's *Historical and
Critical Essays,* Vol. 2 (Boston : Ticknor, 1853), and printed
many times elsewhere. De Quincey's essay is of value in tracing

the ups and downs of rhetoric. The Essay was originally written by De Quincey as a review of Whately's *Elements of Rhetoric*.

Kittredge, George Lyman, *Some Landmarks in the History of Latin Grammars* (Boston : Ginn and Co., 1903). This 16-page booklet on the forerunners of American Latin and English grammars has some illustrations from the collection of George A. Plimpton.

Kittredge, George Lyman, "Some Landmarks in the History of English Grammar" *(Ginn's Text-Book Bulletin,* November, 1906). Continues along the line of the publication listed next above. Was reprinted in *English Grammars of Five Centuries,* issued a few years later by Ginn & Company without date.

Laing, Gordon J., "Quintilliam the Schoolmaster," *Classical Journal,* January, 1920 (Chicago University Press). A clear presentation of conditions in Roman times that formed the basis for the evolution of the modern school rhetoric text, and reveals that the study of literature was already advanced in that era.

Lyman, R. L., "English Grammar in America before 1850" (Washington : *Bulletin Bureau of Education,* 1921, No. 21). An important study that covers thoroughly the beginnings of grammar study in American schools and traces the early development of texts and the influences that led to their appearance. Discusses some of the early textbooks.

Scudder, Horace E., "The Primer and Literature," *Atlantic Monthly,* September, 1892. Little about the primer, but much on the use of collections of literature in schools; an outstanding argument in favor of their use. To quote the author's own words, it is a "pleading for an unbroken, continuous presentation of great literature in the Common Schools." Appearing only six months after Andrew Lang's "Can Literature Be Taught?," mentioned in Chapter 14 of the present work, Scudder's article might have been a rebuttal to the ideas that Lang expressed — a telling one, whether so intended or not.

Scudder, Horace E., *Noah Webster* (Boston : Houghton Mifflin, 1887). The first book-length biography of Webster. Although written by a man of high literary standing, it is not as valuable as the biographies that have appeared in our day.

Shoemaker, Irving C., *Noah Webster, Pioneer of Learning* (New York : Columbia University Press, 1936). The most comprehensive volume on the work of Webster, in particular as pertaining to his schoolbooks. Goes very thoroughly into the lineage of the blue-back spelling book, the grammars, and other texts of Webster. Conveys an understanding of the conditions under which Webster's school-text compiling was done.

Warfel, Henry R., *Noah Webster, Schoolmaster to America* (New York : Macmillan, 1936). A biography of much general interest about Webster and his publications. Treats the history of the Webster spelling book during the nineteenth century especially well. In 1958 Professor Warfel also issued a lengthy volume of Webster's letters, a number of which touch upon his dictionary and schoolbooks.

Anonymous, "Mr. Wolfit Proposes School Ban of Shakespeare," *London Times,* January 29, 1956, general news section. The article relates that the actor, Donald Wolfit, voices opposition to the study of Shakespeare's plays in schools because of their being "above the heads of children." His argument, like much writing along this line, is perhaps as unjustified as the time-worn claim that many adults "hate Shakespeare" because they were forced to study the plays in school.

Arithmetics

Cajori, Florian, *The Teaching and History of Mathematics in the United States* (Washington : Bureau of Education, Circular No. 3, 1890). Contains much useful information and is the first of Professor Cajori's numerous publications on the history of arithmetic. Cajori was never so bibliography-conscious as were Professors Karpinski and Smith in their works enumerated below.

Greenwood, J. M., "Notes on the History of American Textbooks on Arithmetic" (Washington : *Annual Report Bureau of Educa-*

tion, 1897–98), I, 789–868. Valuable data on the subject at the end of the nineteenth century. A further article by the same author is in the 1900 *Annual Report*, pp. 781–837.

Hughes, Raymond Grove, "Joseph Ray, The Mathematician and The Man," (Charleston : *West Virginia Review*, February 1932). A good account of the well-known arithmetic compiler, with analysis of the factors that made his texts successful.

Karpinski, Louis C., *Bibliography of Mathematical Works Printed in America through 1850* (Ann Arbor : University of Michigan Press, 1940). One of the most superb bibliographies ever produced in America. Already mentioned in Chapter 10 of the present volume. Contains more than 900 facsimile title-page and text-page reproductions, and other illustrations. Covers not only mathematical books produced in the United States and Mexico, but includes a 36-page list of journals and newspapers containing mathematical articles.

Karpinski, Louis C., *The History of Arithmetic* (Chicago : Rand McNally, 1925). A terse but comprehensive coverage, incorporating information on several outstanding American texts. Has a list of American arithmetics published before 1800.

Parke, Uriah, *Lectures on the Philosophy of Arithmetic* (Philadelphia : Moss & Brother, 1850). A volume of worth-while material on early arithmetics in our land, written by a resident of the then almost backwoods settlement of Zanesville, Ohio. Scattered through the volume are facts not to be found elsewhere on Bowditch, Oliver Shaw, Collins, and other writers of early American textbooks. Parke has a chapter on mathematical prodigies, being one of the earliest American writers on this subject. He mentions one or two prodigies evidently not mentioned elsewhere.

Smith, D. E., *History of Mathematics*, 2 volumes (Boston : Ginn & Co., 1923). Reprinted by Dover (New York, 1953, 2 vols.) as part of that firm's softbound series. A very long history with quite a lot of material on elementary arithmetics produced in the

United States. Covers particularly well the early mathematical publications of Mexico.

Smith, D. E., *Rara Arithmetica* (Boston : Ginn & Co., 1908). A bibliography of arithmetics prior to 1601 in the collection of George A. Plimpton. Has valuable data on the early Spanish-language arithmetics printed in America.

Simons, Lao Genevra, "Introduction of Algebra into American Schools in the Eighteenth Century" (Washington : *Bureau of Education Bulletin*, 1924, No. 18). Of outstanding value on algebra texts and on the study of the subject in the 1700's. Much on Isaac Greenwood, Pike, Pieter Venema, and one or two other early compilers of mathematical texts. Miss Simons' numerous writings on mathematics are all strong on the bibliographical side.

The volumes of *Scripta Mathematica,* a quarterly sponsored by Yeshiva University of New York, contains numerous studies on American arithmetics, their compilers, and on related subjects. This journal was started in 1933 and has carried some most interesting articles, all in a pithy, direct, down-to-earth style. Many of the articles have been reprinted in pamphlet form and distributed through a department of Yeshiva University. Two of the articles, that on Pieter Venema and the one on "George Fisher, Accomptant," have already been referred to in Chapter 10. Among the other *Scripta Mathematica* pamphlets are "Pennsylvania German Arithmetical Books," "The Place of Mathematics in Modern Education," "Changes in the Elementary Mathematical Terms in the Last Three Centuries," "The Teaching of Mathematics in Schools," "Thomas Jefferson and Mathematics," "Arithmetic Centenarians : Textbooks With a Long Life," and others along kindred lines.

Science Texts and Physiologies

Chancellor, William E., *Theory of Motives, Ideas and Values in Education* (Boston : Houghton Mifflin, 1907). Chapter 17 is useful in the study of certain aspects of progress in physiology texts.

Clendennin, Logan, *The Human Body* (New York : Knopf, 1927). Contains some information on school physiologies. Calls attention to the fact that much of the material was devoted to furthering the anti-liquor movement.

Graves, Frank P., *A History of Education in Modern Times* (New York : Macmillan, 1913). Chapter 10, on "The Modern Scientific Movement," treats of the factors that have led to present-day school science texts, including the influence of Herbert Spencer, Huxley, Youmans, Charles W. Eliot, and others.

Osborn, Henry Fairfield, "Biology and Other Science in the Schools," *Report of Schoolmasters Association of New York, 1893,* pp. 35–42. An able treatment of the subject, as are all the writings of Osborn.

Paget, James, "On the Study of Physiology," in *Culture Demanded by Modern Life,* edited and with introduction by E. L. Youmans (New York : Appleton, 1873). This paper by Dr. Paget is still of value in appraising the contents of school physiologies.

Powers, S. R., *History of the Teaching of Chemistry in Secondary Schools of the United States before 1850* (Minneapolis : University of Minnesota, 1920). Useful in a study of the early chemical manuals. Many of our best-known early scientists and educators had a hand in putting together many of the better school chemistry texts used before the middle of the nineteenth century.

Swann, W. F. G., "Three Centuries of Natural Philosophy," *Annual Report Smithsonian Institution, 1928.* A paper (already referred to in Chapter 18) on the evolution of natural philosophy, giving an idea of the changes that have been necessary in science schoolbooks from time to time. Dr. Swann said, "in speaking of theories being discarded and superseded by others, we must not think of the discarded ones as useless."

Anonymous, "Physiology," *Monroe's Cyclopedia of Education* (New York : Macmillan, 1913), vol. 4. This, although brief, is one of the best delineations of physiology as it appears in American textbooks and the place the study holds in schools.

Anonymous, "Quackery in American Literature" (Baltimore : *Southern Review,* January, 1868). A review of Rufus W. Griswold's *Curiosities of American Literature.* Along with other examples, errors of statement of a scientific nature in schoolbooks of the time are cited. Among the texts mentioned are Woodbridge's "American Geography," Worthington Hooker's "Natural History," Marcus Willson's "Fifth Reader," Goodrich's "Natural History," and J. A. Porter's "Principles of Chemistry." Some of the errors and deviations from fact seem particularly glaring, coming as they did from the pens of well-known educators.

Handwriting, Drawing, Art

Drepperd, C. W., *American Drawing Books* (New York : New York Public Library, 1946). Perhaps the best guide to drawing books. It lists, with bibliographical data, 19 items specifically designed for use in schools.

Goldstein, Harriet and Vetta, *Art in Everyday Life* (New York : Macmillan, 1940), 3rd edition. Intended as a textbook, this volume is an excellent summary of art in the school. Has splendid format and is illustrated in both black and white and in color. There are sections on the esthetics of painting, lettering, script and print from Gutenberg's day, household design, clothing design, and other branches of art taught in schools today.

Nash, Ray, *Some Early American Writing Books and Masters* (Cambridge : Harvard Library Dept. of Graphic Arts, 1943). A splendid monograph on the first American copybook compilers, with eight facsimiles of early handwriting. Nash is the foremost American authority on our early handwriting.

Nash, Ray, *American Writing Master and Copybooks* (Boston : Colonial Society of Massachusetts, 1959). The most extensive publication on early American handwriting, superbly illustrated with 16 facsimiles. Covers "editions and variants of all American publications on handwriting by authors working before the end of the eighteenth century."

Ricketts, C. L., "Penmanship," *Home and Business Instructor* (Chicago. Laird and Lee, 1896). An excellent 37-page treatment of the history and technique of handwriting, well-illustrated with clear plates. It is rather odd to find such an efficiently written history of handwriting in a book of this type — an agent-distributed "home" book of the kind sold by itinerant agents during the nineteenth century.

Spencer, M. C. *Spencerian Key to Practical Penmanship* (New York : Ivision, Phinney, Blakeman & Co., 1867). Twenty-one chapters on handwriting by a son of the founder of the Spencerian system. An introductory chapter is on Platt R. Spencer.

Anonymous, "Handwriting In America," *London Times Literary Supplement,* September 18, 1959. An able review of Professor Nash's *American Writing Masters and Copybooks,* which gives a fair appraisal of the book. The review contains considerable information on American handwriting and copybooks.

Anonymous, *Manual of Writing Founded on Mulhauser's Method Adapted to English Use* (London: John W. Parker & Sons, 1860 and prior). Important data on Mulhauser, whose system had a strong influence on American handwriting; a study of this volume in connection with early American copybooks is profitable.

A number of other items on handwriting have been listed in a footnote to Chapter 14.

Histories and Geographies

Desmond, H. J., "A Grave Omission In American School Histories," *Century Magazine,* October, 1868. Criticizes school histories on several counts, chiefly for not taking note of the vast immigrations from foreign countries since the time of the Revolution. Criticizes "Peter Parleyism" in school histories and takes exception to compilers "servilely imitating their predecessors." Enlightening on the mid-century period.

Fiske, John, *Essays, Historical and Literary, Vol. 2* (New York : Macmillan, 1902). Chapter 1, "Old and New Ways of Treating History," mainly about history above the school level, in places probes deep into our school histories and the methods of compilers. Fiske points out that Sparks in editing Washington's letters, changed "Old Put" to "General Putnam," and "things are in a devil of a state" to "our affairs have reached a deplorable condition."

Guyot, Arnold, "Geography," in Johnson's *New Universal Encyclopedia,* Vol. 2, Part 1 (New York : 1884). A clear definition of geography around mid-nineteenth century as the subject had to do with school texts. Guyot was the advisory editor-in-chief of the Johnson *Encyclopedia,* by all odds the most authoritative reference work produced in America before the end of the nineteenth century. Many of the articles in the work written by Guyot are still highly valuable — that on "Rains," to cite one.

Hall, G. Stanley, Editor, *Methods of Teaching and Studying History* (Boston : Heath, 1896). Studies by various scholars, with 82 pages of bibliography on school history texts and collateral material.

Higham, John, "The Rise of American Intellectual History," *American Historical Review,* April, 1951. About historical writing above the school range, this may be read with profit toward understanding the movement of school history compiling.

Osborn, Henry Fairfield, *Creative Education* (New York : Scribners, 1927). This volume by the noted paleontologist, while casting a great deal of light on education and much of deep interest on the personal experiences of the author, is especially informative on phases of Arnold Guyot's career, bringing out data not generally known. Here we learn that Guyot never fully mastered English and had to employ helpers to put his geographies and other publications in shape for publication. Osborn was a student of Guyot, and reports that the geography compiler's lectures were fascinating for their quaint English.

Smith, Goldwin, "Are Our School Histories Anglophobe?", *North*

American Review, September, 1897. Investigation of and defense against the accusation that American school histories tend "to develop a hatred of Great Britain." A lengthy review of this article appeared in the *Review of Reviews,* October, 1897, under the title, "Our School Histories As a Cause of Anglophobia."

Weiss, Harry B., *Solomon King* (New York : New York Public Library, 1947). Discusses early geographies extensively, and especially that of Jedidiah Morse, at a time when the use of geographies was spreading.

White, Emerson E., *The Art of Teaching* (New York : American Book Co., 1901). Has two chapters on geography in the schools, with estimates of text materials. Touches on the work of Guyot in modernizing our geography texts.

Wright, John Kirkland, *Geography in the Making* (New York : American Geographical Society, 1952). Discusses the ideal content of geography and goes into the history of its study and present-day trends.

Anonymous, *A Few Words about Mitchell's New Series of School Geographies* (Philadelphia : E. H. Butler & Co., n.d. [1870]). A 100-page booklet describing the Mitchell geographies, recording where they were used, and reproducing letters from teachers pertaining to the geographies.

Anonymous, "School Histories," *Southern Review* ' (Baltimore : January, 1868). Reviews (pp. 154–179) covering eleven school histories issued before and during the Civil War; the reviews, although chiefly from the Southern viewpoint contain considerable sound criticism of school histories in general and information on the past treatment of early American history.

Compilers, Publishers, Illustrators, Collectors

Archibald, Mrs. George, *Joel Dorman Steelt, Teacher and Author* (New York : A. S. Barnes, 1900). A biography written by a personal friend of the subject. In general it clearly betrays, perhaps unintentionally, the mental workings and weaknesses of those nineteenth-century professional schoolbook compilers who worked under orders.

Davis, William Harper, "Plimptoniana Or Some Notes On The Plimpton Collections," *American Book Collector,* November, 1932, December, 1932, January, 1933. Comprehensive information on the noted Plimpton schoolbook collection, with fine illustrative plates. Gives data on other material in the collection. The bulk of the Plimpton schoolbook collection is now in the Columbia University Library.

Derby, J. C., *Fifty Years among Authors, Books and Publishers* (New York : Carleton, 1884). One of the source books on many of the early schoolbook publishers, written against a background of close personal contacts and long experience.

Hamilton, Sinclair, *Early American Book Illustrators and Wood Engravers* (Princeton : Princeton University Library, limited edition, 1958). This *catalogue raisonné* contains a great deal of material connected with early schoolbooks, and especially with the work of Alexander Anderson, who had a part in illustrating numerous school texts. Forms a sort of complement to the previous volumes of D. M. Stauffer, Mante Fielding, and F. M. Burr dealing with early engravers.

O'Brien, Joseph M., "Confederate Book Bindings in Wallpaper," (Chicago : *Amateur Book Collector,* September, 1952). One of the few treatments of the subject that discusses schoolbooks; gives definite descriptions of wallpaper bindings utilized.

Oswald, John Clyde, *Printing in the Americas* (New York: Gregg, 1937). Data on first books printed in most of the states, some of which were schoolbooks. Other coverage of early schoolbook printings. A volume of much importance on its subject.

Pulsifer, W. E., *A Brief Account of the Educational Publishing Business in the United States* (Atlantic City : privately printed, 1921). Historical information on several individual textbooks and of considerable value because of brief historical matter on a number of firms established since Derby's day.

Weiss, Harry B., *Printers and Publishers of Children's Books in New York City 1698–1830* (New York : N. Y. Public Library, 1948). A bibliography containing fifty-nine items of direct interest to those studying early American schoolbooks and the producers of them.

Anonymous, "Library Notes," (Alexandria, Virginia : *New Age,* April, 1960). Biographical information on Amos Doolittle, illustrator and map maker, who played a part in the production of numerous school texts after the Revolution and during the early part of the nineteenth century. Some data on Doolittle perhaps not to be found elsewhere.

Anonymous, *One Hundred Notable Engravers* (New York : N. Y. Public Library, 1928). An indexed, annotated 38-page listing of an exhibition of prints held in the New York Public Library late in 1927 and early in 1928. Contains much· bibliographical information on numerous engravers and map makers who had a part in early schoolbook creation.

Anonymous, *Textbooks in Education* (New York : American Textbook Publishers Institute, 1949). Contains a 50-page "Short History of the Textbook in America" written as a "closely-woven fabric of the nation's history"—and written very well considering its limited scope.

Index

Date Due

AP 3'67				